"At last, a simple but complete (and very readable) guide to non-profit accounting for the non-accountant! Invaluable for nonprofit managers and particularly useful for board members who may have no background in this arcane area.

The secrets of *restricted revenue, net assets,* and other terms new to those from the for-profit world are explained straightforwardly and with enough detail to ensure understanding."

—**Lita Nelsen,** *consultant and board of directors member of nonprofit institutions, retired director, MIT Technology Licensing Office*

"Ittelson has done a public service by providing a fast-moving, readable guide to a subject not every board member finds thrilling, yet with which everyone should have at least a nodding acquaintance. Clear, simple examples to illustrate every point is especially useful."

—**David T. Flanagan,** *former President, University of Southern Maine*

"This is the book I have been looking for for two decades! It is clear, practical and breaks down complex information in a way that is relevant to the work all of us in the nonprofit sector do. Highly recommended."

—**Marjorie Schwarzer,** *Professor of Museum Studies, University of San Francisco*

"A must read for grantees. Provides the financial understanding we expect at all levels in supported organizations."

—**Irina Simmons,** *foundation executive, former corporate treasurer, Fortune 500 company*

"Just think of this book as an in-depth, one semester-long course condensed into 220 readable pages."

—**Peter Lowy,** *editor and publisher, Massnonprofit News*

"A clear and effective financial primer for the board and everybody else in the organization."

—**Barbara Kemp,** *former school board chair, Scarsdale, NY, and trustee Occidental College*

D1598139

"Rare that a book on understanding nonprofit financials is actually entertaining—but this one is. A clear, thorough and highly accessible walkthrough of the essentials of nonprofit accounting, this should be required reading for all nonprofit board members."
—**Kate Merritt**, *CEO, KMP Consulting and consultant to nonprofit boards*

"A must-have guide to the nonprofit world. Excellent, highly readable book that all board members should have in their library. Spells out our fiduciary responsibility clearly. Staff would benefit from this book as well."
—**Ed Bailey,** *5-Star Amazon.com review*

"An easy read for conscientious board members. Will be a reference for years to come. Ittelson incorporates a down-to-earth style while demystifying financial reports for newcomer and veteran nonprofit leaders alike."
—**Douglas Long,** *5-Star Amazon.com review*

"Although I have been an entrepreneur for nearly 40 years and took finance and accounting in college, I learned concepts from this book that had never been obvious to me before. Several times I had the "slap the forehead, but of course" reaction. Great book."
—*5-Star Amazon.com review*

"The author has done what most fail to do: explain something to beginners in an understandable way. If you look at a financial statement as a series of unintelligible tables full of meaningless numbers, accompanied by mind numbing prose, this book will help you out immensely."
—*5-Star Amazon.com review*

***Revised & Expanded 3rd Edition***
*with FASB & OMB Accounting Standards Updates,*
*Fund Accounting Methods, and Computer System Design*

# Nonprofit Accounting
# &
# Financial Statements

## Overview for Board, Management, and Staff

**Mercury Group Press**
**Cambridge, MA**

# Other nonprofit books by Thomas R. Ittelson

*A Picture Book of Nonprofit Financial Statements* by Thomas R. Ittelson, 60 pages, 2017.
ISBN: 978-0997108941

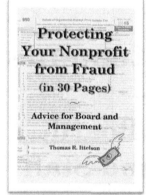

*Understanding Financial Statements (in 30 Pages): A Short tutorial for Board, Management, and Staff* by Thomas R. Ittelson, 30 pages, 2020, ISBN: 978-1970050400

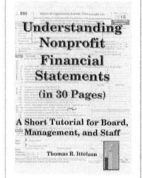

*Protecting Your Nonprofit From Fraud (in 30 Pages): Advice for Board and Management* by Thomas R. Ittelson, 30 pages 2020 ISBN: 978-1-970050-01-1

*Revised & Expanded 3rd Edition*
*with FASB & OMB Accounting Standards Updates,*
*Fund Accounting Methods, and Computer System Design*

# Nonprofit Accounting
# &
# Financial Statements

## Overview for Board, Management, and Staff

**Thomas R. Ittelson**

**Nonprofit Accounting & Financial Statements:
Overview for Board, Management, and Staff (3rd Edition)**

**Copyright © 2020 by Thomas R. Ittelson**

**Available in quantity directly from the publisher.**

Printed and bound in the United States of America.

**ISBN: 978-1-970050-03-5**

**Mercury Group Press**
PO Box 381350
Cambridge, MA 02238
*www.mercurygrouppress.com*
*info@mercurygroup.com*
617-285-1168

**Library of Congress Cataloging-in-Publication Data**
Available upon request.

*VIK0808-4*

To my son, Alesdair.

# Acknowledgements

Many people helped make this book a reality.

First and foremost, I thank my family: Mary, Johnny, Bobbi, Darcy, Sara, Tim and Baby Callie, Brenden, Bryce, and Alesdair for being on my side, at my side.

Special thanks to my editor Kate Osthaus, CPA, for making my words flow and my numbers correct. However, I take full responsibility for errors and misstatements that remain. They are my own. Sigh.

Thanks to my clients and my students, Thanks to my fellow nonprofit board members and finance committee members who showed me the need for such a book and inspired me to write it.

Thanks to Barbarajo Bockenhauer for her valuable conceptual editing of early manuscript drafts, her continuing encouragement, her determination to keep me on target, and her occasional heckling. Thanks to Jean Ann Schulte for her careful review and comments, to Drs. Leann Canty and Rachael Fawcett for keeping me healthy, to Gwen Acton for keeping me mostly sane, to Davis Reid who keeps me laughing, and to Stephen J. Potter for calling me from the road.

# Table of Contents

Nonprofit organizations play a very special role in our society. They are *mission-driven* groups of dedicated people with admirable social goals and without a profit motive, yet they must be managed in a business-like fashion to succeed. Sound financial management within the organization and oversight by the board are essential.

## Section A. Setting the Stage

With over 1.5 million organizations, 10% of the nation's workforce, and approximately $1.7 trillion in annual revenues, nonprofits are a force in the U.S. economy.

The nonprofit organization's board members—often serving without compensation—are stewards of the nonprofit's mission and are ultimately responsible for the organization's mission-driven financial success. Each board member—and especially finance committee members—holds a fiduciary responsibility for the financial viability of the organization.

# Section B. Nonprofit Financial Statements

FASB makes the rules and calls them GAAP. The IRS
and the OMB develop regulations too. Got that?

Shows the organization's revenue and expense, profit
(*surplus*) and loss (*deficit*) for a period of time.

Shows what the organization owns and what it owes at
a snapshot in time. Assets minus liabilities equal "net
assets" indicates the power and scope of the organization.

Shows the movement of cash into the organization and
out. It functions for the organization as your checkbook
register functions for you. Run out of cash to pay the
bills and the organization is bankrupt. Sigh.

Expenses for a period of time are presented separately
for individual projects. The government and foundations like to see this information for the projects they
financially support.

# Section C. The Mechanics of Nonprofit Accounting

A *transaction* in accounting language is any action a
nonprofit organization takes that affects its financial
records, the so-called "books." Future chapters will describe the accounting entries for some common nonprofit financial transactions by our sample 501(c)(3) organization, the Westside Neighborhood Association, or
"WsNA" for short.

Many nonprofit organizations survive and prosper with
philanthropy of many generous community members.
See how revenue transactions are recorded in the financial statements.

- **T1.** A donor contributes $1,000 by check in support of our cause.
- **T2.** We receive a $15,000 gift to write, produce, and distribute a booklet on how to build and grow community gardens.
- **T3.** The Ex-Chair of the board bequeaths $100,000 to the organization to increase our endowment fund.
- **T4.** Knowledgeable friend contributes needed professional services.
- **T5.** Perhaps the most valuable gift of all— volunteers contribute their time.
- **T6.** Local Auto dealer pledges a $5,000 gift to be funded "when sales pick up!"
- **T7.** Prior pledge of $5,000 is funded!

**Chapter 10. Program Services Transactions** ............. 93

Program services revenue is payment received by the nonprofit organization for providing goods and services to clients performed in the advancement of its mission. In this exchange of goods and services for money, the organization often acts like a commercial business— but the purpose of the exchange is the advancement of mission, not the generation of profits.

- **T8.** Receive payment from Medicare. Pay our contracted physician for professional services performed in our clinic.
- **T9.** Pay Senior Center rent. It would be great if we had our own building!
- **T10.** Order supplies for use in the Senior Center.
- **T11.** Receive supplies ordered in **T10**.
- **T12.** Pay for supplies received in **T11**.
- **T13.** Use some purchased supplies from inventory.
- **T14.** Take me out to the Ball Game!

**Chapter 11. Payroll Expense Transactions** ................ 109

Payroll is often by far the largest expense of many nonprofit organizations. Learn how to record these major expense transactions.

- **T15.** Issue $10,780 in payroll checks.

- **T28.** Hire fundraising consultant to plan our annual-fund campaign.
- **T29.** Pay fundraising consultant for preparing her excellent annual campaign plan.
- **T30.** Hold an awards dinner followed by a high-end auction of donated antiques.
- **T31.** Promote "Rainy-Day Club" and give donors an umbrella costing $22.50 as a thank-you gift.
- **T32.** Conduct a trial email fundraising campaign. Money well spent?

- T33. Produce and distribute booklet funded by a purpose-restricted donation.
- T34. Receive donation and place a portion of funds received into board-restricted Net Assets.
- T35. Release board-restricted Net Assets and fund scholarship.
- T36. Accept a contract from the state DHS to provide meals-on-wheels to shut-ins in our community.
- T37. Provide meals-on-wheels services to shut-ins in the community.

- T38. Receive utility bills.
- T39. Pay utility bills.
- T40. Hire accountants and lawyers for performing audits and helping to prepare IRS Form 990.
- T41. Pay WsNA's annual liability insurance premium. Record first quarter's expense.
- T42. Record unrelated business income.

# Section D. Planning, Budgeting, Reporting & Oversight

Some easy ways to keep track of financial performance to mission—both qualitative and quantitative. Both views are important. Presenting data in a way that stakeholders can understand is essential.

Understanding the financial situation of a nonprofit organization usually starts with the financial statements. Using ratios of the numbers therein can provide a "performance score" and help with comparison and benchmarking.

Putting all the information together in a simple, easy to understand "dashboard" is essential for regular stakeholder and board review. Charts and trend lines communicate effectively to those less familiar with numeric financial statements.

"Thanks, but what are you going to do for me in the future?" is a common question clients, donors, staff, and volunteers ask of a nonprofit organization. Here is how to answer and stay true to your mission.

The people, activities, and finances of nonprofit organizations are reported to the government using IRS Form 990. It is like an individual's IRS Form 1040, but for a nonprofit organization. If your organization does not file its Form 990, it could lose nonprofit status. It is important to do it right. Used right, the Form 990 can be a wonderful fundraising tool.

# Section E. Conclusion

A lot can go wrong. Pay attention. Be vigilant. Develop competence. Be prepared. Remember, you are responsible both individually and collectively.

**Chapter 23. Twenty Important Lessons Learned** ...... 225

Act on these 20 most important lessons learned. Actually follow them; really do them; do not just talk about the. *You know.*

**About the Author**

# Foreword

Virtually every decision a nonprofit organization makes has its roots in accounting information. While many board members, managers, and staff may lack a background in finance, they owe it to their organizations to understand its financial underpinnings. They will find this book to be an invaluable resource. Intended as an overview for boards, management, and staff, this guide, free of jargon, will help board members fulfill their fiduciary duties and better equip managers and others to better understand their organization.

Consider questions with which nonprofit organizations often grapple. Can we execute our strategic plan? Are our expenses in line with what we need to do? Are some expense areas rising faster than their sources of income, and, if so, why? Do we have the right checks and balances in place? Are we fulfilling requirements of funders, and effectively fulfilling our mission?

The answers to these and many related questions depend on understanding the organization's finances. Nonprofits may not be profit oriented, but they have a keen interest in maintaining financial stability and possibly generating a surplus with which to fund new programs. Charitable organizations are subject to the laws of economics that apply to everyone else.

This book guides the reader through the fundamentals of nonprofit financial statements, the mechanics of nonprofit accounting, and planning, budgeting, reporting, and oversight. It is an in-depth, semester-long course condensed to 220 readable pages.

Peter Lowy, editor & publisher
*Massnonprofit News*
Brookline, MA

# Preface

The important changes made to nonprofit accounting and financial reporting by FASB in 2017 (the first since 1993) and by the Office of Management and Budget in 2019 are now fully operational. This 3rd edition incorporates these new rules. See **Appendix A.** on page 233.

**Preface to the First Edition:**

I come to accounting through the laboratory, a kind of circuitous route to travel for sure. Armed with my formal training as a PhD-level natural scientist, I was working in a biotechnology lab. My main task was pouring liquid from Test Tube A into the liquid in Test Tube B, shaking and measuring how long it took the mixture to turn blue. I got bored (who would not?) and started a high-tech company instead, learning accounting on the job.

My own "lightening bolt" moment during that learning process? Professional accountants, while very useful in performing audits, had great difficulty teaching me key accounting principles. I am a smart guy, but I consistently became mired in the specialized vocabulary and buried by what seemed unnecessary detail. Being a scientist *and* a businessperson, I recognized a problem—and wrote the book[1] to solve it.

Because of my business background and that wildly popular little business accounting textbook I wrote, I was asked to serve on the finance committee of a mid-sized, nonprofit 501(c)(3) public charity in Boston. Honored, I accepted—being humbled followed soon thereafter. Let me explain.

---

[1] *Financial Statements: A Step-by-Step Guide to Understanding and Creating Financial Reports* by Thomas Ittelson, Career Press, Pompton Plains, 2009.

As happens on many nonprofit boards and the finance committees of those boards, members were bright, committed, and cared passionately about the mission of the organization; but they were simply not financially literate. Collectively, even we professional business members, though successful in the for-profit world, brought little understanding of the special needs of nonprofit accounting, reporting, and financial governance.

We knew that nonprofit accounting and financial reporting is a language that board members, management, and staff *all* needed to learn in order to serve our mission effectively. It was a different bottom line, but no less important than our for-profit measurement models. I decided to write this book.

There are many worthwhile books about nonprofit leadership, stewardship, mission, and operations; reading them will make you a better board member and manager. There are also books to teach you how to be an accountant; but you probably would be one by now if you were interested in doing so. This book is not going to teach you how to be a board member or be an accountant. Stop now if that was your hope.

This book has a much narrower focus: to teach you *how* the financial accounts of your nonprofit organization work. How does money flow into and out of the organization? How do you keep track of it properly? What questions should you ask your organization's accountants, financial officers, and auditors?

In addition, it is presented in a manner that translates complex transactions into practical language "pared down" to the material that is absolutely relevant, leaving the esoteric to the professional accountants. Simply stated, this book will help you fulfill your "fiduciary duty" to your nonprofit organization, its donors, the community, and the government.

As a scientist and a passionate advocate for the nonprofits that play such a vital role in our communities, I wrote this book to meet my need to serve nonprofits. I hope it meets your need to do the same. Read on.

Thomas R. Ittelson
Cambridge, MA

# Introduction

*Welcome to the Board.* We are very happy to have you serve. We have appointed you to the finance committee. To prepare you to meet your fiduciary responsibility for the financial success of the organization, please review:

* last year's audited financial statements,
* the current year's budget, and
* our latest Form 990 filed with the IRS.

———

*What!?* Having to understand accounting and finances was not what you had in mind when you accepted this "honor." Reconciling your checkbook is sometimes a problem. Now you need to analyze the organization's *Statement of Activities, Statement of Financial Position, Statement of Cash Flows* and *Statement of Functional Expenses* then approve next year's budget. They probably expect you to give money as well! Uh-oh...

As a board member, you are a *shepherd* of that organization's financial resources and its financial ability to act in support of its mission. You owe it to your organization's donors and to the people your organization serves, to *steer the boat* wisely. More mixed metaphors to follow.

———

This book, useful for anyone who works in, or with, nonprofit organizations, is written mostly from a board member's perspective, because oversight and financial accountability ultimately rest with the board. If the board does not understand the basics of nonprofit accounting and financial reporting, they will be too dependent on

1

the CEO. If the CEO does not understand, the organization will be headed for financial disaster. If management and staff do not understand, the organization will be inefficiently run and likely be ineffective in meeting mission goals.

Typically, board members are not businesspeople with experience in accounting or financial reporting. They are nominated for other reasons. Also, management and staff are selected because they are focused on a particular mission, rather than on financial resources. A book like this one is needed by all.

### What will you learn; how will you benefit?

We will teach all that nonprofit board members, managers, and staff need as an overview of nonprofit accounting and financial reporting.

- *Accounting* is record keeping; the accounting rules describe how the records should be kept.
- *Financial Reporting* is presenting your accounting records in a way that you and other people can understand.

This book should give everyone involved in nonprofit organizations enough financial understanding to review the financial statements of their organization and ask the questions necessary to fulfill their fiduciary duty and job requirements. The contents herein are simplified, but we teach all that is needed to be a good board member, manager, and staff, while leaving out confusing details that get in the way of a useful conceptual understanding.

> **Most of the important decisions made by nonprofit organizations are based, in some material way, on accounting information.**

It is not that accounting details are unimportant to the success of your organization. They are important, but there are specialist financial officers and accountants within the organization to deal with details. The purpose here is not to turn everyone into number crunchers, but rather, to provide the basic understanding necessary for everyone to review the organization's financial statements with confidence. *It is not that difficult.*

Note that nonprofit accounting and financial reporting is significantly different from that used by for-profit companies. Even those who come to the organization with a business background often do not grasp the special complexities. Nonprofit organizations use different accounting rules and have different IRS compliance requirements than do for-profit companies. Nonprofit organizations are not created to make a profit. This fundamental difference is reflected in the accounting and reporting setup for nonprofits. This book focuses on the special accounting treatments for contributions, gifts, grants, contracts, and program services revenue and expense—highlighting the key differences between accounting in nonprofit organizations and for-profit companies.

**The Bottom Line**

How does the board, management, and staff know that the organization is doing a good financial job furthering the mission? Ask and then answer these four seminal questions using the data collected and presented in financial statements:

- *Are we doing the right things?* Is our spending congruent with our mission? Do we put our money where our mission is, or do we allow misdirection and mission creep?
- *Are we being effective?* Over time, are we reaching our goals? How are we sure? How do we measure and demonstrate our success?
- *Are we being efficient?* Are we getting the most bang for our buck? If not, we are squandering our donors' money—shame on us.
- *Do we have adequate resources?* Are our available financial and human resources sufficient to fully support our mission? Are we biting off more than we can chew?

*Money is most often an organization's scarcest resource and how well money is used is the best measure of board, management, and staff performance.* The organization's financial statements document that performance. By the time you have finished this book, you will understand the importance of the following questions—and how to answer them.[1]

---

[1] Adapted from: *Managing the Nonprofit Organization: Principles and Practices* by Peter F. Drucker, HarperCollins Publishers, New York, 1990, p142.

- Is our financial plan consistent with our strategic plan?
- Is our projected cash flow adequate?
- Do we have sufficient reserves?
- Are any specific expense areas rising faster than their sources of income? Why? A problem for the future?
- Are we performing to plan? Are we regularly comparing our financial activity with what we have budgeted?
- Are our expenses appropriate?
- Do we have in-place the checks and balances necessary to prevent errors, fraud, and abuse?
- Are we meeting guidelines and requirements set by our funders?
- Are we effectively and efficiently promoting our mission for the benefit of our stakeholders?

———

Your worries are over, new board member, management, or staff. Relax and read on!

"*Your 3 wishes are taxable. Donate them to charity and take the write off!*"

# Section A.
# Setting the Stage

# Chapter 1.
# Nonprofits: Big Business in the U.S.A.

With over 1.5 million organizations, almost 10% of the nation's workforce, $3 trillion in assets, and $1.7 trillion in annual revenues (5% of GDP), nonprofit organizations are a major force in the United States economy.[1]

Doing the *right things,* and doing them both *efficiently* and *effectively,* could be worth billions of dollars to nonprofits in America. The ultimate purpose of this book is to improve the financial literacy of nonprofit board members, managers, and staff. The increased productivity coming from applying this new knowledge will significantly increase nonprofit organizations' contributions to the health and happiness of our citizens.

## Nonprofit Efficiency & Effectiveness

Most people, including big donors, think that while nonprofit board members and managers are nice people, they do not manage their organizations very well.

For nonprofit organizations mostly stuck with the stereotype of being warm but not particularly competent, anything that boosts their perceived competence will help them survive and prosper in the donor marketplace. Donors really want to know how well their donations are pushing the peanut forward.

---

[1] Most of the statistical information in this chapter is derived from data presented in *Giving USA 2015: The Annual Report on Philanthropy for the Year 2014,* a publication of Giving USA Foundation, 2015. http://www.givingusa.org.

Using *the numbers* to guide charity work is crucial to ensuring the efficient and effective use of limited resources. The following chapters will give you the knowledge and the tools required!

> ## "Charities have been warmheartedly, but also wastefully, throwing money at problems without good management or market discipline."
>
> *The Creative Climate* by David Brooks,
> **The New York Times**, Jul 7, 2014

### The Nonprofit World

Almost all nonprofit organizations are state-chartered corporations. A few, such as the Boy Scouts of America and American Red Cross, are chartered by Congress. Nonprofit organizations must have a public purpose (mission) and have no "owners" in the traditional sense. They are governed by a board of directors and no individual benefits from net profits (called *surplus* in nonprofit language).

The special operating rules for nonprofit organizations are defined by each state individually and by federal regulations promulgated by the Internal Revenue Service (IRS). Nonprofit organizations are called "exempt organizations" because they are exempt from income taxation.

Nonprofit organizations include everything from neighborhood associations that meet a couple times a year and have minimal assets, to Harvard University and the Gates Foundation, each with tens of billions of dollars in assets. They include soup kitchens, small medical clinics, and traditional charities that serve the poor, as well as your local churches, hospitals, and chambers of commerce. The YMCA, Catholic Charities, Sierra Club, United Steel Workers, and the Metropolitan Opera are some well-known nonprofit organizations.

Note, the designation "nonprofit" does not necessarily mean that donations to these organization are tax deductible to the donor. Only organizations with a charitable public purpose may receive tax-deductible contributions. These organizations are formed under United States Internal Revenue Code Title 26 U.S.C. § 501(c)(3).

## Public Charities (501(c)(3) Organizations

Public charities that can accept tax-deductible donations include most organizations active in the arts, education, health care, and human services. Religious congregations are also considered public charities, but for constitutional reasons they are not required to register with the IRS.

---

### What is a "Public Charity?"

Only certain types of nonprofit organizations are qualified by the IRS as *exempt* from paying income taxes and of those, only ones with specific charitable public purposes may receive tax-deductible contributions from donors.

Most of our discussion in this book will concern nonprofits formed around the Internal Revenue Code Section 501(c)(3) Public Charity Organizations. These organizations—types specifically defined in the tax code—can receive tax-deductible contributions from donors, and include:

- Churches, temples, synagogues, mosques, and religious organizations,
- Fraternal and veterans organizations,
- Charitable organizations such as the American Red Cross, the United Way and the like, big or small,
- Nonprofit educational organizations, colleges, and museums,
- Nonprofit hospitals and medical research organizations,
- Volunteer fire departments,
- Other nonprofit organizations with public missions such as cemetery companies, civil defense organizations, organizations that develop and maintain public parks and recreation facilities.

---

The term *charitable* (as defined in the Internal Revenue Code and/or Treasury Department Code of Regulations) is used in its generally accepted legal sense and includes:

- Relief of the poor, the distressed, or the underprivileged;
- Advancement of religion;
- Advancement of education or science;

- Erecting or maintaining public buildings, monuments, or works;
- Lessening the burdens of government;
- Lessening neighborhood tensions;
- Eliminating prejudice and discrimination;
- Defending human and civil rights secured by law; and
- Combating community deterioration and juvenile delinquency.

Note, under the Code, public charities must not engage in extensive political lobbying or ever endorse or provide funds to candidates for political office. All public charity organizations are "absolutely prohibited from directly or indirectly participating in, or intervening in, any political campaign on behalf of (or in opposition to) any candidate for elective public office." Certain activities and expenditures are okay, such as for voter education conducted in a non-partisan manner.

Nonprofit organizations that are not public charities can also accept contributions, but these are not tax-deductible by donors. These organizations do have public service missions but of a different character than the public charities.

## Lobbying (501(c)(4) Organizations)

Often 501(c)(3) organizations will form a 501(c)(4) organization so that it can be politically active. These nonprofit organizations can lobby in support of their cause and financially support candidates running for public office. Contributions and expenses for the two organizations must be kept totally separate for the 501(c)(3) to maintain its ability to receive tax-deductible contributions. The boards of the two organizations may overlap, but personnel of the 501(c)(3) organization should not do extensive work for the 501(c)(4) organization. It can get messy.

## Charity Statistics & Demographics

There are over 1,500,000 tax-exempt organizations in the U.S. Approximately 400,000 of these cannot accept tax-deductible contributions because while they have a public purpose, they are not charities as defined by the IRS. These types of organizations include civil leagues, fraternal benefit societies, business associations, labor organizations, social clubs, etc.

There are about 1,000,000 tax exempt 501(c)(3) public charities in the U.S. Of these, 400,000 have less than $25,000 in annual revenue and are not required to file reports with the government. In addition, there are 100,000 private foundations. Many times they are 501(c)(3) organizations that a wealthy family has endowed. They often fund other charitable organizations, make grants, or act like a public charity themselves.

As you would expect, the density of nonprofits mirrors population: 100,000 in California, 60,000 in New York down to 3,000 in Delaware, 3,600 in Vermont, and 2,500 in Wyoming.

### Revenue by Source

Unlike for-profit companies, nonprofit organizations have no shareholders or owners and thus no sources of money other than donations, cash generated from service operations, and borrowing.

**Revenue by Source**
**$1.7 trillion**

Approximately half of the $1.7 trillion in total revenue to nonprofits is direct health care billings by nonprofit hospitals ($850 billion), a quarter is contributions and contracts to 501(c)(3) organizations ($390 billion), a third is tuition revenue paid to educational institutions ($265 billion), membership organizations account for $100 billion, and the remaining $100 billion is from other nonprofit organizations.

Again, nonprofit revenue mirrors population: over $150 billion annually for large states like California and New York down to about $1 billion per year in small states such as Delaware, Vermont, and Wyoming.

### Individual & Foundation Giving

In 2016, American households gave over $275 billion to nonhospital charities, an average of 2% of their income after taxes. These charities received additional funds from foundations, bequests, and corporate giving totaling about $115 billion.

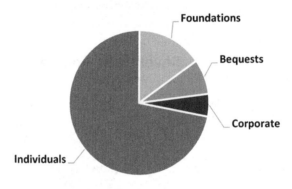

## Donations by Donor Source
### $390 billion

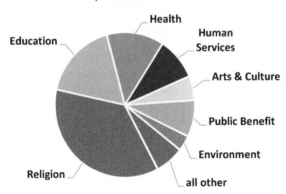

## Donations by Organization Mission
### $390 billion

## Government as a Major Donor

When you think about it, the government does its own charitable giving in the form of allowing tax deductions to individuals when they give to qualified public charities. When an individual donates to a charity, the federal government essentially pays a portion of that donation: A $1,000 donation from a donor in the highest tax bracket costs the donor only about $600 in cash. The federal government kicks in the remaining $400 in the form of a reduction in the donor's taxes. In any case, the nonprofit receives $1,000 in cash.

These charitable donations cost the federal government almost $40 billion a year in lost tax revenues.[2]

---

*Roll-up your sleeves and forge ahead.* There is knowledge and productivity to be gained and opportunities to advance your organization's mission. Despite wide diversity in donors and organizations, there are common threads in the ability to understand a nonprofit's financial picture and the fiduciary obligations of boards, managers, and staff.

Read on!

---

[2] *How the Government Gives* by Ray D. Madoff. New York Times, December 7, 2013.

# Chapter 2.
# Financial Direction, Oversight, & Control

Most of this chapter belongs in a textbook on nonprofit management. However, the topics of nonprofit financial governance and general management are so intertwined, I feel the perspective presented in this chapter is necessary. Bear with me for a while; it is only six pages.

~

Financial direction, oversight, control, and achieving productivity and desired results are team efforts in a nonprofit organization. The board provides purpose and oversight; management provides leadership and direction; staff provides boots-on-the-ground and good efforts. Donors provide money—perhaps the scarcest of resources. Each role is required in order to advance the organization's mission. Here, I am going to focus on the money trail, cowpokes!

## Special Role of the Board

The four principal responsibilities of the board of directors of a 501(c)(3) public charity are:

- **Mission, Goal, & Vision.** Defining the population that the organization will serve and its charitable reason for being;
- **Program Selection.** Determining on what and where the organization spends its money today and in the future;

- *Execution.* Hiring competent management and staff to execute its programs efficiently and effectively; and
- *Planning & Fundraising.* Assuring the organization's rosy future and continuing financial success.

Board members act as trustees of the organization's assets. They must exercise care and diligence to assure that the organization is thriving and that its finances remain sound. Board members hold a financial accountability to both stakeholders and mission. The board of directors of a nonprofit organization retains—and cannot abdicate—the ultimate responsibility for the organization's success.

## Fiduciary Duty

While board service is a voluntary act of social responsibility, board members must devote time, attention, knowledge, and skill to their duties. More than ever before, boards can expect to be held accountable for their decisions and their actions. Each board member—and especially finance committee members—holds a fiduciary responsibility for the financial viability of the nonprofit. A fiduciary is one charged with acting beneficently on behalf of those whose welfare depends on that trust. In fact, the word "fiduciary" comes from the Latin word for "trust."

Fiduciary duty requires board members to stay objective, unselfish, responsible, honest, trustworthy, and efficient in their dealings. Board members need to exercise reasonable care in all decision making, without placing the organization under unnecessary risk. Further, their personal actions should be consistent with the mission and values of the organization.

## Duty of Care, Loyalty, & Obedience[1]

Traditionally, nonprofit board members are said to have three "duties" to their organization: duty of care, duty of loyalty, and duty of obedience. Taken together, they require board members to make careful, good-faith decisions in the best interest of the organization, consistent with its public or charitable mission and independent of undue influence from any party or from their own financial interests. These duties apply to management and staff as well.

---

[1] Adapted from the Association of Governing Boards of Universities and Colleges (AGB) Statement of Fiduciary Duties of Governing Board Members. July 2015.

***Duty of Care.*** Participate in decision making in the organization. Set mission and goals and assure focus on that mission. Make sure the organization has the resources to achieve its goals and strategies. Board members should stay informed, attend meetings, be in-the-loop, and take care to look into any relevant and important information that is available when making a decision or taking an action. *Pay attention!* For example, before voting to approve a new program, board members should have a clear understanding of important issues: who will be served, what will the program cost, where will funds come from, and whether the activity exposes the organization to any special risk.

***Duty of Loyalty.*** Make decisions in the organization's and key stakeholders' best interest, putting aside any conflicting personal interests. *Put the organization and those it serves first!* Board members must make decisions with no self-dealing and with no unannounced conflicts of interest. In general, state laws require that the director disclose all relevant facts about potential conflicts or personal interests. Only noninterested directors participate in votes. If both these requirements are met , then the conflict(s) will have been avoided ("discharged" in legalese).

***Duty of Obedience.*** Honor first the mission and then donors, clients, and the government. Assure the organization complies with all state and federal laws. While dedication to mission is high, management's and staff's livelihoods are at stake. The board has no such conflict and can be more objective with much less dedication to the status quo.

## Financial Oversight

For nonprofit organizations, most everything revolves around money. Starting with a special tax status and a charter of charity, the 501(c)(3) organization assembles financial resources to be used in promoting a social mission.

The board is financially responsible to the organization's stakeholders who include the government, clients, and donors in the community they serve. The board's role is single focused in overseeing thoughtful use of resources (money and other assets) in support of mission.

Not every board member can be a financial wizard. However, every board member needs to be financially awake. It is essential to be able to read financial statements and judge their soundness. Board members are responsible for all oversight of the organization and must have the capacity to recognize the warning signs that things may not be going as hoped.

*The board's ultimate financial tasks are to both: (1) watch how money is being spent by the organization and (2) make sure there is enough of it to go around.*

### Key Elements of Oversight

If you only have a hammer, everything looks like a nail. Accounting has the appropriate tools too, so you do not end up whacking something you should not. Board members need to agree on clear guidelines and standards to measure the effectiveness of organizational accomplishments. Appropriate policies (fiscal controls, financial reports, audits, investments, capital resources, budget practices) must be in place to guide management and board decisions. See Chapters 16 and 17 for further discussions of performance measurement tools.

---

**"Assessing a nonprofit organization's financial health should be under constant review by the board of directors. Gone are the days when board members can proclaim that they do not have the financial background to comment.**

**The liabilities involved with sitting on a nonprofit board are too high to bury one's head in the sand. Every board member must take the initiative to learn how to read the organization's financial statements and reach their own conclusions on the organization's financial health."**

Adapted from *Zone of Insolvency: How Nonprofits Avoid Hidden Liabilities & Build Financial Strength* by Ron Mattocks, Wiley, 2008.

---

***Budgets.*** The board assures that budgets are in place that reflect the financial realities the organization faces. The board also assures that the budget is congruent with, and advances, the organization's mission. Approving the annual budget is a major responsibility of the board. The budget creates the framework for program management and overall administrative decisions. Securing necessary funding is part of a viable budget.

Examining financial statements regularly and comparing actual figures to the projected ones allows the board to verify that the organization stays on track. The board should question any major variances as the year progresses and take corrective action if necessary.

***Guarding Assets with Adequate Controls.*** Financial control mechanisms are not intended to detect fraud, but rather to prevent it. Ensuring clarity in job descriptions and responsibilities; defining financial and accounting procedures (signing checks, handling cash, approving expenses, outlining parameters for credit card usage); managing potential conflicts of interest with a clear policy; and requesting regular external audits are all manifestations of fiduciary responsibility.

***Overseeing Legal Obligations.*** The board verifies that all filing requirements and tax obligations (federal, state, and local) are completed. The organization must fill out Form 990 completely, and file it on time. It must regularly withhold and pay employment taxes. To avoid sanctions, the board must document and justify its executive compensation and any financial transactions.

Note, normal legal shields of corporate structure of the organization may not protect your personal assets from being seized. Directors and Officers (D&O) insurance purchased by the organization may not be adequate. You can be personally sued by other board members, clients of your organization, the government, and others for certain negligent behavior while a board member. Sorry, but see box on the next page. *It is not as bad as it sounds.*

## Role of the Finance Committee

Nonprofit boards typically create committees to focus on specific areas or complicated issues. Once the committee makes progress, these issues are brought to the entire board membership for approval or to give further guidance. Board committees should serve the needs of the board, not management or staff.

Most boards have a *finance committee* to review budgets and the organization's performance compared to budget, ensure that financial reports prepared by staff are timely and accurate, make financial policy recommendations, and report on financial conditions to the full board. In addition, larger organizations may have an *investment committee* to set investment priorities and to hire and manage investment managers, and an *audit committee* to hire outside auditors and monitor their performance and report audit results to the board. *Finance Committee members rock!*

---

# Cal Corp Code § 5231(a)

"A director shall perform the duties of a director, including duties as a member of any committee of the board upon the director may serve, in good faith, in a manner such director believes to be in the best interests of the corporation and with such care, including reasonable inquiry, as an ordinarily prudent person in a like position would use under similar circumstances."

California law and similar federal rules provide that if a volunteer director: (1) acts within the scope of his or her duties as a director, (2) does not commit gross negligence or act in wanton or reckless ways, and (3) does not engage in any self-dealing, *then a director is provided strong protections from personal liability for his/her actions.*

---

# Section B.
# Nonprofit Financial
# Statements

# Chapter 3.
# Nonprofit Accounting Rules

Why do we need accounting rules? Simply, we need a common understanding of how an organization's financial records are assembled and then reported to serve as a basis for making informed business decisions. This clarity is important in for-profit companies so that the government can collect taxes on profits. In nonprofit organizations, tax deductions that are taken by donors are the main concern, as well as assuring the public purpose.

So, who makes these rules? An alphabet soup of folks: FASB, an organization of prestigious CPAs, writes the rules called GAAP. The IRS enforces the laws and regulations that qualify organizations for nonprofit status and requires these organizations to fill out special public disclosure forms (Form 990) each year. The OMB issues auditing circulars (A-133) with auditing procedures used by organizations receiving government grants and contracts.

Need a cheat-sheet of acronyms?

- **CPA**—Certified Public Accountant
- **FASB**—Financial Accounting Standards Board
- **GAAP**—Generally Accepted Accounting Principles
- **ASU**—Accounting Standards Update
- **IRS**—U.S. Internal Revenue Service
- **OMB**—U.S. Office of Management and Budget
- **A-133**—OMB Circular A-133 Federal Audit Procedures
- **Form 990**—IRS Return of Organization Exempt from Income Tax

These rules and their proper implementation are complex. People go to college to learn them and spend years of apprenticeship figuring out how to use them. Board members, managers, and staff need a simple overview—leave the details for the professionals.

## FASB & GAAP

The Financial Accounting Standards Board (FASB) mission is "to establish and improve standards of financial accounting and reporting for guidance and education of the public, including issuers, auditors, and users of financial information."

FASB is a private, nonprofit organization made up of certified public accountants (CPAs) whose purpose is to develop generally accepted accounting principles (GAAP) for use by both nonprofit organizations and for-profit companies in the U.S. The Securities and Exchange Commission (SEC) designates FASB as the organization responsible for setting accounting standards. Periodically, FASB issues Statements of Financial Accounting Standards (SFAS), guidance documents specifically for nonprofits. *Sorry you asked?* Other countries use different rules.

## 12 Principles

What follows are the 12 most important accounting principles established by FASB and codified in GAAP. The accounting profession holds these rules as if they were commandments carved on granite tablets, so they are worth a glance.

1. *The Accounting Entity.* There is an entity—a fictional person—separate from its owners, board, management, and staff, for which financial reports can be written. The entity is often called a "company," if it is for-profit and an "organization," if it is a nonprofit.

2. *Going Concern.* Accountants assume that the lifespan of the entity will be infinite. This assumption simplifies the presentation of the financial statements, but is seldom true. If, during the review of an organization's books, the accountant has reason to believe that the organization may go bankrupt, he must issue a "qualified opinion," stating the potential for the organization's demise. Sort of an R.I.P. notice.

3. *Measurement.* Accounting counts only things that can be quantified—resources and obligations upon which there is an agreed-upon value. Perversely, this assumption leaves

out many very valuable organizational attributes, such as loyal donors, repeat clients, hard-working volunteers, and so forth.

4. *Units of Measure.* U.S. dollars are the units of value reported in the financial statements of U.S. companies. Results of any foreign operations are translated into U.S. dollars for consolidated reporting of results.

5. *Historical Cost.* What an organization owns and what it owes are recorded at their original (historical) cost with no adjustment for inflation or rise in value. The nonprofit organization can own a building valued at $50 million, yet carry it on the books at its $5 million original purchase price (less accumulated depreciation), a gross understatement of value.

Why do accountants demand that we obviously under-state assets? Well it is an "accounting fiction," but the easiest thing to do. You do not have to appraise and reap-praise.

6. *Materiality.* Materiality refers to the relative importance of different financial information. All transactions that "materially" affect the financial condition of the organiza-tion must be reported. Materiality is typically calculated as a percentage of total assets, revenue, or expenses. What is material for a local food pantry is merely a rounding error for the American Red Cross.

7. *Estimates and Judgments.* Complexity and uncertainty make any measurement less than exact. Estimates and judgments must often be made in financial reporting. It is okay to make a reasonable and conservative estimate if: (a) that is the best you can do and (b) any expected error would not matter much anyway. However, accountants should use the same estimating methods all the time. *Pick a horse and ride it.*

8. *Consistency.* Sometimes identical transactions can be accounted for differently. You could do it this way or that way, depending upon some preference. The principle of con-sistency states that each individual enterprise must choose a single method of reporting, state it explicitly, and then use it consistently over time. You cannot switch back and forth. *Same horse issue.*

9. *Conservatism.* Accountants have a measurement bias, preferring understatement of assets and overvaluation of liabilities. They are glass half-empty kind of folks.

10. *Periodicity.* Accountants assume that the life of a corporation can be divided into convenient periods of time for which financial transactions can be recorded, reviewed, and reported. Convenient periods are usually a month, quarter or year. These periods are called fiscal periods. Many nonprofit's fiscal year start on April, July or October 1, not on January 1, which is most common for profit-making companies. Why? Midyear audits are cheaper because accounting firms have more time on their hands during the summer than at year-end.

11. *Substance Over Form.* Accountants report the economic substance of a transaction rather than its form. For example, an equipment lease that is really a purchase dressed in a "lease costume" must be recorded as a purchase and not as a lease on financial statements. This substance over form rule requires that: if it looks like a duck and quacks like a duck—then accountants must report it as a duck.

12. *Basis of Presentation.* The accounting "basis" of a set of financial statements is defined by the rules that determine how and when revenue and expense are reported on the Statement of Activities. Choose either cash or accrual basis.

   In *cash-basis accounting*, the organization reports revenue in the period received and deducts expenses in the period paid. The financial statements work just like a check register; cash in, cash out.

   In *accrual-basis accounting* the organization reports revenue in the period earned although it may not receive actual payment until a later period. Expenses are recorded when they are incurred, not when the actual cash is paid.

~

   In for-profit accounting, revenue is recorded when a product is shipped to a customer or services are rendered. Expenses (cost of goods) are recorded at the same time thus "matched" with revenue. The matching principle allows for a more objective analysis of profitability. By recognizing revenue and costs together, the business can see how much money was spent to generate that revenue.

In nonprofit accounting, revenue is recognized when contributions and gifts are made and the cash arrives. Pledges are recognized as revenue when they are committed even though cash may not arrive until a later period. See Chapter 4.

Nonprofit program services revenue and expense and revenue and expense from grants and contracts are recorded in a similar fashion to that in for-profit companies. Other expenses are not matched to revenue and are recorded when the organization has incurred the obligation to pay, not when actual payment is made. Again, see Chapter 4 and also Chapter 5.

Most medium-sized and all large nonprofits are required to use the accrual basis of accounting to maintain their books. Small nonprofits often use a cash basis. It is simpler than accrual bookkeeping and requires less accounting knowledge—which may be scarce in small organizations. However, accrual basis accounting often provides a better representation of the financial status of an organization.

### Goals of Nonprofit vs. For-Profit Accounting

The basic accounting differences between nonprofit organizations and for-profit companies are:

- For-profit accounting is designed to properly compute profit so that the government can tax it. A for-profit company's financial statements are structured to provide owners and investors with useful information, while not giving away competitive secrets.

- Nonprofit accounting and financial reporting is designed so that donors, the government, and other stakeholders can see how monies are spent in pursuit of mission goals. Nonprofit financial reports are public record for all to see.

- Profits and retained earnings are "owned" by a for-profit company's shareholders and can be distributed to them as dividends, whereas surplus and total net assets are owned by the nonprofit organization itself, as an entity, and can be used only for the advancement of its mission.

There are different expectations when buying widgets versus helping the homeless. If you buy a product from a manufacturer, you do not care what they do with the money if the selling price is right. They can spend it on salaries, research, marketing, or even administration. It does not matter.

However, in the nonprofit world, donors and other funders want to know exactly what happens to their money. Sometimes it feels within the organization that every dollar has to have a flag attached to it so donors (and the government) can follow it through the system. Not only do donors care, but they may even sue the charity if funding gets used differently from their stated desires when making a restricted contribution.

## Donation Records

For all cash, check, or credit card donations, the nonprofit organization must provide the donor a written communication as a record of the contribution. Written records prepared by the donor (such as check registers or personal notations) are not sufficient to support charitable contribution tax deductions. However, bank records (canceled checks, or credit card statements) are sufficient provided they show the date paid, the name of the charity, and the amount of the payment.

A donor claiming a deduction of $250 or more is required to obtain and keep a contemporaneous written acknowledgment for a charitable contribution. For claimed contribution of property valued at over $5,000, generally an appraisal prepared by a qualified appraiser must be obtained.

If a donor gives a charity $100 and receives a concert ticket valued at $40, the donor has made a *quid pro quo* contribution. In this example, the charitable contribution portion of the payment is $60. A charitable organization must provide a written disclosure statement to donors of a *quid pro quo* contribution in excess of $75.

## Staff Responsibilities

Simply, follow the rules. Have a system of checks and balances, policies, and procedures to help you do so. Enter each transaction at the right time. Enter the right amount. Enter in the right account. Keep detailed records supporting each and every transaction. Summarize and present records of accounts correctly. Moreover, do all of this consistently.

Maybe not so simple, but your organization depends on you. The next chapters will give you all of the information and the knowledge to do it right. Really!

*"And this is our department of experimental accounting."*

# Chapter 4.
# Statement of Activities

A nonprofit's *Statement of Activities* shows money coming into the organization (revenue) and money going out (expenses). The money left over when you subtract expenses from revenue is called *surplus* or, more formally, the organization's *change in net assets* over a specified time period (for example, a month, a three-month quarter, or a year). All financial revenue-generating or expense-making transactions are summarized in the *Statement of Activities* using the accounting equation shown in the box below.

A nonprofit organization's *Statement of Activities* is analogous to a for-profit company's *Income Statement* (sometimes called the company's *Profit & Loss Statement)*. GAAP defines the structure and content presented in the statement structure, for both nonprofit organizations and for-profit companies.

---

*— Statement of Activities —*

**REVENUE − EXPENSES = CHANGE IN NET ASSETS**

*...for a specified time period*

Generating revenue increases *change in net assets* and incurring expenses lowers *change in net assets. Change in net assets* is recorded for a specified time period and can be a *surplus* (profit) or a *deficit* (loss).

---

In nonprofit organizations, if revenue is greater than expenses, then *net assets* increases (good); if revenue is less than expenses, *net assets* decreases (bad). In for-profit companies, if revenue is greater than expenses, then the company makes a *profit* (good); if revenue is less than expenses, then the company suffers a *loss* (bad). Both nonprofit organizations and for-profit companies need an excess of revenue over expenses to (1) stay solvent (have cash in the bank to pay bills) and (2) provide capital for investments required to grow.

The IRS and individual states *do not* collect taxes on a nonprofit organization's *change in net assets* (surplus). Being subject-to income tax is the major financial difference between a for-profit company and a nonprofit organization.

*Net assets* and *profits* differ in that the *net assets* of a nonprofit organization belong to the organization itself and may only be used in support of the organization's public mission. In contrast, all the *profits* made by a for-profit company belong to its owners (shareholders). These *profits* are available for distribution as dividends to these shareholders. Nonprofit organizations have no owners and can make no such distributions. Nonprofit organizations are required by IRS rules to serve a public purpose, whereas a for-profit company serves its owners.

$\sim$

Using information presented in the organization's *Statement of Activities*, board members and management should ask:

- Is there a growing demand for our products and services?

- Are our programs financially sustainable? Do they provide us with the necessary surplus required for growth?

- Are our fundraising efforts effective and efficient?

- Are our management and overhead expenses appropriate for the tasks at hand or are they excessive?

$\sim$

See the simplified "family" example on the facing page. Then read the line-by-line discussion of the *Statement of Activities* of a nonprofit organization beginning on the page following.

# Statement of Activities

One day (the specified time period), you give your son $2.50 in cash to take to school to buy a nutritious morning snack and a wholesome lunch. That amount is *revenue* on your son's *Statement of Activities* for the period. In fact, it is *restricted revenue* since the donor (you) has placed conditions on how the money is to be used. No candy!

Your son does not buy a snack that day, but he does spend $2.00 for lunch. This $2.00 is his *expense* for the period and we post the amount on his *Statement of Activities*.

In summary, your son has received $2.50 in revenue and has $2.00 in expense for the period. He has 50¢ left in his pocket. Nonprofit accountants call this left over 50¢ the *change in net asset*s for the period (also called *surplus*).

Your son's *Statement of Activities* for the period looks like this (simplified):

| | |
|---|---|
| **REVENUE** | **$2.50** |
| **EXPENSES** | **2.00** |
| **CHANGE IN NET ASSETS** | **$0.50** |
| **BEGINNING NET ASSETS** | **$0.00** |
| **ENDING NET ASSETS** | **$0.50** |

Note: REVENUE minus EXPENSES equals CHANGE IN NET ASSETS. BEGINNING NET ASSETS plus CHANGE IN NET ASSETS equals ENDING NET ASSETS. Voilà!

Another note: See page 37 for what the single and double lines mean.

35

# STATEMENT OF ACTIVITIES

*for the period*

|  | Ⓑ WITHOUT DONOR RESTRICTIONS | Ⓒ WITH DONOR RESTRICTIONS |  |
|---|---|---|---|
| Ⓐ **REVENUE** | | | |
| Ⓓ CONTRIBUTIONS & GIFTS | | | $ 0 |
| Ⓔ PROGRAM SERVICES REVENUE | | | 0 |
| Ⓕ GRANTS & CONTRACTS | | | 0 |
| Ⓖ OTHER REVENUE | | | 0 |
| Ⓗ **TOTAL REVENUE** | $ 0 | $ 0 | $ 0 |
| Ⓘ **EXPENSES** | | | |
| Ⓙ FUNDRAISING | | | 0 |
| Ⓚ PROGRAM SERVICES | | | 0 |
| Ⓛ GRANTS & CONTRACTS | | | 0 |
| Ⓜ MANAGEMENT & GENERAL | | | 0 |
| Ⓝ **TOTAL EXPENSES** | $ 0 | | $ 0 |
| Ⓞ **CHANGE IN NET ASSETS** | | | $ 0 |
| Ⓟ **BEGINNING NET ASSETS** | | | 0 |
| Ⓠ **ENDING NET ASSETS** | | | $ 0 |

Note, entries are made only into the boxed elements. The other statement lines are just additions or subtractions of boxed entry lines.

## Statement Structure & Function

Review the sample *Statement of Activities* structure on the facing page. Match the letters on each line of the sample statement with the letters and definitions that follow. By the time you have reviewed each line and read each definition, you will have achieved a basic understanding of this financial statement.

∼

Note that entries are made on the *Statement of Activities* only into the boxed elements shown on the facing page. The other statement lines are just additions and subtractions of boxed entry lines. A single line in the statement means that the above grouped numbers are added and the resulting subtotal is shown below that line. See the lines above both TOTAL REVENUE and TOTAL EXPENSES.

The line above CHANGE IN NET ASSETS indicates that the above section TOTAL EXPENSES is subtracted from the section TOTAL REVENUE to yield CHANGE IN NET ASSETS. The double line below ENDING NET ASSETS shows the end of the statement. The lines clarify where arithmetic calculations have been made.

 **REVENUE** is both: (1) money coming into the organization during the period, and (2) promises to give to the organization (pledges) made during the period, but to be actually paid in cash in a future period. REVENUE—the top line on the *Statement of Activities*—lists money by source (for example, contributions, program services revenue, grants, and so forth) and by any type of restriction placed by donors dictating a specific use for the funds.

Different nonprofit organizations have different sources of revenue. A museum would have membership and admission fees, whereas, a university would have tuition payments and research grants and a hospital would have room and medical services charges. These major revenue sources would have separate lines on the *Statement of Activities*.

***Revenue Recognition.*** Accounting standards dictate when revenue is recognized (*recorded* or *posted*) on the *Statement of Activities*. For contributions and gifts, revenue is recorded when: (1) cash actually comes in the door, or (2) a donor makes an irrevocable pledge to fund a specific dollar donation at a specified date in the future. Expenses, on the other hand, are most often recorded when they occur. More later.

***Donated Services.*** Accounting standards dictate that if a donated service would need to be purchased if it had not been donated, then the fair market value of the service should be simultaneously recorded: (1) as gift revenue and (2) an equal expense on the organization's *Statement of Activities.* Recording both revenue and expense is a *wash transaction* that does not change the value of NET ASSETS. Note, the value of these services is not tax-deductible by professionals or tradespeople donating services. Otherwise, the IRS thinks too much hanky-panky tax deductions would be possible.

Examples of donated services include: (1) a software professional helping to program the organization's computer systems, (2) a carpenter helping to configure offices, (3) a lawyer donating essential legal work, and so forth. Note, the value of work performed by nonprofessional volunteers assisting with events, answering telephones, stuffing envelopes for a marketing campaign, performing general office duties, distributing food, and so forth, is **NOT** recorded as revenue on the nonprofit organization's *Statement of Activities.*

***Donated Goods.*** Donations of goods (such as furniture, a car, a computer, and so forth) are recorded as gifts at fair market value on the *Statement of Activities* and may be tax-deductible at that value by the donor.

**Ⓑ** **REVENUE WITHOUT DONOR RESTRICTIONS** means contributions (or pledges) that the organization can use for any purpose the organization so chooses (but then only in furtherance of its mission). REVENUE W/O DONOR RESTRICTIONS is the *unconditional, nonreciprocal transfer of assets* by a donor to a nonprofit organization. Once given, the donor cannot take the money back or dictate the money's use.

**Ⓒ** **REVENUE WITH DONOR RESTRICTIONS** means that the *donor* has placed either a short-term use restriction on the money donated or a permanent use restriction (endowment). A use restriction most often specifies how and when the donor wants the money spent. An example would be restrictions to spend the contributed funds by delivering a specified social service over the next three years.

REVENUE WITH DONOR RESTRICTIONS for CONTRIBUTIONS & GIFTS must be reported as REVENUE in the period received (or pledged) even though the spending conditions imposed are not yet fulfilled. Most often, the expenses associated with programs are recorded in the EXPENSES section of the *Statement of Activities* when they are spent, perhaps in the later period. Not "matching" revenue with its associated expenses is a unique accounting convention for nonprofit organizations. For-profit companies must match revenue with expense on their *Income Statement* by reporting both revenue and associated expenses in the same period.

The FASB decided that clearly presenting the restrictions on revenue donated to nonprofit organizations is more important than is matching that revenue with expense. Revenue and associated expense matching is very important in calculating taxable profit in a for-profit company, but is not an issue for nontaxed nonprofits.

Donors can give funds to be maintained in perpetuity as an investment (endowment) for the benefit of the organization and its mission. These donations may not be spent. However, any interest generated by endowment funds may become REVENUE W/O DONOR RESTRICTIONS for spending at the organization's discretion. Some nonprofit organizations have very large endowments (for example Harvard University at $32 billion); some have small endowments (for example the Cambridge, Massachusetts Historical Society at $489 thousand); and some have none at all.

 CONTRIBUTIONS & GIFTS REVENUE made to the organization are recorded on the *Statement of Activities* either when: (1) cash is received from a donor or (2) a promise to give cash at a later date is made by a donor. These pledges are formal and specific *promises to give*. Both contributions and pledges are made expecting nothing in return (except there may be restrictions on use).

This recognition of pledges as revenue in the period the promise to give is made is very different from for-profit company accounting where revenue is recorded, *not* when an "order" for products is placed, but rather when the goods are actually shipped to the customer.

 PROGRAM SERVICES REVENUE comes in when the nonprofit organization provides a product or service to the public. The money received is recorded on the *Statement of Activities* as PROGRAM SERVICES REVENUE, and often called an *exchange transaction*. In effect, the nonprofit organization "exchanges" its products or services for cash paid by the receiver of the products or services. *Exchange transactions*

are purchases of goods or services and, thus, are not contributions or gifts. Remember, contributions and gifts are nonreciprocal, meaning the donor makes the contribution expecting nothing in return.

Just because goods and services are purchased from a nonprofit organization, it does not mean that the nonprofit organization is jeopardizing its nonprofit status. Nonprofit organizations often sell goods and services that support their public missions. The nonprofit organizations may even generate an increase in net assets (surplus) from the transaction, analogous to profit for a for-profit company.

Different nonprofits have different revenue types. Nonprofit organizations such as hospitals, receive most of their revenue as PROGRAM SERVICES REVENUE (patient fees), whereas scientific research organizations receive most of their revenue as GRANTS & CONTRACTS REVENUE.

Both program services revenue and expenses are recorded on the *Statement of Activities* when the services are rendered (and the customer receives an invoice) or the expenses are incurred (due as payable) regardless of when cash is received or the bills are paid. These invoiced amounts become ACCOUNTS RECEIVABLE and the expense amounts become ACCOUNTS PAYABLE in the *Statement of Financial Position*. The wonders of accrual-based accounting! See the next chapter.

⒡ GRANTS & CONTRACTS REVENUE comes mostly from governmental agencies and other charitable organizations and foundations. These grants and contracts are usually: (1) for a specific purpose, (2) to be performed in a specific time period, and (3) directly related to the recipient nonprofit organization's skills and charitable mission.

The way revenue and expense for grants and contracts is recorded in financial statements depends on the fine print in the agreements. Some grants are really an outright gift of funds and are recorded as contributions. Other grants and contracts are best regarded as *fee-for-service* exchange transactions where the grantor gives money to the nonprofit organization to provide specific goods or to perform specific services with a public purpose.

But, most often, GRANTS & CONTRACT REVENUE is recorded on the *Statement of Activities* when the terms and conditions have been fulfilled (i.e. the work has been performed satisfactorily). Expenses associated with the work are then "matched" to revenue and recorded. Note contract conditions are different from gift restrictions and thus the different accounting treatments of revenue and expense restrictions between the two types of revenue.

Special compliance audits (called *Single Audits* or *A-133 Audits*) are required if the organization receives sizable federal government grants (over $500,000 per year). Foundation donors may impose their own reporting requirements on the nonprofit organization as specified as part of the contract.

---

# Restrictions vs. Conditions

Contract *terms and conditions* are different from gift *restrictions* and thus the different accounting treatments of revenue and expense recording between these two types of revenue.

**Restrictions.** Big donors—bless their generous hearts—often put restrictions on how their contributions may be spent. These restrictions *must be honored* by the nonprofit organization. It is a commitment. Further, the organization must set up systems and procedures to make sure that restricted contributions are actually used as the donor wishes. This record keeping is mandated by accounting standards as well as the IRS, so you really have to do it right. But, since the contributions are fully funded and cannot be taken back, accounting standards require that you record contributions and gifts when received.

**Conditions.** Terms and conditions are different than restrictions. Contract conditions must be met before payment is due and can be received. Revenue is contingent on performance. Accounting standards say that this revenue can only be recorded when it is a sure thing, that is, after you have performed the work and satisfied the contract conditions.

---

**OTHER REVENUE** is revenue received from sources not listed as separate line items. If revenue from a source type is large, it really should have its own line on the *Statement of Activities*. Examples of other types of revenue lines that could be included separately in statements are membership fees, ticket sales, auction proceeds, revenue from special events, advertisement sales, contributed goods or services (at fair market value), and so forth.

**TOTAL REVENUE** is the sum of all the different types of revenue. Note, a horizontal line on financial statements means that the items above the line are added and presented as a total below the line.

TOTAL REVENUE ⒣ = ⒟ + ⒠ + ⒡ + ⒢

**EXPENSES** are money spent by the organization. In *accrual basis accounting* (used in most medium and all large nonprofit organizations), expenses are recorded on the *Statement of Activities* when the organization incurs an "obligation to pay," not when the cash is actually paid. Expenses recorded, but to be paid in the future, are shown on an additional financial statement, the *Statement of Financial Position,* as ACCOUNTS PAYABLE or ACCRUED EXPENSES. More later in Chapter 5.

In *cash basis accounting*, expenses are recorded in the *Statement of Activities* when paid in cash, irrespective of when goods or services were received by the organization—just like your checkbook.

———

EXPENSES shown on the *Statement of Activities* are categorized by expense type. See the following:

**FUNDRAISING EXPENSES** are all the money (including human resources costs) that the organization spent soliciting contributions, gifts, grants, and contracts. Fundraising is often called *organizational development* to mask its real purpose—to raise money from donors.

**PROGRAM SERVICES EXPENSE** aggregates the expenditures the organization makes to provide goods and services in fulfillment of its mission. The biggest expense type in PROGRAM SERVICES EXPENSE is often human resources for salaries, wages, and benefits.

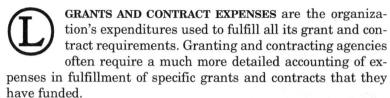

**GRANTS AND CONTRACT EXPENSES** are the organization's expenditures used to fulfill all its grant and contract requirements. Granting and contracting agencies often require a much more detailed accounting of expenses in fulfillment of specific grants and contracts that they have funded. Generally, GRANTS & CONTRACT EXPENSES are "matched," that is, recorded at the same time as the associated revenue.

**MANAGEMENT, ADMINISTRATIVE & GENERAL EXPENSES** are money spent on management, accounting, finance, computer operations, rent, utilities, and other expenses that are difficult to assign to the specific functions. MANAGEMENT, ADMINISTRATIVE & GENERAL EXPENSES are often referred to as *overhead*. Sometimes it is necessary to allocate a portion of overhead to certain program services reporting, especially for government grants and contracts. There is an ongoing debate in nonprofit circles about what constitutes appropriate levels of overhead expense. See how overhead is reported in the *Statement of Functional Expenses* discussed in Chapter 7.

**TOTAL EXPENSES** is the sum of all expenses for the period. Just as with TOTAL REVENUE, the horizontal line means the items above the line are added and presented as a total below the line.

TOTAL EXPENSES Ⓝ = Ⓙ + Ⓚ + Ⓛ + Ⓜ

**CHANGE IN NET ASSETS** is simply the difference between the organization's TOTAL REVENUE and TOTAL EXPENSES for the period (a surplus or a deficit). In a for-profit company, this is call profit or loss. Note, small increases in expenses or small decreases in revenue can turn a surplus into a deficit.

CHANGE IN NET ASSETS Ⓞ = Ⓗ - Ⓝ

The circle diagrams shown on the next page, represent by area, REVENUE (here for example $100) minus EXPENSES (here for example, set at $98). Thus, CHANGE IN NET ASSETS (what is left over) is a $2 "crescent" peeking out of the revenue-sized circle.

If expenses were only $2 higher, there would be no surplus for the period. If expenses were $3 higher, there would be a loss. Achieving a positive CHANGE IN NET ASSETS is very sensitive to small changes in TOTAL REVENUE and TOTAL EXPENSES.

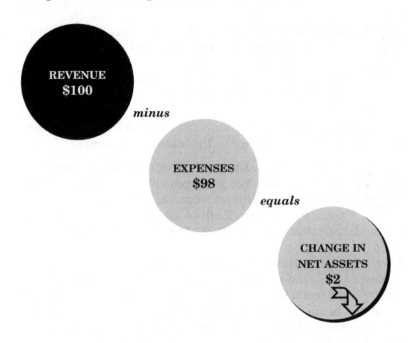

BEGINNING NET ASSETS is the accumulated annual CHANGE IN NET ASSETS of the organization since its inception. This amount is the sum of NET ASSETS W/O RESTRICTIONS and NET ASSETS WITH DONOR RESTRICTIONS shown on the *Statement of Financial Position* written for the prior accounting period. See Chapter 5.

ENDING NET ASSETS shown in this period's *Statement of Activities* is simply the sum of the BEGINNING NET ASSETS at the start of the accounting period plus the CHANGE IN NET ASSETS generated by the organization during the period. The double line below ENDING NET ASSETS indicates that the line item is a final summary.

$$\text{ENDING NET ASSETS } \textcircled{Q} = \textcircled{O} + \textcircled{P}$$

Form 990 Return of Organization Exempt from Income Tax, a nonprofit organization's publicly available annual IRS tax filing, shows (in aggregate) the nonprofit organization's *Statement of Activities* for the year including schedules Part VIII Statement of Revenue, Part IX Expenses, and Part XI Reconciliation of Net Assets. See Chapter 20 for more details.

Two more major statements and one specialized one to go! Later chapters in this section will define the *Statement of Financial Position, the Statement of Cash Flows,* and the *Statement of Functional Expenses.*

# Chapter 5.
# Statement of Financial Position

A nonprofit's *Statement of Financial Position* summarizes the organization's financial strength at a point in time, such as a month end, quarter end, or year end. The statement reports what the organization:

- owns today...its *assets,*
- owes today...its *liabilities* and,
- the accumulated annual surpluses and deficits since the organization's inception...its so-called *net assets.*

---

*— Statement of Financial Position —*

**ASSETS = LIABILITIES + NET ASSETS**

*...at a specified moment in time.*

A nonprofit organization's *Statement of Financial Position* is analogous in structure and content to a for-profit company's *Balance Sheet.* The major difference between the two types of statements is that *net assets* are reported on the nonprofit's *Statement of Financial Position* while *shareholders' equity* is reported on the *Balance Sheet.* Nonprofit organizations have no shareholders and thus no shareholders' equity.

---

The *Statement of Financial Position* describes the resources (*assets*) the nonprofit organization has available to employ in support of its mission. Further, the statement shows the allocation of those resources by type and amount. The statement also shows what it owes to others (*liabilities*). *Net assets* is what is left over. By definition, the *Statement of Financial Position* must always be in balance with *assets* equaling *liabilities* plus *net assets*.

Note, the *Statement of Activities* (described in Chapter 4) shows the organization's CHANGE IN NET ASSETS for a time period, the *Statement of Financial Position* described in this chapter, sums all prior periods' CHANGE IN NET ASSETS since the organization's inception.

## What does "strong" mean?

A "strong" financial position is at the core of all successful nonprofit organizations (and all for-profit companies, for that matter). A financially strong organization has the resources to reinvent itself as required by circumstances. Very few organizations remain stagnant for long. They either grow or decline.

Using information presented on the organization's *Statement of Financial Position*, the Board can ask and then answer:

- How risky is the financial structure of the organization?
- Does it have excess debt?
- Does the organization have enough cash on hand to pay its bills when they come due?
- Is the organization efficiently collecting debts it is owed?
- Is the organization's inventory bloated and potentially out-of-date?
- Are the organization's net assets growing with time and making the organization better able to invest in its future and so forth?

∼

See the simplified "family" example of the *Statement of Financial Position* on the facing page. Then, read on.

## *Statement of Financial Position*

Remember, you gave your son $2.50 in cash one day (the specified *period*) to take to school to buy a nutritious morning snack and a very wholesome lunch. He only spent $2.00, so his *Statement of Activities* (see Chapter 4) shows an *increase in net assets* (sometimes called *surplus*) of 50¢ for the period (the day). Further, in his *Statement of Cash Flows* (see Chapter 6) his ending cash was that leftover 50¢. Now let us look at his *Statement of Financial Position* (always written as of the end of the period, in your son's case, bedtime that evening).

At the end of the period, your son's *Statement of Financial Position* looks like this (simplified):

*ASSETS* ————— *LIABILITIES & NET ASSETS* ——

   CASH    50¢     NET ASSETS    50¢

By definition, the *Statement of Financial Position* must be in-balance, with TOTAL ASSETS equal to TOTAL LIABILITIES plus NET ASSETS.

# STATEMENT OF FINANCIAL POSITION

*as of the period ending date*

## Ⓐ ASSETS

- Ⓑ CASH
- Ⓒ ACCOUNTS RECEIVABLE
- Ⓓ INVENTORIES
- Ⓔ PREPAID EXPENSES
- Ⓕ PLEDGES RECEIVABLE
- Ⓖ INVESTMENTS
- Ⓗ PP&E (NET)

Ⓘ TOTAL ASSETS          $ 0

## Ⓙ LIABILITIES & NET ASSETS

- Ⓚ ACCOUNTS PAYABLE
- Ⓛ SHORT TERM DEBT
- Ⓜ LONG TERM DEBT
- Ⓝ ACCRUED EXPENSES
- Ⓞ NET ASSETS:
  - Ⓟ W/O DONOR RESTRICTIONS
  - Ⓠ WITH DONOR RESTRICTIONS

Ⓡ TOTAL LIABILITIES & NET ASSETS          $ 0

Note, entries are made only into the boxed elements. The other statement lines are just additions or subtractions of boxed entry lines.

## Statement Structure & Function

Review the sample *Statement of Financial Position* structure on the facing page. Match the letters on each line of the sample statement with the letters and definitions that follow below. By the time you have reviewed each line and read each definition, you will have achieved a basic understanding of this financial statement.

～

Note that entries are made on the *Statement of Financial Position* only into the boxed elements shown on the facing page. The other statement lines are just subtotals and totals. A single line in the statement means that the above grouped numbers are added and the resulting subtotal is shown below that line.

The three main financial statements all interact. Some entries on the *Statement of Financial Position* come from one of the other financial statements. For example, CASH here on this *Statement of Financial Position* comes from ENDING CASH on *the Statement of Cash Flows* discussed in the next chapter.

～

 ASSETS are everything the organization owns—cash in the bank, inventory, equipment, buildings—all of it. Assets are also certain "rights" of the company that have a monetary value, such as the right to collect cash from clients who owe money to the organization (ACCOUNTS RECEIVABLE). Assets also include PLEDGES RECEIVABLE from donors who have pledged contributions but have yet to fund them. PREPAID EXPENSES (services paid for by the organization but not yet used) also are included in assets.

The different asset types are listed on the *Statement of Financial Position* in order of descending liquidity—the speed with which each type of asset can be turned into actual dollars and cents. CASH is at the top of the liquidity list. Land and buildings are at the bottom of the list, taking the longest to turn into CASH.

 CASH is the ultimate "liquid asset," and includes on-demand deposits in a bank as well as any stray change hanging around in the petty-cash drawer. When the organization's treasurer writes a check to pay a bill, the money comes out of CASH assets.

**C** ACCOUNTS RECEIVABLE is money owed to the organization from its clients and customers (the "accounts") who were provided goods or services on credit and who have yet to pay. Organizations that charge fees for their services usually provide those services before payments are made. The monies owed by clients and customers are aggregated and shown here as ACCOUNTS RECEIVABLE.

**D** INVENTORIES include products ready for sale to customers and also any materials that will be used in performing services for clients. As INVENTORY is sold, the amounts sold reduce INVENTORY and is added to CASH. As INVENTORY is used by the organization in performing service, that value is subtracted from INVENTORY and added as a program expense in the *Statement of Activities*.

**E** PREPAID EXPENSES represent bills for services that the organization has paid with CASH, but for which the services have yet to be provided. For example, in January we paid with CASH the entire year's insurance premium. Now, it is the first of April, and we have received only three months of the benefit of protection. This cost (one-fourth of the premium paid) will be recorded on the *Statement of Activities* as an EXPENSE. The remaining nine months of premium would be presented here as the asset PREPAID EXPENSE.

**F** PLEDGES RECEIVABLE represent contributions and gifts amounts that have been committed (pledged) to the organization by outside donors, but not yet paid by the donor in cash. In nonprofit accounting, these PLEDGES RECEIVABLE have already been listed as REVENUE on the *Statement of Activities* when pledged, and NET ASSETS have been increased by that amount in the *Statement of Financial Position*.

When money is received, CASH will increase and PLEDGES RECEIVABLE will decrease by the same amount, thus keeping the *Statement of Financial Position* in balance.

～

Note, other asset types that are expected to become actual cash through the organization's regular business operations within the next twelve months, such as ACCOUNTS RECEIVABLE, INVENTORIES, PREPAID EXPENSES, and PLEDGES RECEIVABLE—plus CASH are called the organization's *current assets*.

**INVESTMENTS** is the value of any stock, bonds, or other property held for financial gain by the organization. Usually any funds held in the endowment are included here.

 **PP&E (NET)** is the organization's property, plant, and equipment, valued at: (a) original purchase prices (*historic cost*) of any land owned by the organization plus (b) the *net book value* of the organization's long lived physical assets. Note, land is not depreciated under GAAP.

*Net book value* is computed as *historic cost* minus the accumulated depreciation for the item since its date of purchase. Depreciation is an annual charge to the *Statement of Activities* that lowers net asset value for a physical asset by an amount accounting for the drop in value of the asset during the year.

Note, depreciation is a *non-cash expense* meaning that, while it is shown in the *Statement of Activities* as an expense for the period, no cash actually leaves the organization during that reported period. The organization paid-in-full for the item when it was originally purchased and the total amount of cash spent was posted at that time in the *Statement of Cash Flows*.

 **TOTAL ASSETS** are everything the organization owns. The *Statement of Financial Position* must always be in balance so TOTAL ASSETS equals TOTAL LIABILITIES plus NET ASSETS.

**TOTAL ASSETS** Ⓘ = Ⓑ + Ⓒ + Ⓓ + Ⓔ + Ⓕ + Ⓖ + Ⓗ

 **LIABILITIES** are financial obligations of the organization, such as money it owes to lenders, to suppliers, to employees, and to others. LIABILITIES are listed by type in the LIABILITIES & NET ASSETS section of the *Statement of Financial Position* and ordered by how soon they will need to be paid. If the values of individual categories are large, they would be shown on a separate line.

**ACCOUNTS PAYABLE** are amounts owed by the organization to vendors or creditors for goods and services rendered. Unpaid bills, wages, taxes, and so forth are listed in this line.

**SHORT-TERM DEBT** is money owed by the organization to a bank or other creditors scheduled to be repaid within 12 months from the date of the *Statement of Financial Position.* The principal plus interest due within 12 months is included in the current liabilities section of the *Statement of Financial Position.*

Debt may allow the organization to amplify its activities in support of its mission. However, interest is an added expense and it—plus some of the original loan amount—needs to be repaid according to a schedule. The organization must have the money available when these loans come due.

ACCOUNTS PAYABLE and SHORT-TERM DEBT are referred to as the organization's *current liabilities.* Current liabilities will be paid-off within the next 12 months with cash generated by the organization collecting *current assets* (CASH, ACCOUNTS RECEIVABLES, INVENTORIES, PREPAID EXPENSES, and PLEDGES RECEIVABLE).

---

## *Net Working Capital*

The organization's "net working capital" is its *current assets* minus its *current liabilities.* Having an adequate amount of working capital is an indication the organization will be able to pay its regular operating bills when they come due. If the organization cannot pay its bills when due, it is *bankrupt, insolvent, tapped-out.* Can happen. Watch out!

---

**LONG-TERM DEBT** is the portion a loan due later than 12 months from the date of the *Statement of Financial Position.* Mortgages are the most common form of long-term debt.

**ACCRUED EXPENSES** is money owed by the organization to employees and others whose services have been rendered but for which the organization has yet to pay. Examples include wages and salaries owed but not yet paid, legal and accounting fees incurred but not yet billed us by the service provider, and so forth. If billed, these ACCRUED EXPENSES would be ACCOUNTS PAYABLE.

**NET ASSETS** is the excess of revenue over expenses (CHANGE IN NET ASSETS from the *Statement of Activities*) accumulated for all the years that the organization has been operating. This amount would be called the "retained earnings" on a for-profit company's *Balance Sheet.* NET ASSETS are shown in two basic classes, Ⓞ and Ⓟ.

**NET ASSETS WITHOUT DONOR RESTRICTIONS** are contributions (or pledges) that the organization can use for any purpose to further its mission. CONTRIBUTIONS & GIFTS REVENUE donated without donor restrictions (the source of NET ASSETS W/O DONOR RESTRICTIONS from the *Statement of Activities*) is the *unconditional, nonreciprocal transfer of assets* by a donor to a nonprofit organization. Once given, the donor cannot take the money back and cannot dictate its use.

**NET ASSETS WITH DONOR RESTRICTIONS** is the portion of NET ASSETS of the organization the use of which is limited by any donor-imposed restrictions or contract terms and conditions.

Donor-imposed use restrictions most often specify how the donor wants the money spent. These restrictions are requirements that an organization perform a specific program at a specific time in the future. An example would be spending the contributed funds by delivering a specified social service over the next three years. Once the organization fulfills these use restrictions and spends the money, CASH and NET ASSETS WITH DONOR RESTRICTIONS are lowered by the same amount keeping the *Statement of Financial Position* in balance.

This category also includes donations made to the organization's *endowment.* Donors give funds (or other assets such as a building) to be maintained in perpetuity as investments for the benefit of the organization. These donations may not be spent, but most often any interest generated by endowment funds becomes unrestricted revenue able to be spent.

**TOTAL LIABILITIES & NET ASSETS** are everything the organization owes and owns. The *Statement of Financial Position* must always be in balance so that TOTAL LIABILITIES & NET ASSETS always equals TOTAL ASSETS.

**TOTAL LIABILITIES & NET ASSETS** Ⓡ = Ⓚ + Ⓛ + Ⓜ + Ⓝ + Ⓟ + Ⓠ

One more major statement to go! The following chapter in this section will describe the *Statement of Cash Flows*. Then, we will discuss the specialized *Statement of Functional Expenses*, an especially useful tool in assessing the financial viability of the organization's individual programs and in collecting the data required for government audits of grants and contracts.

~

The organization's publicly available annual IRS tax filing "Form 990 Return of Organization Exempt from Income Tax: Part X Bal*ance Sheet shows a nonprofit organization's Statement of Financial Position* at year-end. See Chapter 21 for more details.

*"By God, gentlemen, I believe we've found it—the Fountain of Funding!"*

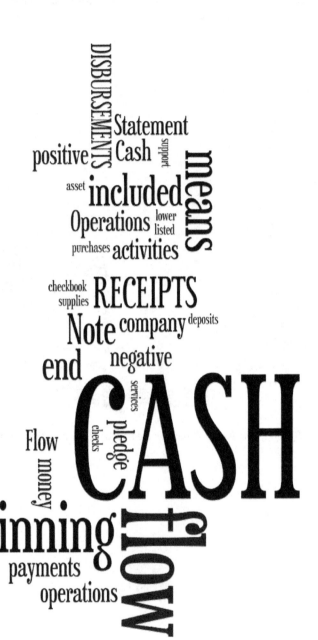

# Chapter 6.
# Statement of Cash Flows

The *Statement of Cash Flows* is just like your checkbook register. You subtract an amount when you spend money and add an amount when you deposit money. Every month (hopefully!) you tally all your entries and reconcile the checkbook.

The *Statement of Cash Flows* summarizes the organization's payments (cash outflows) and deposits (cash inflows) for a period of time. A *positive* cash flow for a period means that the organization has more cash at the end of the period than at its beginning. A *negative* cash flow for a period means that the organization has less cash at the end of the period than at its beginning.

---

*— Statement of Cash Flows —*

**BEGINNING CASH + CASH-IN – CASH OUT
= ENDING CASH**

*...at the end of the period*

*Sources* of cash include cash receipts, gifts, program revenue, grants, investment income, and increases in debt. *Uses* of cash include cash disbursements for salaries, materials, and the like, repayment of debt, and any purchase of new property, plant, and equipment. The ENDING CASH amount becomes the BEGINNING CASH amount for the next period.

---

If an organization actually runs totally out of cash, it is broke — a sorry state that will greatly interfere with progress towards its mission. Sigh.

Review the sample *Statement of Cash Flows* structure shown below. Match the letters on each line of the sample statement with the letters and definitions that follow. By the time you have reviewed each line and read each definition, you will have achieved a basic understanding of this financial statement.

## STATEMENT OF CASH FLOWS  *for the period*

| | | |
|---|---|---|
| Ⓐ **BEGINNING CASH** | $ | 0 |
|     Ⓑ CASH RECEIPTS | | |
|     Ⓒ CASH DISBURSEMENTS | | |
| Ⓓ **CASH FLOW FROM OPERATIONS** | $ | 0 |
| | | |
| Ⓔ PP&E PURCHASES | | |
| Ⓕ NET BORROWINGS | | |
| Ⓖ INVESTMENT INCOME | | |
| Ⓗ **ENDING CASH** | $ | 0 |

Note, make entries on the *Statement of Cash Flows* only into the boxed elements shown above. The other statement lines are just additions and subtractions of boxed entry lines. A drawn single line in the statement means that the above grouped numbers are added or subtracted and the summation is shown below that drawn line. The lines are drawn for clarity showing where arithmetic calculations have been made.

The three main financial statements all interact. ENDING CASH here on the *Cash Flow Statement* is shown as CASH in the *Statement of Financial Position* for the same period.

Using information presented on the organization's *Statement of Cash Flows*, the Board and management can ask and then answer:

• Are we overspending?

• Will we have enough money in the bank to pay our upcoming bills? Are we now and will we remain solvent?

**BEGINNING CASH** is the money on hand in the organization's bank accounts and petty-cash drawer at the beginning of the accounting period.

 **CASH RECEIPTS** (from operations) is new cash that has come into the organization since the beginning of the period. This cash comes from CONTRIBUTIONS & GIFTS, plus any cash payments from PROGRAM SERVICES REVENUE, and GRANTS & CONTRACTS. Only cash coming in from the organization's "operations" is included here. CASH RECEIPTS do not include DEBT, PP&E, or INTEREST INCOME transactions.

Note, a pledge is not a CASH RECEIPT and does not increase CASH at the time of the pledge. No actual money changes hands when a pledge is made. However, when the pledge is funded, the incoming cash is a CASH RECEIPT for that period and included here.

 **CASH DISBURSEMENTS** (from operations) is cash that goes out of the organization since the beginning of the period as payments for salaries, supplies, and so forth. These payments reduce cash on-hand. CASH DISBURSEMENTS do not include any DEBT, PP&E or interest transactions.

 **CASH FLOW FROM OPERATIONS** is CASH RECEIPTS minus CASH DISBURSEMENTS—the flow of money into and out of the organization from its "operating activities." Operating activities do not include any DEBT, PP&E, or INVESTMENT INCOME transactions.

**CASH FLOW FROM OPERATIONS ⑩ = ⑧ − ©**

The following line items show financing and investment cash flows of the organization during the period. Only cash coming into the organization from financing and investing activities is included here.

 **PROPERTY & EQUIPMENT PURCHASES** (PP&E) is money spent to buy property, plant, and equipment. For example, spending to purchase a building would be listed here.

 **NET BORROWINGS** is the difference between any new borrowing in the period and the amount paid back. These are "financing activities" of the organization.

**INVESTMENT INCOME** is primarily interest and dividends coming from the organization's investments and is considered unrestricted revenue.

 **ENDING CASH** is computed as BEGINNING CASH plus or minus CASH FLOW FROM OPERATIONS minus PROPERTY & EQUIPMENT PURCHASES plus NET BORROWINGS plus INVESTMENT INCOME.

$$\text{ENDING CASH } Ⓗ = Ⓐ + Ⓓ + Ⓔ + Ⓕ + Ⓖ$$

Shown below is a commonly used alternative *Statement of Cash Flows* structure and presentation format. Also, review our simplified "family" cash flow example on the facing page.

## STATEMENT OF CASH FLOWS *for the period*

**CASH USED (GENERATED) BY**

| | | |
|---|---|---|
| Ⓓ OPERATING ACTIVITIES | | |
| Ⓘ INVESTING ACTIVITIES | | |
| Ⓕ FINANCING ACTICITIES | | |
| Ⓙ **NET CHANGE IN CASH** | $ | 0 |
| Ⓐ **BEGINNING CASH** | | 0 |
| Ⓗ **ENDING CASH** | $ | 0 |

 **INVESTING ACTIVITIES** include PP&E PURCHASES and INVESTMENT INCOME.

$$\text{INVESTING ACTIVITIES } Ⓘ = Ⓔ + Ⓖ$$

 **NET CHANGE IN CASH** is the net cash inflows and outflows of the organization.

$$\text{NET CHANGE IN CASH } Ⓙ = Ⓓ + Ⓘ + Ⓕ$$

~

We have now reviewed the structure of the three major financial statements of the organization, the *Statement of Activities* (analogous to the *Income Statement* of a for-profit company), the *Statement of Financial Position* (analogous to the *Balance Sheet* of a for-profit company), and the *Statement of Cash Flows.*

---

## Statement of Cash Flows

Remember, you gave your son $2.50 in cash one day (the specified period), to take to school to buy a nutritious morning snack and a very wholesome lunch. At the start of the day, your son was broke (no money at all) so his *beginning cash* was zero. The $2.50 you gave him is his *cash receipts* for the day. He then spent $2.00 for lunch (*cash disbursements*) leaving an *ending cash* balance of 50¢.

His *Statement of Cash Flows* for the period looks like this (simplified):

| | |
|---|---|
| **BEGINNING CASH** | **$0.00** |
| **CASH RECEIPTS** | **2.50** |
| **CASH DISBURSEMENTS** | **2.00** |
| **CASH FLOW FROM OPERATIONS** | **$0.50** |
| **ENDING CASH** | **$0.50** |

---

One more specialty statement to go, the *Statement of Functional Expenses.*

# Chapter 7.
# Statement of
# Functional Expenses

The *Statement of Functional Expenses* of a nonprofit organization presents in great detail, the organization's expenses for a time period. A matrix format is used showing:

- **natural expenses** in rows grouped by salaries, benefits, supplies, and so forth, versus

- **functional expenses** grouped by specific program services projects and internal support service types in columns.

*Natural expenses* are grouped according to type. *Functional expenses* are grouped according to the purpose for which costs are incurred. This particular matrix presentation highlights overhead expenses, both direct and indirect, in a very straightforward and informative way. See ‡ (twice) in the chart on the next page.

Also, adding the revenue totals to the matrix will allow us to compute any absolute dollar surplus generated by a specific program and also a program-spending ratio for the program.

$$\text{Program Spending Ratio} = \frac{Program\ Revenue}{Program\ Expenses}$$

## Nonprofit Accounting & Financial Statements

Match the small-circled letters on each line of the sample *Statement of Functional Expenses* with the large-circled letters and definitions that follow.

### Statement of Functional Expenses

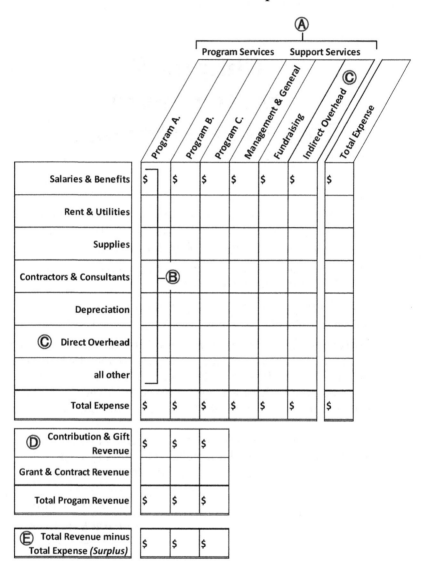

*Functional Expense Groups.* Reporting by these groupings show the organization's expenditures by major programs. Is the organization's spending congruent with its mission? Is it putting its money where its mouth is?

 *Natural Expense Groups.* Reporting by these groupings show the organization's expenditures by the type of expense, how it spends its money to get desired results. Is this allocation the most efficient and effective mix?

*Direct & Indirect Overhead. Indirect overhead* is an expense type that is difficult to assign to a specific project or function. An example of indirect overhead would be the chief financial officer's salary—difficult to assign to a specific project and better viewed as a expense necessary for all projects.

*Direct overhead* can easily be assigned to a project, but does not fit into one of the natural expense groups. For example, purchasing a special liability insurance policy required by the nature of a specific program.

Overhead expense is often viewed with suspicion by donors and other funders as a potential waste of money. However, these expenses are real (rent, utilities, audits, finance, insurance, staff training and so forth) and are required in a well-managed organization. Classification of overhead by direct or indirect provides more information and additional clarity to these expenses. Government audits like to see this clarity.

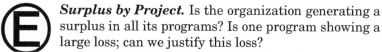 *Revenue by Program.* Revenue may come in with specific restrictions on its use. For other projects, the board must decide, as it budgets, what monies will be used where. This data line summarizes the revenue dedicated for specific project use.

*Surplus by Project.* Is the organization generating a surplus in all its programs? Is one program showing a large loss; can we justify this loss?

The board needs to see this information to gauge the performance of the organization and its projects. The IRS thinks that donors and other stakeholders need to see this information too. With the new FASB 2017 regulations, this statement is now required of all nonprofit organizations.

Form 990 Part III Statement of Program Service Accomplishments shows Revenue and Expenses (in total) for each one of the three largest programs, plus the total for "other" programs. The total program services expenses must equal Total Program Services Expense in Part IX. Part IX is the Statement of Functional Expenses. The Form 990 presents lots of information but can be complex and difficult to read.

～

Note that for-profit companies do not have to issue a *Statement of Functional Expenses*. The sort of data presented—profitability by product line—is a closely kept competitive secret.

# Section C.
# The Mechanics of
# Nonprofit Accounting

# Chapter 9.
# Contribution, Gift, & Pledge Transactions

Many nonprofit organizations survive and prosper with the philanthropy of generous community members. See how these contribution, gift, and pledge transactions are recorded in the three main nonprofit financial statements: the *Statement of Activities, Statement of Financial Position,* and *Statement of Cash Flows.*

**Transaction 1.** Kind donor contributes $1,000 by check in support of our cause.

**Transaction 2.** Receive a $15,000 gift to write, print, and distribute a booklet.

**Transaction 3.** Ex-chair of the board bequeaths $100,000 to increase our endowment fund.

**Transaction 4.** Knowledgeable friend contributes needed professional services.

**Transaction 5.** Perhaps the most valuable gift of all— volunteers contribute their time.

**Transaction 6.** Local auto dealer pledges a $5,000 gift to be funded "when sales pick up!"

**Transaction 7.** Prior pledge of $5,000 is funded.

# T1. Kind donor contributes $1,000 by check in support of our cause.

Mary Worthwell, long-time patron of the WsNA, is due to make her annual contribution. It is not a done deal, but it is as close as it gets. Our CEO makes a telephone call to Mary and sets up a lunch for the two of them plus the chairperson of the board for next Friday.

Lunch is delicious and Mary seems genuinely excited to hear about the goals we have for next year. She shares that she appreciates being able to play a small part in WsNA's success, and hands us a check for $1,000. Woo woo! We thank her for being so generous.

The CEO returns to the office and hands the check to the accounting department staff. They deposit it in the bank *pronto* and then enter the contribution into our computerized accounting system. We send Mary a thank you letter that acknowledges the contribution and provides her with a receipt for her tax return.

---

**Transaction:** Receive by check a $1,000 contribution and deposit in WsNA's bank account. The donor has placed no restrictions on how we may use this gift, so it is recorded as unrestricted revenue.

**1** Record the $1,000 donation as **CONTRIBUTION & GIFT REVENUE** in the **WITHOUT DONOR RESTRICTIONS COLUMN** on the *Statement of Activities*.

**2** Deposit the $1,000 check in WsNA's bank account. Now we have $1,000 more cash. Record this increase in **CASH** as a **CASH RECEIPT** on the *Statement of Cash Flows*.

**3** **ENDING CASH** on the *Statement of Cash Flows* is always the same as **CASH** on the *Statement of Financial Position,* so add $1,000 to **CASH** on that statement.

**4** **ENDING NET ASSETS** has increased by $1,000 on the *Statement of Activities* so add this amount to the **NET ASSETS W/O RESTRICTION** line on the *Statement of Financial Position*.

Now, **TOTAL ASSETS** equals **TOTAL LIABILITIES & NET ASSETS** on the *Statement of Financial Position.*

## STATEMENT OF ACTIVITIES  *for the period*

| REVENUE | WITHOUT DONOR RESTRICTIONS | WITH DONOR RESTRICTIONS | |
|---|---|---|---|
| CONTRIBUTIONS & GIFTS | ❶ $ 1,000 | | $ 1,000 |
| PROGRAM SERVICES REVENUE | | | 0 |
| GRANTS & CONTRACTS | | | 0 |
| OTHER REVENUE | | | 0 |
| **TOTAL REVENUE** | **$ 1,000** | **$ 0** | **$ 1,000** |
| EXPENSES | | | |
| FUNDRAISING | | | $ 0 |
| PROGRAM SERVICES | | | 0 |
| GRANTS & CONTRACTS | | | 0 |
| MANAGEMENT & GENERAL | | | 0 |
| **TOTAL EXPENSES** | **$ 0** | | **$ 0** |
| | CHANGE IN NET ASSETS | | $ 1,000 |
| | BEGINNING NET ASSETS | | 0 |
| | ENDING NET ASSETS | ❹ | $ 1,000 |

## STATEMENT OF FINANCIAL POSITION  *as of the period ending date*

| ASSETS | | LIABILITIES & NET ASSETS | |
|---|---|---|---|
| CASH | ❸ $ 1,000 | ACCOUNTS PAYABLE | |
| ACCOUNTS RECEIVABLE | | SHORT TERM DEBT | |
| INVENTORIES | | LONG TERM DEBT | |
| PREPAID EXPENSES | | ACCRUED EXPENSES | |
| PLEDGES RECEIVABLE | | NET ASSETS: | |
| INVESTMENTS | | W/O DONOR RESTRICTIONS | ❹ 1,000 |
| PP&E (NET) | | WITH DONOR RESTRICTIONS | |
| **TOTAL ASSETS** | **$ 1,000** | **TOTAL LIABILITIES & NET ASSETS** | **$ 1,000** |

## STATEMENT OF CASH FLOWS  *for the period*

| | | |
|---|---|---|
| BEGINNING CASH | | $ 0 |
| CASH RECEIPTS | ❷ | $ 1,000 |
| CASH DISBURSEMENTS | | |
| **CASH FLOW FROM OPERATIONS** | | **$ 1,000** |
| PP&E PURCHASES | | |
| NET BORROWINGS | | |
| INVESTMENT INCOME | | |
| **ENDING CASH** | ❸ | **$ 1,000** |

Transaction 1.
Statement
Entries

# T2. Receive a $15,000 gift to write, print, and distribute a booklet.

The local nursery company, Growell Flowers and Plants, Inc., donates $15,000 for us to write and distribute to the community a booklet on how to design, build, plant, grow, and harvest healthy vegetables in a city garden. It is our decision whether to have a list at the back of the brochure of local suppliers of soil, plants, and necessary equipment (including Growell).

All things considered, we regard the brochure to be of real benefit to the community. This $15,000 is a donation from Growell and is recorded as restricted revenue to WsNA. Sure, Growell may benefit from the donation, but not directly. We write them a donation acknowledgement for use when preparing their tax return as required by the IRS.

With this transaction, our net assets have increased until we begin to spend the funds working on the booklet. GAAP requires that contributions & gifts be recorded in the period received or pledged, and that expenses be recorded in the period incurred. Revenue and expenses are not necessarily "matched" in time in nonprofit financial statements as they are in for-profit accounting.

---

**Transaction:** Receive by check a $15,000 contribution and deposit in WsNA's bank account. The donor has placed restrictions on how we may use this gift, so it is recorded as restricted revenue.

**1** Record the $15,000 donation as **CONTRIBUTION & GIFTS WITH DONOR RESTRICTIONS** on the *Statement of Activities*.

**2** Deposit the $15,000 check in WsNA's bank account. Now we have $15,000 more **CASH**. Record this increase in cash as a **CASH RECEIPT** on the *Statement of Cash Flows*.

**3** **ENDING CASH** on the *Statement of Cash Flows* is always the same as **CASH** on the *Statement of Financial Position*, so add $15,000 to **CASH** on that statement.

**4** On the *Statement of Activities*, **ENDING NET ASSETS** has increased by $15,000. Add this amount to the **NET ASSETS WITH DONOR RESTRICTIONS** line on the *Statement of Financial Position*.

## STATEMENT OF ACTIVITIES
*for the period*

| REVENUE | WITHOUT DONOR RESTRICTIONS | WITH DONOR RESTRICTIONS | |
|---|---|---|---|
| CONTRIBUTIONS & GIFTS | | ❶ $ 15,000 | $ 15,000 |
| PROGRAM SERVICES REVENUE | | | 0 |
| GRANTS & CONTRACTS | | | 0 |
| OTHER REVENUE | | | 0 |
| **TOTAL REVENUE** | $ 0 | $ 15,000 | $ 15,000 |
| **EXPENSES** | | | |
| FUNDRAISING | | | $ 0 |
| PROGRAM SERVICES | | | 0 |
| GRANTS & CONTRACTS | | | 0 |
| MANAGEMENT & GENERAL | | | 0 |
| **TOTAL EXPENSES** | $ 0 | | $ 0 |

CHANGE IN NET ASSETS ❹ $ 15,000
BEGINNING NET ASSETS 0
ENDING NET ASSETS $ 15,000

## STATEMENT OF FINANCIAL POSITION
*as of the period ending date*

| ASSETS | | LIABILITIES & NET ASSETS | |
|---|---|---|---|
| CASH | ❸ $ 15,000 | ACCOUNTS PAYABLE | |
| ACCOUNTS RECEIVABLE | | SHORT TERM DEBT | |
| INVENTORIES | | LONG TERM DEBT | |
| PREPAID EXPENSES | | ACCRUED EXPENSES | |
| PLEDGES RECEIVABLE | | NET ASSETS: | |
| INVESTMENTS | | W/O DONOR RESTRICTIONS | |
| PP&E (NET) | | WITH DONOR RESTRICTIONS ❹ | 15,000 |
| **TOTAL ASSETS** | $ 15,000 | **TOTAL LIABILITIES & NET ASSETS** | $ 15,000 |

## STATEMENT OF CASH FLOWS *for the period*

| | | |
|---|---|---|
| BEGINNING CASH | | $ 0 |
| CASH RECEIPTS | ❷ | $ 15,000 |
| CASH DISBURSEMENTS | | |
| **CASH FLOW FROM OPERATIONS** | | $ 15,000 |
| PP&E PURCHASES | | |
| NET BORROWINGS | | |
| INVESTMENT INCOME | | |
| **ENDING CASH** | ❸ | $ 15,000 |

**Transaction 2.
Statement
Entries**

81

# T3. Ex-chair of the board bequeaths $100,000 to increase our endowment fund.

Barbara Stiff, a former chairperson of the WsNA board, passes away after a long illness. Our CEO visited her home many times, sharing news of the organization's flourishing. Hearing about WsNA's positive impact on the community filled Barbara with joy and brought tears to her eyes.

Barbara bequeathed $100,000—WOW!—to the organization for use as an endowment fund, never to be spent. The $100,000 is recorded as restricted revenue. Her will did not stipulate what to do with the interest and dividend earnings from the endowment fund, so we can consider the earnings from the endowment as unrestricted revenue to be used as the Board sees fit.

---

**Transaction:** Receive from the executor of Barbara's estate, a check for $100,000 as a contribution to WsNA's endowment.

**1** Record the $100,000 donation as CONTRIBUTIONS & GIFTS WITH DONOR RESTRICTIONS on the *Statement of Activities.*

**2** Deposit the $100,000 check in WsNA's bank account. Now we have $100,000 more CASH. Record this increase in cash as a CASH RECEIPT on the *Statement of Cash Flows.*

**3** ENDING CASH on the *Statement of Cash Flows* is always the same as CASH on the *Statement of Financial Position,* so add $100,000 to CASH on that statement.

**4** ENDING NET ASSETS has increased by $100,000 on the *Statement of Activities,* so add this amount to the NET ASSETS WITH DONOR RESTRICTIONS line on the *Statement of Financial Position.*

Now, TOTAL ASSETS equals TOTAL LIABILITIES & NET ASSETS on the *Statement of Financial Position,* as by definition, they must.

## STATEMENT OF ACTIVITIES                                   *for the period*

| REVENUE | WITHOUT DONOR RESTRICTIONS | WITH DONOR RESTRICTIONS | |
|---|---|---|---|
| CONTRIBUTIONS & GIFTS | | ❶ $ 100,000 | $100,000 |
| PROGRAM SERVICES REVENUE | | | 0 |
| GRANTS & CONTRACTS | | | 0 |
| OTHER REVENUE | | | 0 |
| **TOTAL REVENUE** | $ 0 | $100,000 | $100,000 |
| **EXPENSES** | | | |
| FUNDRAISING | | | $ 0 |
| PROGRAM SERVICES | | | 0 |
| GRANTS & CONTRACTS | | | 0 |
| MANAGEMENT & GENERAL | | | 0 |
| **TOTAL EXPENSES** | $ 0 | | $ 0 |

|  |  |
|---|---|
| CHANGE IN NET ASSETS | $100,000 |
| BEGINNING NET ASSETS | 0 |
| ENDING NET ASSETS ❹ | $100,000 |

## STATEMENT OF FINANCIAL POSITION          *as of the period ending date*

| ASSETS | | LIABILITIES & NET ASSETS | |
|---|---|---|---|
| CASH ❸ | $ 100,000 | ACCOUNTS PAYABLE | |
| ACCOUNTS RECEIVABLE | | SHORT TERM DEBT | |
| INVENTORIES | | LONG TERM DEBT | |
| PREPAID EXPENSES | | ACCRUED EXPENSES | |
| PLEDGES RECEIVABLE | | NET ASSETS: | |
| INVESTMENTS | | W/O DONOR RESTRICTIONS | |
| PP&E (NET) | | WITH DONOR RESTRICTIONS ❹ | 100,000 |
| **TOTAL ASSETS** | **$100,000** | **TOTAL LIABILITIES & NET ASSETS** | **$100,000** |

## STATEMENT OF CASH FLOWS   *for the period*

| | |
|---|---|
| BEGINNING CASH | $ 0 |
| CASH RECEIPTS ❷ | $ 100,000 |
| CASH DISBURSEMENTS | |
| **CASH FLOW FROM OPERATIONS** | **$100,000** |
| PP&E PURCHASES | |
| NET BORROWINGS | |
| INVESTMENT INCOME | |
| **ENDING CASH** ❸ | **$100,000** |

---

**Transaction 3.
Statement
Entries**

# T4. Knowledgeable friend contributes needed professional services.

The CEO and the Board Chair have concerns about the long-term vitality and viability of the WsNA. Will people still want and need our services five years from now? How will the drop-off in governmental grants affect us? Will our current donor base continue to support our efforts? How can we attract younger donors? We need a strategic plan that gives us a clear pathway to follow and we need help to formulate that plan.

The CEO immediately thinks of Rob Writewell. He is a senior partner in a large multinational strategic planning consulting firm and an ideal person to help develop and document our strategic plan. They are friends since college (they briefly dated!), and Rob is a regular contributor to the organization.

The CEO takes Rob out to lunch and pops the question: Will he help? Rob immediately agrees and says he is honored to be asked. Rob estimates his work on the project will be extensive; about $20,000 worth of his time if he were billing this effort as a professional service provider. Rob agrees to donate his services and he is more than happy to do so in furtherance of our organization's mission. Rob pays for lunch too.

Rob will not receive a donation acknowledgement letter from WsNA. Donated professional services are not tax-deductible to the donor. Too large a potential for fraud says the IRS.

---

**Transaction:** Donated personal professional services to a nonprofit organization must be recorded as revenue at an estimated cost and as a matching expense.

**❶** Record the $20,000 professional services donation as OTHER REVENUE on the *Statement of Activities*.

**❷** Record the $20,000 estimated cost of the professional services donation as MANAGEMENT & GENERAL EXPENSE on the *Statement of Activities*.

NOTE: No cash changes hands so no entries on the *Statement of Cash Flows*. No entries on the *Statement of Financial Position* either.

## STATEMENT OF ACTIVITIES                                              *for the period*

| REVENUE | WITHOUT DONOR RESTRICTIONS | WITH DONOR RESTRICTIONS | | |
|---|---|---|---|---|
| CONTRIBUTIONS & GIFTS | | | $ | 0 |
| PROGRAM SERVICES REVENUE | | | | 0 |
| GRANTS & CONTRACTS | | | | 0 |
| OTHER REVENUE | ❶ 20,000 | | | 20,000 |
| **TOTAL REVENUE** | **$ 20,000** | **$ 0** | **$** | **20,000** |
| **EXPENSES** | | | | |
| FUNDRAISING | | | $ | 0 |
| PROGRAM SERVICES | | | | 0 |
| GRANTS & CONTRACTS | | | | 0 |
| MANAGEMENT & GENERAL | ❷ 20,000 | | | 20,000 |
| **TOTAL EXPENSES** | **$ 20,000** | | **$** | **20,000** |
| | CHANGE IN NET ASSETS | | $ | 0 |
| | BEGINNING NET ASSETS | | | 0 |
| | ENDING NET ASSETS | | $ | 0 |

## STATEMENT OF FINANCIAL POSITION                      *as of the period ending date*

| ASSETS | | | LIABILITIES & NET ASSETS | | |
|---|---|---|---|---|---|
| CASH | | | ACCOUNTS PAYABLE | | |
| ACCOUNTS RECEIVABLE | | | SHORT TERM DEBT | | |
| INVENTORIES | | | LONG TERM DEBT | | |
| PREPAID EXPENSES | | | ACCRUED EXPENSES | | |
| PLEDGES RECEIVABLE | | | NET ASSETS: | | |
| INVESTMENTS | | | W/O DONOR RESTRICTIONS | | |
| PP&E (NET) | | | WITH DONOR RESTRICTIONS | | |
| **TOTAL ASSETS** | **$** | **0** | **TOTAL LIABILITIES & NET ASSETS** | **$** | **0** |

## STATEMENT OF CASH FLOWS    *for the period*

| | | | |
|---|---|---|---|
| | BEGINNING CASH | $ | 0 |
| | CASH RECEIPTS | | |
| **Transaction 4.** | CASH DISBURSEMENTS | | |
| **Statement** | **CASH FLOW FROM OPERATIONS** | **$** | **0** |
| **Entries** | | | |
| | PP&E PURCHASES | | |
| | NET BORROWINGS | | |
| | INVESTMENT INCOME | | |
| | **ENDING CASH** | **$** | **0** |

# T5. Perhaps the most valuable gift of all—volunteers contribute their time.

How does nonprofit GAAP recommend accounting for volunteers contributing their time?

As we described in Transaction 4, contributions of services to nonprofits must be recognized as revenue (and as a coordinated expense) if the volunteer services received meet all three conditions below:

- require specialized skills,
- are provided by individuals possessing those skills, and
- would typically need to be purchased if not provided by donation.

Such services requiring specialized skills are often provided by accountants, architects, carpenters, doctors, electricians, lawyers, nurses, plumbers, teachers, and other professionals and craftspeople.

Volunteer services that do not involve specialized skills, including much of the volunteer help nonprofits receive for program activities, office tasks, special events, and so forth, GAAP does not allow value recognition on financial statements. However, expenses incurred by volunteers when performing services for the nonprofit are deductible as contributions on the individual's federal tax returns.

These nonspecialized volunteer services may be unrecognized by accounting standards, but they are highly valued by nonprofit organizations. WsNA supporters contribute thousands of hours of their time each year doing volunteer work advancing our mission. Our organization is not alone in receiving volunteer support. According to the Bureau of Labor Statistics at the U.S. Department of Labor, about 65 million Americans (almost 25% of the adult population) gave almost 8 billion hours of volunteer service worth over $175 billion in 2015. Wow!

---

**Transaction:** No changes are made on the financial statements to account for non-specialized contribution of volunteer's time to WsNA's good works.

## STATEMENT OF ACTIVITIES  *for the period*

| REVENUE | WITHOUT DONOR RESTRICTIONS | WITH DONOR RESTRICTIONS | | |
|---|---|---|---|---|
| CONTRIBUTIONS & GIFTS | | | $ | 0 |
| PROGRAM SERVICES REVENUE | | | | 0 |
| GRANTS & CONTRACTS | | | | 0 |
| OTHER REVENUE | | | | 0 |
| **TOTAL REVENUE** | $ 0 | $ 0 | $ | 0 |
| **EXPENSES** | | | | |
| FUNDRAISING | | | $ | 0 |
| PROGRAM SERVICES | | | | 0 |
| GRANTS & CONTRACTS | | | | 0 |
| MANAGEMENT & GENERAL | | | | 0 |
| **TOTAL EXPENSES** | $ 0 | | $ | 0 |
| | **CHANGE IN NET ASSETS** | | $ | 0 |
| | **BEGINNING NET ASSETS** | | | 0 |
| | **ENDING NET ASSETS** | | $ | 0 |

## STATEMENT OF FINANCIAL POSITION  *as of the period ending date*

| ASSETS | | LIABILITIES & NET ASSETS | |
|---|---|---|---|
| CASH | | ACCOUNTS PAYABLE | |
| ACCOUNTS RECEIVABLE | | SHORT TERM DEBT | |
| INVENTORIES | | LONG TERM DEBT | |
| PREPAID EXPENSES | | ACCRUED EXPENSES | |
| PLEDGES RECEIVABLE | | NET ASSETS: | |
| INVESTMENTS | | W/O DONOR RESTRICTIONS | |
| PP&E (NET) | | WITH DONOR RESTRICTIONS | |
| **TOTAL ASSETS** | $ 0 | **TOTAL LIABILITIES & NET ASSETS** | $ 0 |

## STATEMENT OF CASH FLOWS  *for the period*

| | | |
|---|---|---|
| BEGINNING CASH | $ | 0 |
| CASH RECEIPTS | | |
| CASH DISBURSEMENTS | | |
| **CASH FLOW FROM OPERATIONS** | $ | 0 |
| PP&E PURCHASES | | |
| NET BORROWINGS | | |
| INVESTMENT INCOME | | |
| **ENDING CASH** | $ | 0 |

**Transaction 5.
Statement
Entries**

# T6. Local auto dealer pledges a $5,000 gift to be funded "when sales pick up!"

Margery Friendly, our director of development, has been courting Sam DeLay, a wealthy car dealer in town, trying to bring him into the fold as a major donor. Margery takes the chairperson of the board to make her next pitch down at the dealership.

Our chairperson and Mr. DeLay have gone to the same synagogue for years, and she attended DeLay's eldest son's bar mitzvah last year. The time is right for Sam to contribute, and our chairman has the perfect hook. When she says that she is considering buying a new car, DeLay's eyes light up and he takes them onto the display-room floor and shows them all the latest models.

Right on the spot, Sam takes a new car brochure and jots down and signs a note pledging a contribution of $5,000 to WsNA. He says he will fund the donation after President's Day when car sales pick-up considerably. Margery and our chairperson thank him profusely.

---

**Transaction:** Donor signs a written pledge to make a $5,000 unrestricted donation to WsNA next year. Under nonprofit GAAP, pledges are recognized as revenue in the period they are made.

**❶** Record the $5,000 pledge as CONTRIBUTIONS & GIFTS W/O DONOR RESTRICTIONS on the *Statement of Activities*

**❷** ENDING NET ASSETS has increased by $5,000 on the *Statement of Activities* so add this amount to NET ASSETS W/O RESTRICTIONS line on the *Statement of Financial Position.*

**❸** Add $5,000 to PLEDGES RECEIVABLE in the asset section of the *Statement of Financial Position.*

**Note:** WsNA has generated a surplus (profit) from this transaction and NET ASSETS has increased, yet no cash has come in. This accounting treatment of revenue in nonprofits is very different than revenue recognition in for-profit GAAP.

For-profit accounting focuses on profits, matching, timing, and taxation. Nonprofit accounting focuses more on accountability within the organization and to donors.

*Contributions, Gifts & Pledges*

## STATEMENT OF ACTIVITIES
*for the period*

| REVENUE | WITHOUT DONOR RESTRICTIONS | WITH DONOR RESTRICTIONS | |
|---|---|---|---|
| CONTRIBUTIONS & GIFTS | ❶ $ 5,000 | | $ 5,000 |
| PROGRAM SERVICES REVENUE | | | 0 |
| GRANTS & CONTRACTS | | | 0 |
| OTHER REVENUE | | | 0 |
| TOTAL REVENUE | $ 5,000 | $ 0 | $ 5,000 |
| EXPENSES | | | |
| FUNDRAISING | | | $ 0 |
| PROGRAM SERVICES | | | 0 |
| GRANTS & CONTRACTS | | | 0 |
| MANAGEMENT & GENERAL | | | 0 |
| TOTAL EXPENSES | $ 0 | | $ 0 |
| CHANGE IN NET ASSETS | | | $ 5,000 |
| BEGINNING NET ASSETS | | | 0 |
| ENDING NET ASSETS | | | $ 5,000 |

## STATEMENT OF FINANCIAL POSITION
*as of the period ending date*

| ASSETS | | LIABILITIES & NET ASSETS | |
|---|---|---|---|
| CASH | | ACCOUNTS PAYABLE | |
| ACCOUNTS RECEIVABLE | | SHORT TERM DEBT | |
| INVENTORIES | | LONG TERM DEBT | |
| PREPAID EXPENSES | | ACCRUED EXPENSES | |
| PLEDGES RECEIVABLE ❸ | 5,000 | NET ASSETS: | |
| INVESTMENTS | | W/O DONOR RESTRICTIONS ❷ | 5,000 |
| PP&E (NET) | | WITH DONOR RESTRICTIONS | |
| TOTAL ASSETS | $ 5,000 | TOTAL LIABILITIES & NET ASSETS | $ 5,000 |

## STATEMENT OF CASH FLOWS *for the period*

**Transaction 6.**
**Statement**
**Entries**

| BEGINNING CASH | $ 0 |
|---|---|
| CASH RECEIPTS | |
| CASH DISBURSEMENTS | |
| CASH FLOW FROM OPERATIONS | $ 0 |
| PP&E PURCHASES | |
| NET BORROWINGS | |
| INVESTMENT INCOME | |
| ENDING CASH | $ 0 |

89

# T7. Prior pledge of $5,000 is funded.

True to his word, Sam Delay (the car dealer) sends us a check funding his prior $5,000 pledge. It is always a relief when the money for a pledge actually comes in. We send Mr. DeLay a thank you note and a receipt for his records. Our development director also puts Mr. DeLay's name on the list of those to contact next year hoping for another significant donation.

Our Chairperson buys a new car from the dealership. Maybe we should ask Sam to join the board?

---

**Transaction:** Receive by check a $5,000 contribution funding a donor's prior pledge. Deposit the check in WsNA's bank account. Send donor a receipt for his files and the IRS.

**1** Deposit the $5,000 check in WsNA's bank account. Now we have $5,000 more cash. Record this increase in cash as a **CASH RECEIPT** on the *Statement of Cash Flows*.

**2** Move the $5,000 **PLEDGES RECEIVABLE** into **CASH** on the *Statement of Financial Position* (which is still in balance).

**Note:** Receiving cash in this transaction does not affect the *Statement of Activities* and no net asset change is made on the *Statement of Financial Position* either.

**NET ASSETS** were increased when we received the pledge, not when we received the actual cash. So says nonprofit GAAP.

## STATEMENT OF ACTIVITIES                    *for the period*

| REVENUE | WITHOUT DONOR RESTRICTIONS | WITH DONOR RESTRICTIONS | |
|---|---|---|---|
| CONTRIBUTIONS & GIFTS | | | $ 0 |
| PROGRAM SERVICES REVENUE | | | 0 |
| GRANTS & CONTRACTS | | | 0 |
| OTHER REVENUE | | | 0 |
| **TOTAL REVENUE** | $ 0 | $ 0 | $ 0 |
| **EXPENSES** | | | |
| FUNDRAISING | | | $ 0 |
| PROGRAM SERVICES | | | 0 |
| GRANTS & CONTRACTS | | | 0 |
| MANAGEMENT & GENERAL | | | 0 |
| **TOTAL EXPENSES** | $ 0 | | $ 0 |
| CHANGE IN NET ASSETS | | | $ 0 |
| BEGINNING NET ASSETS | | | 0 |
| ENDING NET ASSETS | | | $ 0 |

## STATEMENT OF FINANCIAL POSITION          *as of the period ending date*

| ASSETS | | LIABILITIES & NET ASSETS | |
|---|---|---|---|
| CASH ❷ | $ 5,000 | ACCOUNTS PAYABLE | |
| ACCOUNTS RECEIVABLE | | SHORT TERM DEBT | |
| INVENTORIES | | LONG TERM DEBT | |
| PREPAID EXPENSES | | ACCRUED EXPENSES | |
| PLEDGES RECEIVABLE ❷ | (5,000) | NET ASSETS: | |
| INVESTMENTS | | W/O DONOR RESTRICTIONS | |
| PP&E (NET) | | WITH DONOR RESTRICTIONS | |
| **TOTAL ASSETS** | $ 0 | **TOTAL LIABILITIES & NET ASSETS** | $ 0 |

## STATEMENT OF CASH FLOWS          *for the period*

**Transaction 7.
Statement
Entries**

| | |
|---|---|
| BEGINNING CASH | $ 0 |
| CASH RECEIPTS ❶ | $ 5,000 |
| CASH DISBURSEMENTS | |
| **CASH FLOW FROM OPERATIONS** | $ 5,000 |
| PP&E PURCHASES | |
| NET BORROWINGS | |
| INVESTMENT INCOME | |
| **ENDING CASH** | $ 5,000 |

# Chapter 10.
# Program Services
# Transactions

Program services revenue is payment (and pledges) received by the organization for providing goods and services to clients. Our program services expenses are our costs in providing these goods and services. In this exchange of goods and services for money, the organization often acts just like a commercial business—but the purpose of the exchange is the advancement of mission, not the generation of profits.

**Transaction 8.** Receive payment from Medicare and pay our contracted physician for her professional services performed in our clinic.

**Transaction 9.** Pay Senior Center rent. It would be great if we owned our own building.

**Transaction 10.** Order supplies for use in the Senior Center.

**Transaction 11.** Receive the supplies ordered in T10.

**Transaction 12.** Pay for supplies received in T11.

**Transaction 13.** Use some of the newly purchased supplies.

**Transaction 14.** Take me out to the Ball Game!

# T8. Receive payment from Medicare and pay our contracted physician for her professional services performed in our clinic.

We contract with Dr. Agnes Feelgood, a local physician specializing in gerontology, to administer annual Medicare physicals to our clients at the Friday morning Senior Center clinic. Everybody likes "Dr. Agnes" and it is a real convenience for our seniors.

We bill Medicare $180 per exam. The going rate in town for such services is $280, but Medicare will only pay us the lower amount (sigh). We pay Dr. Feelgood $500 for the half-day. This week she does four exams. We can still make a surplus (profit) if we are efficient in our exam scheduling.

---

**Transaction:** Bill Medicare for $720 and receive payment. Pay physician $500 for a one-half day of contracted professional services in the clinic.

**❶** A. Record the $720 Medicare reimbursement check as **PROGRAM SERVICES REVENUE** on the *Statement of Activities.*

B. Deposit the $720 check in the WsNA's bank account. Record this increase **CASH** as a **CASH RECEIPT** on the *Statement of Cash Flows.*

**❷** A. Issue a check to Dr. Feelgood for $500 in payment of her professional services rendered in the clinic. Record this payment as a **PROGRAM SERVICES EXPENSE** on *the Statement of Activities.*

B. Record this payment as a **CASH DISBURSEMENT** on the *Statement of Cash Flows.*

**❸** **ENDING CASH** on the *Statement of Cash Flows* is always the same as **CASH** on the *Statement of Financial Position,* so add $220 to **CASH** on that statement.

**❹** **CHANGE IN NET ASSETS** has increased by $220 on the *Statement of Activities* so add this amount to the **NET ASSETS W/O DONOR RESTRICTIONS** line on the *Statement of Financial Position.*

## STATEMENT OF ACTIVITIES                    *for the period*

| REVENUE | WITHOUT DONOR RESTRICTIONS | WITH DONOR RESTRICTIONS | | |
|---|---|---|---|---|
| CONTRIBUTIONS & GIFTS | | | $ | 0 |
| PROGRAM SERVICES REVENUE | ❶ 720 | | | 720 |
| GRANTS & CONTRACTS | | | | 0 |
| OTHER REVENUE | | | | 0 |
| **TOTAL REVENUE** | **$ 720** | **$ 0** | **$** | **720** |
| EXPENSES | | | | |
| FUNDRAISING | | | $ | 0 |
| PROGRAM SERVICES | ❷ 500 | | | 500 |
| GRANTS & CONTRACTS | | | | 0 |
| MANAGEMENT & GENERAL | | | | 0 |
| **TOTAL EXPENSES** | **$ 500** | | **$** | **500** |

| | | |
|---|---|---|
| CHANGE IN NET ASSETS | $ | 220 |
| BEGINNING NET ASSETS | | 0 |
| ENDING NET ASSETS | $ | 220 |

## STATEMENT OF FINANCIAL POSITION              *as of the period ending date*

| ASSETS | | | LIABILITIES & NET ASSETS | | |
|---|---|---|---|---|---|
| CASH | ❸ $ | 220 | ACCOUNTS PAYABLE | | |
| ACCOUNTS RECEIVABLE | | | SHORT TERM DEBT | | |
| INVENTORIES | | | LONG TERM DEBT | | |
| PREPAID EXPENSES | | | ACCRUED EXPENSES | | |
| PLEDGES RECEIVABLE | | | NET ASSETS: | | |
| INVESTMENTS | | | W/O DONOR RESTRICTIONS | ❹ | 220 |
| PP&E (NET) | | | WITH DONOR RESTRICTIONS | | |
| **TOTAL ASSETS** | **$** | **220** | **TOTAL LIABILITIES & NET ASSETS** | **$** | **220** |

## STATEMENT OF CASH FLOWS   *for the period*

| | | |
|---|---|---|
| BEGINNING CASH | $ | 0 |
| CASH RECEIPTS | ❶ $ | 720 |
| CASH DISBURSEMENTS | ❷ | 500 |
| **CASH FLOW FROM OPERATIONS** | **$** | **220** |
| PP&E PURCHASES | | |
| NET BORROWINGS | | |
| INVESTMENT INCOME | | |
| **ENDING CASH** | ❸ **$** | **220** |

**Transaction 8.**
**Statement**
**Entries**

# T9. Pay Senior Center rent. It would be great if we owned our own building!

Our Senior Center and WsNA's corporate offices on the second floor occupy an 11,000 sq. ft. building on an attractive block near the center of town. We pay $18,500 in rent each month with building utilities costing us another $2,000 (more in the summer when the air conditioning is running).

We would like to make some renovations and improvements to the property. Our landlord would make us pay for them which does not seem a good investment for just a rental property. WsNA's chairperson (the *vision* lady) dreams of owning our own building. We think the landlord would be willing to sell, but at what price and, more important, where would we get all that money? Gadzooks, a capital campaign perhaps?

**Note:** For nonprofit organizations, occupancy costs are usually the second largest expense category, just after salaries and wages. Occupancy costs are often regarded as *overhead* expenses. More discussion of *overhead* later.

---

**Transaction:** Pay this month's rent of $18,500 on our leased building. Pay the $2,000 utilities bill too.

**1** Write an $18,500 check for rent and mail it to our landlord. Write a $2,000 check and mail it to the utility company. Record $20,500 as **MANAGEMENT & GENERAL EXPENSE** on the *Statement of Activities.*

**2** Record the written checks as **CASH DISBURSEMENTS** on the *Statement of Cash Flows.*

**3** **ENDING CASH** on the *Statement of Cash Flows* is always the same as **CASH** on the *Statement of Financial Position,* so subtract $20,500 in **CASH** on that statement.

**4** **CHANGE IN NET ASSETS** has decreased by $20,500 on the *Statement of Activities,* so subtract this amount from **NET ASSETS W/O DONOR RESTRICTIONS** on the *Statement of Financial Position.*

**Note:** **CASH** on the *Statement of Financial Position* will really never be negative. It is here, because we are only looking at a single transaction. It will be balanced by a later transaction.

## STATEMENT OF ACTIVITIES $\qquad$ *for the period*

| REVENUE | WITHOUT DONOR RESTRICTIONS | WITH DONOR RESTRICTIONS | |
|---|---|---|---|
| CONTRIBUTIONS & GIFTS | | | $ 0 |
| PROGRAM SERVICES REVENUE | | | 0 |
| GRANTS & CONTRACTS | | | 0 |
| OTHER REVENUE | | | 0 |
| **TOTAL REVENUE** | $ 0 | $ 0 | $ 0 |
| **EXPENSES** | | | |
| FUNDRAISING | | | $ 0 |
| PROGRAM SERVICES | | | 0 |
| GRANTS & CONTRACTS | | | 0 |
| MANAGEMENT & GENERAL | ❶ 20,500 | | 20,500 |
| **TOTAL EXPENSES** | $ 20,500 | | $ 20,500 |
| | **CHANGE IN NET ASSETS** | | $ (20,500) |
| | **BEGINNING NET ASSETS** | | 0 |
| | **ENDING NET ASSETS** | | $ (20,500) |

## STATEMENT OF FINANCIAL POSITION $\qquad$ *as of the period ending date*

| ASSETS | | LIABILITIES & NET ASSETS | |
|---|---|---|---|
| CASH | ❸ $ (20,500) | ACCOUNTS PAYABLE | |
| ACCOUNTS RECEIVABLE | | SHORT TERM DEBT | |
| INVENTORIES | | LONG TERM DEBT | |
| PREPAID EXPENSES | | ACCRUED EXPENSES | |
| PLEDGES RECEIVABLE | | NET ASSETS: | |
| INVESTMENTS | | W/O DONOR RESTRICTIONS | ❹ (20,500) |
| PP&E (NET) | | WITH DONOR RESTRICTIONS | |
| **TOTAL ASSETS** | $ (20,500) | **TOTAL LIABILITIES & NET ASSETS** | $ (20,500) |

## STATEMENT OF CASH FLOWS *for the period*

| Transaction 9. Statement Entries | | |
|---|---|---|

| | | |
|---|---|---|
| BEGINNING CASH | | $ 0 |
| CASH RECEIPTS | | |
| CASH DISBURSEMENTS | ❷ | 20,500 |
| **CASH FLOW FROM OPERATIONS** | | $ (20,500) |
| PP&E PURCHASES | | |
| NET BORROWINGS | | |
| INVESTMENT INCOME | | |
| **ENDING CASH** | ❸ | $ (20,500) |

# T10. Order supplies for use in the Senior Center

Once a month we place an order with Speedy Office Supply (SOS) for the miscellaneous "stuff" that keeps WsNA operating. SOS is local and offers us a special nonprofit discount. It is win-win as a contribution to the local economy and to the community. We have used them for years. Bob Speedy, the owner, is on our vendor council.

We telephone in an order for $1,230 worth of goods. Delivery is an additional $25.

---

**Transaction:** Placing an order for supplies does not affect the financial statements in any way. However, when we receive the goods, our inventory will increase, as will our accounts receivable. See the next transaction.

## STATEMENT OF ACTIVITIES                        *for the period*

| REVENUE | WITHOUT DONOR RESTRICTIONS | WITH DONOR RESTRICTIONS | | |
|---|---|---|---|---|
| CONTRIBUTIONS & GIFTS | | | $ | 0 |
| PROGRAM SERVICES REVENUE | | | | 0 |
| GRANTS & CONTRACTS | | | | 0 |
| OTHER REVENUE | | | | 0 |
| TOTAL REVENUE | $ 0 | $ 0 | $ | 0 |
| EXPENSES | | | | |
| FUNDRAISING | | | $ | 0 |
| PROGRAM SERVICES | | | | 0 |
| GRANTS & CONTRACTS | | | | 0 |
| MANAGEMENT & GENERAL | | | | 0 |
| TOTAL EXPENSES | $ 0 | | $ | 0 |
| | CHANGE IN NET ASSETS | | $ | 0 |
| | BEGINNING NET ASSETS | | | 0 |
| | ENDING NET ASSETS | | $ | 0 |

## STATEMENT OF FINANCIAL POSITION            *as of the period ending date*

| ASSETS | | LIABILITIES & NET ASSETS | |
|---|---|---|---|
| CASH | | ACCOUNTS PAYABLE | |
| ACCOUNTS RECEIVABLE | | SHORT TERM DEBT | |
| INVENTORIES | | LONG TERM DEBT | |
| PREPAID EXPENSES | | ACCRUED EXPENSES | |
| PLEDGES RECEIVABLE | | NET ASSETS: | |
| INVESTMENTS | | W/O DONOR RESTRICTIONS | |
| PP&E (NET) | | WITH DONOR RESTRICTIONS | |
| TOTAL ASSETS | $ 0 | TOTAL LIABILITIES & NET ASSETS | $ 0 |

## STATEMENT OF CASH FLOWS  *for the period*

| | | |
|---|---|---|
| BEGINNING CASH | $ | 0 |

**Transaction 10. Statement Entries**

| | | |
|---|---|---|
| CASH RECEIPTS | | |
| CASH DISBURSEMENTS | | |
| CASH FLOW FROM OPERATIONS | $ | 0 |
| PP&E PURCHASES | | |
| NET BORROWINGS | | |
| INVESTMENT INCOME | | |
| ENDING CASH | $ | 0 |

# T11. Receive the supplies ordered in T10.

The supplies we ordered in the last transaction arrive. Eric Speedy, Bob's son and deliveryman, helps us store them in the supply room. Eric hands us an invoice for $1,255. Yikes, stuff is expensive, even with a discount.

We give Eric a cup of coffee and chat for a while. Eric is one of the coaches for our Little League team, the "WsBats," further discussed in T14.

---

**Transaction:** Receive ordered supplies and place them in the supply room. Receive invoice from vendor for $1,255 including delivery.

**❶** Increase **INVENTORIES** by $1,255 in the **ASSETS** section of the *Statement of Financial Position.*

**❷** Increase **ACCOUNTS PAYABLE** by $1,255 in the **LIABILITIES & NET ASSETS** section of the *Statement of Financial Position.*

Now, **TOTAL ASSETS** equals **TOTAL LIABILITIES & NET ASSETS**.

**Note:** No cash has (yet) to change hands, so there are no entries on the *Statement of Cash Flows*. When we actually pay for the goods, cash flow entries will be recorded. See **T12** on page 103.

No expenses have been incurred (yet) so there are no entries on the *Statement of Activities* from this transaction. When we take supplies out of inventory and use them, entries will be made in the EXPENSES section on the *Statement of Activities*. See **T13** on page 105.

## STATEMENT OF ACTIVITIES                                   *for the period*

| REVENUE | WITHOUT DONOR RESTRICTIONS | WITH DONOR RESTRICTIONS | | |
|---|---|---|---|---|
| CONTRIBUTIONS & GIFTS | | | $ | 0 |
| PROGRAM SERVICES REVENUE | | | | 0 |
| GRANTS & CONTRACTS | | | | 0 |
| OTHER REVENUE | | | | 0 |
| **TOTAL REVENUE** | $ 0 | $ 0 | $ | 0 |
| **EXPENSES** | | | | |
| FUNDRAISING | | | $ | 0 |
| PROGRAM SERVICES | | | | 0 |
| GRANTS & CONTRACTS | | | | 0 |
| MANAGEMENT & GENERAL | | | | 0 |
| **TOTAL EXPENSES** | $ 0 | | $ | 0 |
| | | CHANGE IN NET ASSETS | $ | 0 |
| | | BEGINNING NET ASSETS | | 0 |
| | | ENDING NET ASSETS | $ | 0 |

## STATEMENT OF FINANCIAL POSITION          *as of the period ending date*

| ASSETS | | LIABILITIES & NET ASSETS | | |
|---|---|---|---|---|
| CASH | | ACCOUNTS PAYABLE | ❷ $ | 1,255 |
| ACCOUNTS RECEIVABLE | | SHORT TERM DEBT | | |
| INVENTORIES ❶ | 1,255 | LONG TERM DEBT | | |
| PREPAID EXPENSES | | ACCRUED EXPENSES | | |
| PLEDGES RECEIVABLE | | NET ASSETS: | | |
| INVESTMENTS | | W/O DONOR RESTRICTIONS | | |
| PP&E (NET) | | WITH DONOR RESTRICTIONS | | |
| **TOTAL ASSETS** | $ 1,255 | **TOTAL LIABILITIES & NET ASSETS** | $ | 1,255 |

## STATEMENT OF CASH FLOWS  *for the period*

| | | |
|---|---|---|
| BEGINNING CASH | $ | 0 |
| CASH RECEIPTS | | |
| CASH DISBURSEMENTS | | |
| **CASH FLOW FROM OPERATIONS** | $ | 0 |
| PP&E PURCHASES | | |
| NET BORROWINGS | | |
| INVESTMENT INCOME | | |
| **ENDING CASH** | $ | 0 |

**Transaction 11.
Statement
Entries**

101

# T12. Pay for supplies received in T11.

Once a month our accounting staff reviews all the outstanding bills (invoices) we will need to pay soon. We try to keep current on our bills and pay all within 30 days of receipt, or we pay them as soon as we have enough cash.

The Speedy Office Supply $1,255 invoice is due to be paid at the end of this month.

---

**Transaction:** Write a check for $1,255 to Speedy Office Supply in payment for the office supplies received last month.

**❶** Record check payment of $1,255 as a CASH DISBURSEMENT on the *Statement of Cash Flows.*

**❷** Reduce ACCOUNTS PAYABLE by the same amount on the *Statement of Financial Position*

**❸** ENDING CASH on the *Statement of Cash Flows* is always the same as CASH on the *Statement of Financial Position,* so add ($1,255) to CASH on that statement.

Now, TOTAL ASSETS equals TOTAL LIABILITIES & NET ASSETS on the *Statement of Financial Position,* as they must by definition.

**Note:** Paying a bill for goods or services purchased on credit has no effect on the *Statement of Activities.* No increase or decrease in NET ASSETS has occurred. However, when we *use* the supplies, their cost will be moved into the *Statement of Activities* as an expense. Then, NET ASSETS will be lowered. See **T13** on the next page.

## STATEMENT OF ACTIVITIES    *for the period*

| REVENUE | WITHOUT DONOR RESTRICTIONS | WITH DONOR RESTRICTIONS | |
|---|---|---|---|
| CONTRIBUTIONS & GIFTS | | | $ 0 |
| PROGRAM SERVICES REVENUE | | | 0 |
| GRANTS & CONTRACTS | | | 0 |
| OTHER REVENUE | | | 0 |
| **TOTAL REVENUE** | $ 0 | $ 0 | $ 0 |
| **EXPENSES** | | | |
| FUNDRAISING | | | $ 0 |
| PROGRAM SERVICES | | | 0 |
| GRANTS & CONTRACTS | | | 0 |
| MANAGEMENT & GENERAL | | | 0 |
| **TOTAL EXPENSES** | $ 0 | | $ 0 |
| **CHANGE IN NET ASSETS** | | | $ 0 |
| **BEGINNING NET ASSETS** | | | 0 |
| **ENDING NET ASSETS** | | | $ 0 |

## STATEMENT OF FINANCIAL POSITION    *as of the period ending date*

| ASSETS | | LIABILITIES & NET ASSETS | |
|---|---|---|---|
| CASH ❸ | $ (1,255) | ACCOUNTS PAYABLE ❷ | $ (1,255) |
| ACCOUNTS RECEIVABLE | | SHORT TERM DEBT | |
| INVENTORIES | | LONG TERM DEBT | |
| PREPAID EXPENSES | | ACCRUED EXPENSES | |
| PLEDGES RECEIVABLE | | NET ASSETS: | |
| INVESTMENTS | | W/O DONOR RESTRICTIONS | |
| PP&E (NET) | | WITH DONOR RESTRICTIONS | |
| **TOTAL ASSETS** | $ (1,255) | **TOTAL LIABILITIES & NET ASSETS** | $ (1,255) |

## STATEMENT OF CASH FLOWS    *for the period*

| | | |
|---|---|---|
| **BEGINNING CASH** | | $ 0 |
| CASH RECEIPTS | | |
| CASH DISBURSEMENTS ❶ | | 1,255 |
| **CASH FLOW FROM OPERATIONS** | | $ (1,255) |
| PP&E PURCHASES | | |
| NET BORROWINGS | | |
| INVESTMENT INCOME | | |
| **ENDING CASH** | ❸ | $ (1,255) |

**Transaction 12.
Statement
Entries**

# T13. Use some of the newly purchased supplies from our inventory.

One quarter of the supplies we ordered are going to be used at a large meeting we will be holding with representatives of other charities in the state. We take what we need out of the supply room and fill out the name tags, stuff the binders, and get ready for the meeting. We used $350 worth of inventory.

---

**Transaction:** Record the use of $350 worth of supplies from our inventory.

**1** Reduce **INVENTORY** in the asset section of the *Statement of Financial Position* by $350 worth of supplies.

**2** Record the cost of the supplies used as a **MANAGEMENT & GENERAL EXPENSE** on the *Statement of Activities*.

**3** **CHANGE IN NET ASSETS** on the *Statement of Activities* has decreased by $350 since we used inventory of that value. Subtract this amount from **NET ASSETS W/O DONOR RESTRICTIONS** on the *Statement of Financial Position*.

**Note:** Under accrual accounting, using already "paid for" inventory has no effect on the *Statement of Cash Flows*. However, when we use these supplies, their cost is moved from **INVENTORY** on the *Statement of Financial Position* to the *Statement of Activities* as an **EXPENSE**.

## STATEMENT OF ACTIVITIES — *for the period*

| REVENUE | WITHOUT DONOR RESTRICTIONS | WITH DONOR RESTRICTIONS | |
|---|---|---|---|
| CONTRIBUTIONS & GIFTS | | | $ 0 |
| PROGRAM SERVICES REVENUE | | | 0 |
| GRANTS & CONTRACTS | | | 0 |
| OTHER REVENUE | | | 0 |
| **TOTAL REVENUE** | $ 0 | $ 0 | $ 0 |
| EXPENSES | | | |
| FUNDRAISING | | | $ 0 |
| PROGRAM SERVICES | | | 0 |
| GRANTS & CONTRACTS | | | 0 |
| MANAGEMENT & GENERAL | ❷ 350 | | 350 |
| **TOTAL EXPENSES** | $ 350 | | $ 350 |
| | CHANGE IN NET ASSETS ❸ | | $ (350) |
| | BEGINNING NET ASSETS | | 0 |
| | ENDING NET ASSETS | | $ (350) |

## STATEMENT OF FINANCIAL POSITION — *as of the period ending date*

| ASSETS | | LIABILITIES & NET ASSETS | |
|---|---|---|---|
| CASH | | ACCOUNTS PAYABLE | |
| ACCOUNTS RECEIVABLE | | SHORT TERM DEBT | |
| INVENTORIES ❶ | (350) | LONG TERM DEBT | |
| PREPAID EXPENSES | | ACCRUED EXPENSES | |
| PLEDGES RECEIVABLE | | NET ASSETS: | |
| INVESTMENTS | | W/O DONOR RESTRICTIONS ❸ | (350) |
| PP&E (NET) | | WITH DONOR RESTRICTIONS | |
| **TOTAL ASSETS** | $ (350) | **TOTAL LIABILITIES & NET ASSETS** | $ (350) |

## STATEMENT OF CASH FLOWS — *for the period*

**Transaction 13.
Statement
Entries**

| | |
|---|---|
| BEGINNING CASH | $ 0 |
| CASH RECEIPTS | |
| CASH DISBURSEMENTS | |
| **CASH FLOW FROM OPERATIONS** | $ 0 |
| PP&E PURCHASES | |
| NET BORROWINGS | |
| INVESTMENT INCOME | |
| **ENDING CASH** | $ 0 |

# T14. Take me out to the Ball Game!

We sponsor several little league baseball teams (9-12 year-olds) in our service area. Costs aren't high (custom uniform t-shirts) and the kids (and parents) love the program. At the end of the season, we put everybody who wants to go in yellow school buses and take them to the local AAA ballpark to watch a Boston Red Sox farm team game. Tickets are donated to the kids by the Sox.

WsNA pays all the other expenses out of general revenue. Two buses cost $400 for the afternoon. Everybody has 2 hotdogs at $3.50 each, a soft drink at $2.50, plus a bag of popcorn at $2.75 for a total of $12.25 per person for forty-two kids, three parent chaperones and two seniors. Our total cost for the event is $976 and well worth it. Why? We like to maintain an active profile in the community, and sometimes our seniors like to go to the games with the kids. Not sure who has the most fun!

---

**Transaction:** Our expenses for the ball-game outing are $976 total. We pay the bus people by check. We will need to pay cash for the food, so we lift the funds from our petty cash drawer (and leave a note to the book-keeper so that she can properly record the expense when she reconciles the drawer).

**1** Record $976 spent as a **PROGRAM SERVICES EXPENSE** on the *Statement of Activities.*

**2** Reduce cash on the *Statement of Cash Flows* by $976 as a **CASH DISBURSEMENT.**

**3** **ENDING CASH** on the *Statement of Cash Flows* is always the same as **CASH** on the *Statement of Financial Position,* so subtract $976 from **CASH** on that statement.

**4** **CHANGE IN NET ASSETS** has decreased by $976 on the *Statement of Activities,* so subtract this amount from the **NET ASSETS W/O DONOR RESTRICTION** line on the *Statement of Financial Position.*

## STATEMENT OF ACTIVITIES
*for the period*

| REVENUE | WITHOUT DONOR RESTRICTIONS | WITH DONOR RESTRICTIONS | | |
|---|---|---|---|---|
| CONTRIBUTIONS & GIFTS | | | $ | 0 |
| PROGRAM SERVICES REVENUE | | | | 0 |
| GRANTS & CONTRACTS | | | | 0 |
| OTHER REVENUE | | | | 0 |
| **TOTAL REVENUE** | $ 0 | $ 0 | $ | 0 |
| **EXPENSES** | | | | |
| FUNDRAISING | | | $ | 0 |
| PROGRAM SERVICES | ❶ 976 | | | 976 |
| GRANTS & CONTRACTS | | | | 0 |
| MANAGEMENT & GENERAL | | | | 0 |
| **TOTAL EXPENSES** | $ 976 | | $ | 976 |

| | | |
|---|---|---|
| CHANGE IN NET ASSETS | ❹ $ | (976) |
| BEGINNING NET ASSETS | | 0 |
| ENDING NET ASSETS | $ | (976) |

## STATEMENT OF FINANCIAL POSITION
*as of the period ending date*

| ASSETS | | | LIABILITIES & NET ASSETS | | |
|---|---|---|---|---|---|
| CASH | ❸ $ | (976) | ACCOUNTS PAYABLE | | |
| ACCOUNTS RECEIVABLE | | | SHORT TERM DEBT | | |
| INVENTORIES | | | LONG TERM DEBT | | |
| PREPAID EXPENSES | | | ACCRUED EXPENSES | | |
| PLEDGES RECEIVABLE | | | NET ASSETS: | | |
| INVESTMENTS | | | W/O DONOR RESTRICTIONS | ❹ | (976) |
| PP&E (NET) | | | WITH DONOR RESTRICTIONS | | |
| **TOTAL ASSETS** | $ | (976) | **TOTAL LIABILITIES & NET ASSETS** | $ | (976) |

## STATEMENT OF CASH FLOWS
*for the period*

**Transaction 14. Statement Entries**

| | | |
|---|---|---|
| BEGINNING CASH | $ | 0 |
| CASH RECEIPTS | | |
| CASH DISBURSEMENTS | ❷ | 976 |
| **CASH FLOW FROM OPERATIONS** | $ | (976) |
| PP&E PURCHASES | | |
| NET BORROWINGS | | |
| INVESTMENT INCOME | | |
| **ENDING CASH** | ❸ $ | (976) |

# Chapter 11.
# Payroll Expense
# Transactions

Payroll is often by far the largest expense category for many non-profit organizations. Learn how to record these expense transactions. Although, most nonprofits use a payroll service company to compute tax payments, manage check writing, and pay employees and the government their due, it is useful for everyone to understand the process. Note, board members may be *personally liable* for any errors!

**Transaction 15.** Issue $10,780 in payroll checks.

**Transaction 16.** Record payroll-related fringe-benefit expenses and withheld payroll taxes.

**Transaction 17.** Pay payroll-related accrued expenses to the government and insurance companies.

# T15. Issue $10,780 in payroll checks.

WsNA's dedicated employees are our greatest asset—and our biggest single expense—as is the case for most nonprofits. We send a list of salaries to CompuRight, Inc., our payroll service. They will calculate paycheck amounts to be issued, the payroll related taxes due to the government, as well as fringe benefits expense due insurance companies. CompuRight will get it right! The service asks us to

| | PAY TO EMPLOYEES | PAY TO OTHERS |
|---|---|---|
| MONTHLY SALARIES & WAGES | $16,000 | $0 |
| EMPLOYEES' SHARE OF FICA | (1,220) | 1,220 |
| FEDERAL/STATE WITHHOLDING | (3,450) | 3,450 |
| EMPYOYER'S SHARE OF FICA | 0 | 1,220 |
| WORKMANS' COMPENSATION | 0 | 500 |
| UNEMPLOYMENT INSURANCE | 0 | 650 |
| EMPLOYEE-PAID HEALTH & LIFE | (550) | 550 |
| WsNA PAID FRINGE BENEFITS | 0 | 3,230 |
| TOTALS PER MONTH | $10,780 | $10,820 |
| PAID BY WsNA TO EMPLOYEES & TO OTHERS | | $21,600 |

send an electronic funds transfer for the total employee check amounts. CompuRight will pay employees via direct deposit or printed checks.

See table above: Monthly payroll costs total $21,600 but, in this transaction, the checks issued to employees total only $10,780. WsNA uses the rest for payment of the employees' share of government taxes and health and life insurance.

---

**Transaction:** Use payroll service to issue salary and wage checks totaling $10,780 to employees: $1,867 for the fundraising staff, $5,990 for the program services staff, and $2,923 for management and general staff.

**1** Send the payroll service an electronic transfer for $10,780. Record this transfer as a **CASH DISBURSEMENT** on the *Statement of Cash Flows*. The Payroll service will issue checks from their own account.

**2** Record the appropriate department amounts in the **EXPENSES** section of the *Statement of Activities*.

**3** **ENDING CASH** on the *Statement of Cash Flows* is always the same as **CASH** on the *Statement of Financial Position*, so reduce **CASH** by $10,780 on that statement.

**4** **ENDING NET ASSETS** has decreased by $10,780 on the *Statement of Activities*. Subtract this amount from the **NET ASSETS W/O RESTRICTIONS** line on the *Statement of Financial Position*.

## STATEMENT OF ACTIVITIES                                    *for the period*

| REVENUE | WITHOUT DONOR RESTRICTIONS | WITH DONOR RESTRICTIONS | | |
|---|---|---|---|---|
| CONTRIBUTIONS & GIFTS | $ 0 | $ 0 | $ | 0 |
| PROGRAM SERVICES REVENUE | | | | 0 |
| GRANTS & CONTRACTS | | | | 0 |
| OTHER REVENUE | | | | 0 |
| **TOTAL REVENUE** | **$ 0** | **$ 0** | **$** | **0** |
| **EXPENSES** | | | | |
| FUNDRAISING | ❷ $ 1,867 | | $ | 1,867 |
| PROGRAM SERVICES | ❷ 5,990 | | | 5,990 |
| GRANTS & CONTRACTS | | | | 0 |
| MANAGEMENT & GENERAL | ❷ 2,923 | | | 2,923 |
| **TOTAL EXPENSES** | **$ 10,780** | | **$** | **10,780** |
| | CHANGE IN NET ASSETS | | $ | (10,780) |
| | BEGINNING NET ASSETS | | | 0 |
| | ENDING NET ASSETS | ❹ | $ | (10,780) |

## STATEMENT OF FINANCIAL POSITION            *as of the period ending date*

| ASSETS | | LIABILITIES & NET ASSETS | | |
|---|---|---|---|---|
| CASH | ❸ $ (10,780) | ACCOUNTS PAYABLE | | $ 0 |
| ACCOUNTS RECEIVABLE | | SHORT TERM DEBT | | |
| INVENTORIES | | LONG TERM DEBT | | |
| PREPAID EXPENSES | | ACCRUED EXPENSES | | |
| PLEDGES RECEIVABLE | | NET ASSETS: | | |
| INVESTMENTS | | W/O DONOR RESTRICTIONS | ❹ | (10,780) |
| PP&E (NET) | | WITH DONOR RESTRICTIONS | | |
| **TOTAL ASSETS** | **$ (10,780)** | **TOTAL LIABILITIES & NET ASSETS** | | **$ (10,780)** |

## STATEMENT OF CASH FLOWS   *for the period*

| | | | |
|---|---|---|---|
| | BEGINNING CASH | $ | 0 |
| | CASH RECEIPTS | | |
| **Transaction 15** | CASH DISBURSEMENTS ❶ | | 10,780 |
| **Statement** | **CASH FLOW FROM OPERATIONS** | **$** | **(10,780)** |
| **Entries** | | | |
| | PP&E PURCHASES | | |
| | NET BORROWINGS | | |
| | INVESTMENT INCOME | | |
| | **ENDING CASH** | ❸ **$** | **(10,780)** |

# T16. Record payroll-related fringe-benefit expenses and withheld payroll taxes.

When we issued payroll checks in **T15**, we only recorded the cash expense for the actual checks issued. Now we must record *all* the payroll-related obligations: fringe benefits, withholding taxes, and FICA. These additional amounts (see the table on page 110) will total $10,820 and will be paid by WsNA—not right now—but later:

- $3,450 for employees' withholding taxes and $1,220 for the employees' share of FICA.

- $550 for the employees' withheld share of health insurance plus WsNA's contribution of $3,230.

- $500 for workers' compensation, $1,220 for the employer's share of FICA, and $650 for unemployment insurance.

Add all these amounts and the total is $10,820. Note, if an expense is recorded in the *Statement of Activities*, but is not paid immediately (satisfying the obligation), then we must record that expense as *accrued* (to be paid later) on the *Statement of Financial Position*.

---

**Transaction:** Accrue $10,820 in payroll-related withholding taxes, employment taxes, and fringe benefit expenses.

**1** Record the appropriate department amounts in the **EXPENSES** section of the *Statement of Activities*.

**2** Add $10,820 to **ACCRUED EXPENSES** on the *Statement of Financial Position*.

**3** **CHANGE IN NET ASSETS** has decreased by $10,820 on the *Statement of Activities*. Subtract this amount from the **UNRESTRICTED NET ASSETS** line on the *Statement of Financial Position*.

Now, **TOTAL ASSETS** and **TOTAL LIABILITIES & NET ASSETS** have not changed and are equal.

## STATEMENT OF ACTIVITIES — *for the period*

| REVENUE | WITHOUT DONOR RESTRICTIONS | WITH DONOR RESTRICTIONS | |
|---|---|---|---|
| CONTRIBUTIONS & GIFTS | | | $  0 |
| PROGRAM SERVICES REVENUE | | | 0 |
| GRANTS & CONTRACTS | | | 0 |
| OTHER REVENUE | | | 0 |
| **TOTAL REVENUE** | $  0 | $  0 | $  0 |
| **EXPENSES** | | | |
| FUNDRAISING | ❶ $  1,874 | | $  1,874 |
| PROGRAM SERVICES | ❶ 6,012 | | 6,012 |
| GRANTS & CONTRACTS | | | 0 |
| MANAGEMENT & GENERAL | ❶ 2,934 | | 2,934 |
| **TOTAL EXPENSES** | $  10,820 | | $  10,820 |
| | CHANGE IN NET ASSETS | ❸ | $  (10,820) |
| | BEGINNING NET ASSETS | | 0 |
| | ENDING NET ASSETS | | $  (10,820) |

## STATEMENT OF FINANCIAL POSITION — *as of the period ending date*

| ASSETS | | LIABILITIES & NET ASSETS | |
|---|---|---|---|
| CASH | | ACCOUNTS PAYABLE | |
| ACCOUNTS RECEIVABLE | | SHORT TERM DEBT | |
| INVENTORIES | | LONG TERM DEBT | |
| PREPAID EXPENSES | | ACCRUED EXPENSES | ❷ 10,820 |
| PLEDGES RECEIVABLE | | NET ASSETS: | |
| INVESTMENTS | | W/O DONOR RESTRICTIONS | ❸ (10,820) |
| PP&E (NET) | | WITH DONOR RESTRICTIONS | |
| **TOTAL ASSETS** | $  0 | **TOTAL LIABILITIES & NET ASSETS** | $  0 |

## STATEMENT OF CASH FLOWS — *for the period*

**Transaction 16. Statement Entries**

| | |
|---|---|
| BEGINNING CASH | $  0 |
| CASH RECEIPTS | |
| CASH DISBURSEMENTS | |
| **CASH FLOW FROM OPERATIONS** | $  0 |
| PP&E PURCHASES | |
| NET BORROWINGS | |
| INVESTMENT INCOME | |
| **ENDING CASH** | $  0 |

# T17. Pay payroll-related accrued expenses to the government & insurance companies.

WsNA owes $10,820 in payroll-related tax, insurance, and other fringe benefit obligations. We recorded the accrual of these obligations in **T16**; now we will pay them.

Or else! If we do not, our employees' health insurance may be cut off. In addition, the government gets very testy if the organization does not pay all withholding and FICA premiums when they are due.

The IRS holds board members personally liable if these payments are not made accurately and on time. They will, quite literally, take your house!

---

**Transaction:** Write checks to the government and to our various insurance companies totaling $10,820 in payment of payroll-related accrued expenses.

**①** Issue checks in payment of payroll-related accrued expenses. Record the $10,820 amount as a **CASH DISBURSEMENT** on the *Statement of Cash Flows*.

**②** Now paid, reduce the amount of **ACCRUED EXPENSES** in the **LIABILITIES & NET ASSETS** section of the *Statement of Financial Position*.

**③** **ENDING CASH** on the *Statement of Cash Flows* is always the same as **CASH** on the *Statement of Financial Position*, so subtract $10,820 from that statement.

**Note:** Handling payroll properly can be difficult. Getting it wrong irritates employees. Also, the government is seriously not amused. Many nonprofit organizations choose to use commercial payroll services to get it right.

## STATEMENT OF ACTIVITIES                    *for the period*

| REVENUE | WITHOUT DONOR RESTRICTIONS | WITH DONOR RESTRICTIONS | | |
|---|---|---|---|---|
| CONTRIBUTIONS & GIFTS | | | $ | 0 |
| PROGRAM SERVICES REVENUE | | | | 0 |
| GRANTS & CONTRACTS | | | | 0 |
| OTHER REVENUE | | | | 0 |
| **TOTAL REVENUE** | $ 0 | $ 0 | $ | 0 |
| **EXPENSES** | | | | |
| FUNDRAISING | | | $ | 0 |
| PROGRAM SERVICES | | | | 0 |
| GRANTS & CONTRACTS | | | | 0 |
| MANAGEMENT & GENERAL | | | | 0 |
| **TOTAL EXPENSES** | $ 0 | | $ | 0 |
| | CHANGE IN NET ASSETS | | $ | 0 |
| | BEGINNING NET ASSETS | | | 0 |
| | ENDING NET ASSETS | | $ | 0 |

## STATEMENT OF FINANCIAL POSITION          *as of the period ending date*

| ASSETS | | | LIABILITIES & NET ASSETS | | |
|---|---|---|---|---|---|
| CASH | ❸ $ (10,820) | | ACCOUNTS PAYABLE | | |
| ACCOUNTS RECEIVABLE | | | SHORT TERM DEBT | | |
| INVENTORIES | | | LONG TERM DEBT | | |
| PREPAID EXPENSES | | | ACCRUED EXPENSES | ❷ | (10,820) |
| PLEDGES RECEIVABLE | | | NET ASSETS: | | |
| INVESTMENTS | | | W/O DONOR RESTRICTIONS | | |
| PP&E (NET) | | | WITH DONOR RESTRICTIONS | | |
| **TOTAL ASSETS** | $ (10,820) | | **TOTAL LIABILITIES & NET ASSETS** | $ (10,820) | |

## STATEMENT OF CASH FLOWS  *for the period*

| | | | |
|---|---|---|---|
| | BEGINNING CASH | $ | 0 |
| **Transaction 17.** | CASH RECEIPTS | | |
| **Statement** | CASH DISBURSEMENTS | ❶ | 10,820 |
| **Entries** | **CASH FLOW FROM OPERATIONS** | $ (10,820) | |
| | PP&E PURCHASES | | |
| | NET BORROWINGS | | |
| | INVESTMENT INCOME | | |
| | **ENDING CASH** | ❸ $ (10,820) | |

115

# Chapter 12.
# Contracts & Grants
# Transactions

It is a tough market for seasoned workers, aged 50 or older. Many of these folks come into the Senior Center looking for help in finding a job. We submit a grant proposal to the U.S. Department of Labor to develop a training course and website to assist workers re-entering the job market.

$\sim$

Nonprofit contract and grant revenue comes mostly from governmental agencies and other charitable organizations and foundations. These grants and contracts are usually: (1) for a specific purpose, (2) to be performed in a specific time period, and (3) directly related to the recipient nonprofit organization's skills and charitable mission.

The accounting treatment of contract and grant revenue can differ greatly depending on the classification of either a contract or grant, the fine print in the agreements, and the desires of the parties. Some grants are really an outright gift of funds and are recorded as CONTRIBUTIONS & GIFTS REVENUE. Other contract and grant revenue is best regarded as *fee-for-service* exchange transactions where the grantor gives money to the nonprofit organization to provide specific goods or to perform specific services with a public purpose; there is a *deliverable*.

Generally, revenue from a grant is treated as a contribution and is reported as revenue when received or pledged and NET ASSETS are increased; expenses to fulfil the grant are reported whenever they occur, even in a different accounting period. No matching of revenue and expense is required. NET ASSETS will increase when revenue is first recorded and fall as expenses are booked.

In contrast, revenues from exchange transaction contracts are recognized *as earned* when associated expenses are recorded. No change in NET ASSETS.

∼

Special governmental compliance audits (called a *Single Audit* or an *A-133 Audit*) are required if the organization receives sizable federal government grants (over $750,000 in a single year). Foundation donors may impose their own reporting requirements on the nonprofit organization as specified as part of the contract.

∼

Contrary to public perception, nonprofit organizations are not designed to lose money and must not if they intend to survive. For nonprofit organizations, *profit* is not a dirty word—even though we sanitize using the word *surplus*. The government and most funders expect a well-run nonprofit organization to produce a small profit from its activities necessary to sustain their long-term viability. Profitable, successful public 501(c)(3) charities should not be suspect.

The following are examples of the accounting treatment of a training contract WsNA has with the federal government.

**Transaction 18.** U.S. Department of Labor awards us a $100,000 contract. Whoopee!

**Transaction 19.** Receive 20% prepayment from the government and record expenses so far.

**Transaction 20.** Finish training program contract. Submit all necessary paperwork for final payment from the government.

**Transaction 21.** The government pays (late)!

**Transaction 22.** Review summary presentation of nonprofit contract accounting.

*"These are magic beans, my boy. Their value comes from growth and scale, not revenue."*

# T18. U.S. Department of Labor awards us a $100,000 contract. Whoopee!

We are awarded a $100,000 contract from the U.S. Department of Labor (DOL) to develop a training course for workers re-entering the job market. Financially, accepting this contract is a mixed blessing. Some grants and contracts can cause liquidity problems for nonprofits. WsNA may need to spend our own cash reserves *before* receiving cash payments from the government. We will have to manage costs carefully, for sure.

There is no change in the financial statements just because we are awarded this contract. As project costs are incurred, we will record revenue and also the corresponding expenses. Cash that we spend before receiving payment from the DOL is out-of-pocket—it hurts now but, we believe in the project.

To start things up quickly, we hire a consultant, Getta Rite, as the project manager and pay her $5,000 as a retainer. Here we go!

---

**Transaction:** Send consultant $5,000 retainer check.

**1** Send the consultant a $5,000 retainer and record on the *Statement of Cash Flows* as a CASH DISBURSEMENT.

**2** ENDING CASH on the *Statement of Cash Flows* is always the same as CASH on the *Statement of Financial Position,* so subtract $5,000 from CASH on that statement.

**3** We regard this prepayment to our consultant as an asset for now. Means we will not have to pay it in the future. Add it to PREPAID EXPENSES in the asset section of the *Statement of Financial Position.*

Now, TOTAL ASSETS equals TOTAL LIABILITIES & NET ASSETS on the *Statement of Financial Position*

**Note:** WsNA has used its own cash to make this payment. Some contracts require a large commitment of a nonprofit's cash prior to any reimbursement. If the needed cash were not available, the nonprofit organization would be *financially unable* to accept the contract without incurring debt and would lose the opportunity. Sigh. Having strong financials is important to mission.

## STATEMENT OF ACTIVITIES    *for the period*

| REVENUE | WITHOUT DONOR RESTRICTIONS | WITH DONOR RESTRICTIONS | | |
|---|---|---|---|---|
| CONTRIBUTIONS & GIFTS | | | $ | 0 |
| PROGRAM SERVICES REVENUE | | | | 0 |
| GRANTS & CONTRACTS | | | | 0 |
| OTHER REVENUE | | | | 0 |
| **TOTAL REVENUE** | $ 0 | $ 0 | $ | 0 |
| **EXPENSES** | | | | |
| FUNDRAISING | | | $ | 0 |
| PROGRAM SERVICES | | | | 0 |
| GRANTS & CONTRACTS | | | | 0 |
| MANAGEMENT & GENERAL | | | | 0 |
| **TOTAL EXPENSES** | $ 0 | | $ | 0 |
| CHANGE IN NET ASSETS | | | $ | 0 |
| BEGINNING NET ASSETS | | | | 0 |
| ENDING NET ASSETS | | | $ | 0 |

## STATEMENT OF FINANCIAL POSITION    *as of the period ending date*

| ASSETS | | | LIABILITIES & NET ASSETS | |
|---|---|---|---|---|
| CASH | ❷ $ (5,000) | | ACCOUNTS PAYABLE | |
| ACCOUNTS RECEIVABLE | | | SHORT TERM DEBT | |
| INVENTORIES | | | LONG TERM DEBT | |
| PREPAID EXPENSES | ❸ 5,000 | | ACCRUED EXPENSES | |
| PLEDGES RECEIVABLE | | | NET ASSETS: | |
| INVESTMENTS | | | W/O DONOR RESTRICTIONS | |
| PP&E (NET) | | | WITH DONOR RESTRICTIONS | |
| **TOTAL ASSETS** | $ 0 | | **TOTAL LIABILITIES & NET ASSETS** | $ 0 |

## STATEMENT OF CASH FLOWS *for the period*

**Transaction 18.**
**Statement**
**Entries**

| | | |
|---|---|---|
| BEGINNING CASH | | $ 0 |
| CASH RECEIPTS | | |
| CASH DISBURSEMENTS | ❶ | 5,000 |
| **CASH FLOW FROM OPERATIONS** | | $ (5,000) |
| PP&E PURCHASES | | |
| NET BORROWINGS | | |
| INVESTMENT INCOME | | |
| **ENDING CASH** | ❷ | $ (5,000) |

121

# T19. Receive 20% prepayment from the government and record expenses so far.

Upon signing the contract with the DOL, they make a prepayment of $20,000 (20% of the award) to help WsNA with startup expenses. We will receive the remainder of the monies due after we submit: (a) the final product for approval and also, (b) our invoice with documented costs.

We just hired a project manager and already have an on-staff writer, W.R. Cleary. We will need to contract with an expert web designer and a training consultant too.

Our selected web designer, Bobbie Flash, charges $35 per hour and quotes 60 hours needed to complete the project. She says we will also need to purchase a computer software training platform license for $10,000. Our own part-time trainer, Clair Bell, will help with the program message. We have budgeted about $97,500 in total to complete the work, leaving us $2,500 for contingencies.

---

**Transaction:** Receive a $20,000 prepayment from the DOL and deposit the check into our bank account.

**1** Deposit the $20,000 check in WsNA's bank account and record as a CASH RECEIPT on the *Statement of Cash Flows*. ENDING CASH on the *Statement of Cash Flows* is always the same as CASH on the *Statement of Financial Position*, so add $20,000 to CASH on that statement.

**2** The project manager has earned the $5,000 we paid in T18, so we can reduce PREPAID EXPENSE on the *Statement of Financial Position* and record the expense in GRANTS & CONTRACTS EXPENSE on the *Statement of Activities*. With $5,000 of expense recorded, we can record the same amount of GRANT & CONTRACT REVENUE on the *Statement of Activities*.

**3** Now that we have received the $20,000 from the DOL and spent $5,000 on project management, we still owe the DOL $15,000 of work to be done on the project. We will record that obligation as ACCRUED EXPENSES on the *Statement of Financial Position*.

Since the revenue and expense are the same amount, there is no change in NET ASSETS.

## STATEMENT OF ACTIVITIES  *for the period*

| REVENUE | WITHOUT DONOR RESTRICTIONS | WITH DONOR RESTRICTIONS | |
|---|---|---|---|
| CONTRIBUTIONS & GIFTS | | | $ 0 |
| PROGRAM SERVICES REVENUE | | | 0 |
| GRANTS & CONTRACTS | ❷ 5,000 | | 5,000 |
| OTHER REVENUE | | | 0 |
| **TOTAL REVENUE** | $ 5,000 | $ 0 | $ 5,000 |
| **EXPENSES** | | | |
| FUNDRAISING | | | $ 0 |
| PROGRAM SERVICES | | | 0 |
| GRANTS & CONTRACTS | ❷ 5,000 | | 5,000 |
| MANAGEMENT & GENERAL | | | 0 |
| **TOTAL EXPENSES** | $ 5,000 | | $ 5,000 |

| | |
|---|---|
| CHANGE IN NET ASSETS | $ 0 |
| BEGINNING NET ASSETS | 0 |
| ENDING NET ASSETS | $ 0 |

## STATEMENT OF FINANCIAL POSITION  *as of the period ending date*

| ASSETS | | LIABILITIES & NET ASSETS | |
|---|---|---|---|
| CASH | ❶ $ 20,000 | ACCOUNTS PAYABLE | |
| ACCOUNTS RECEIVABLE | | SHORT TERM DEBT | |
| INVENTORIES | | LONG TERM DEBT | |
| PREPAID EXPENSES | ❷ (5,000) | ACCRUED EXPENSES | ❸ 15,000 |
| PLEDGES RECEIVABLE | | NET ASSETS: | |
| INVESTMENTS | | W/O DONOR RESTRICTIONS | |
| PP&E (NET) | | WITH DONOR RESTRICTIONS | |
| **TOTAL ASSETS** | $ 15,000 | **TOTAL LIABILITIES & NET ASSETS** | $ 15,000 |

## STATEMENT OF CASH FLOWS  *for the period*

**Transaction 19. Statement Entries**

| | |
|---|---|
| BEGINNING CASH | $ 0 |
| CASH RECEIPTS | ❶ $ 20,000 |
| CASH DISBURSEMENTS | |
| **CASH FLOW FROM OPERATIONS** | $ 20,000 |
| PP&E PURCHASES | |
| NET BORROWINGS | |
| INVESTMENT INCOME | |
| **ENDING CASH** | ❶ $ 20,000 |

# T20. Finish training program contract. Submit all necessary paperwork for final payment from the government.

Everyone loves our training program. We submit a final project report, teaching materials, the website URL, and our invoice for the program director to approve. She is quite happy we are on time, on budget.

Our direct expenses for the project are $85,338. We add a 13.8% overhead rate making $97,115 our total project expense. WsNA has negotiated this overhead rate with the DOL and have data to back up these costs. Otherwise, the government caps overhead payment at 10%. It is important to keep track; that extra 3.8% can be a meaningful chunk of change.

Overhead expenses (*indirect costs*) are real costs to WsNA—real money out—for rent, heat/light/power, insurance, accounting/legal services, fundraising, and so forth. These costs are difficult to assign directly to specific projects, so we use the 13.8% rate to assign them to our programs across-the-board.

---

**Transaction:** Close out the project and record our expected $95,000 in additional revenue ($100,000 less the $5,000 already recorded). Record our additional expenses of $92,115 ($97,115 less the $5,000 already recorded). Submit a final $80,000 invoice ($100,000 total contract amount less the $20,000 in prior payments.

**1** Record the remaining contract amount by increasing GRANTS & CONTRACTS REVENUE by $95,000 on the *Statement of Activities* and increasing ACCOUNTS RECEIVABLE by $80,000 (invoice amount that they owe us) and reducing ACCRUED EXPENSES by $15,000 (we don't owe; the project is complete) on the *Statement of Financial Position.*

**2** Record GRANTS AND CONTRACTS EXPENSE of $92,115 for newly paid expenses. Record this amount as CASH DISBURSEMENTS on the *Statement of Cash Flows.*

**3** *OMG.* We make a surplus (profit) of $2,885. Add this amount to NET ASSETS W/O DONOR RESTRICTIONS.

## STATEMENT OF ACTIVITIES                                *for the period*

| REVENUE | WITHOUT DONOR RESTRICTIONS | WITH DONOR RESTRICTIONS | | |
|---|---|---|---|---|
| CONTRIBUTIONS & GIFTS | | | $ | 0 |
| PROGRAM SERVICES REVENUE | | | | 0 |
| GRANTS & CONTRACTS | ❶ 95,000 | | | 95,000 |
| OTHER REVENUE | | | | 0 |
| **TOTAL REVENUE** | **$ 95,000** | **$ 0** | **$** | **95,000** |
| **EXPENSES** | | | | |
| FUNDRAISING | | | $ | 0 |
| PROGRAM SERVICES | | | | 0 |
| GRANTS & CONTRACTS | ❷ 92,115 | | | 92,115 |
| MANAGEMENT & GENERAL | | | | 0 |
| **TOTAL EXPENSES** | **$ 92,115** | | **$** | **92,115** |
| CHANGE IN NET ASSETS | | | $ | 2,885 |
| BEGINNING NET ASSETS | | | | 0 |
| ENDING NET ASSETS | | | $ | 2,885 |

## STATEMENT OF FINANCIAL POSITION              *as of the period ending date*

| ASSETS | | | LIABILITIES & NET ASSETS | | |
|---|---|---|---|---|---|
| CASH | ❷ | $ (92,115) | ACCOUNTS PAYABLE | | |
| ACCOUNTS RECEIVABLE | ❶ | 80,000 | SHORT TERM DEBT | | |
| INVENTORIES | | | LONG TERM DEBT | | |
| PREPAID EXPENSES | | | ACCRUED EXPENSES | ❶ | (15,000) |
| PLEDGES RECEIVABLE | | | NET ASSETS: | | |
| INVESTMENTS | | | W/O DONOR RESTRICTIONS | ❸ | 2,885 |
| PP&E (NET) | | | WITH DONOR RESTRICTIONS | | |
| **TOTAL ASSETS** | | **$ (12,115)** | **TOTAL LIABILITIES & NET ASSETS** | | **$ (12,115)** |

## STATEMENT OF CASH FLOWS  *for the period*

| | | |
|---|---|---|
| BEGINNING CASH | $ | 0 |
| CASH RECEIPTS | | |
| CASH DISBURSEMENTS | ❷ | 92,115 |
| **CASH FLOW FROM OPERATIONS** | **$** | **(92,115)** |
| PP&E PURCHASES | | |
| NET BORROWINGS | | |
| INVESTMENT INCOME | | |
| **ENDING CASH** | ❷ **$** | **(92,115)** |

**Transaction 20. Statement Entries**

# T21. The government pays (late)!

We have spent a total of $97,115 in cash to fulfill our obligations under the contract. The government paid us $20,000 at the beginning of the project and now owes us a completion payment. We are $77,115 in the hole until the government pays us. Sigh. If we did not have the cash available in the cash account on our strong *Statement of Financial Position*, we would be in a full-blown liquidity crisis!

Happily, we have a strong *Statement of Financial Position* and can carry the governmental accounts payable (our accounts receivable). Many nonprofit organizations are not so lucky and cannot accept slow-paying contracts. They would run out of cash. Bankrupt. Gulp and sigh.

---

**Transaction:** Receive a check for $80,000 from the Department of Labor in final payment of our contract to produce the training program.

**❶** Deposit the $80,000 check in WsNA's bank account. Now we have $80,000 more cash. Record this increase in cash as a **CASH RECEIPT** on the *Statement of Cash Flows*.

**❷** Reduce **ACCOUNTS RECEIVABLE** by $80,000 on the *Statement of Financial Position*.

**❸** **ENDING CASH** on the *Statement of Cash Flows* is always the same as **CASH** on the *Statement of Financial Position,* so add $80,000 to **CASH** on that statement.

Party! The chairperson of the board invites the whole crew to a celebratory barbeque dinner at her home. Yea! A good time is had by all. It is a personal gift from her to our staff; no donation, not on the books.

## STATEMENT OF ACTIVITIES  *for the period*

| REVENUE | WITHOUT DONOR RESTRICTIONS | WITH DONOR RESTRICTIONS | |
|---|---|---|---|
| CONTRIBUTIONS & GIFTS | | | $ 0 |
| PROGRAM SERVICES REVENUE | | | 0 |
| GRANTS & CONTRACTS | | | 0 |
| OTHER REVENUE | | | 0 |
| **TOTAL REVENUE** | $ 0 | $ 0 | $ 0 |
| EXPENSES | | | |
| FUNDRAISING | | | $ 0 |
| PROGRAM SERVICES | | | 0 |
| GRANTS & CONTRACTS | | | 0 |
| MANAGEMENT & GENERAL | | | 0 |
| **TOTAL EXPENSES** | $ 0 | | $ 0 |
| CHANGE IN NET ASSETS | | | $ 0 |
| BEGINNING NET ASSETS | | | 0 |
| ENDING NET ASSETS | | | $ 0 |

## STATEMENT OF FINANCIAL POSITION  *as of the period ending date*

| ASSETS | | LIABILITIES & NET ASSETS | |
|---|---|---|---|
| CASH ❶ | $ 80,000 | ACCOUNTS PAYABLE | |
| ACCOUNTS RECEIVABLE ❷ | (80,000) | SHORT TERM DEBT | |
| INVENTORIES | | LONG TERM DEBT | |
| PREPAID EXPENSES | | ACCRUED EXPENSES | |
| PLEDGES RECEIVABLE | | NET ASSETS: | |
| INVESTMENTS | | W/O DONOR RESTRICTIONS | |
| PP&E (NET) | | WITH DONOR RESTRICTIONS | |
| **TOTAL ASSETS** | $ 0 | **TOTAL LIABILITIES & NET ASSETS** | $ 0 |

## STATEMENT OF CASH FLOWS  *for the period*

**Transaction 21.**
**Statement**
**Entries**

| | |
|---|---|
| BEGINNING CASH | $ 0 |
| CASH RECEIPTS ❶ | $ 80,000 |
| CASH DISBURSEMENTS | |
| **CASH FLOW FROM OPERATIONS** | $ 80,000 |
| PP&E PURCHASES | |
| NET BORROWINGS | |
| INVESTMENT INCOME | |
| **ENDING CASH** ❶ | $ 80,000 |

# T22. Review summary presentation of nonprofit contract accounting.

Review the transactions in this chapter:

- In **Transaction 18**, WsNA received the contract and paid a $5,000 retainer to a program manager consultant.

- In **Transaction 19**, we received a $20,000 prepayment from the government to help us with start-up expenses.

- In **Transaction 20** we finished the project spending a total of $97,115, and billed the DOL for the additional $80,000 owed to us.

- In **Transaction 21** the government pays us our due.

Add all these entries made in WsNA's financial statements and you have the summary financial statements shown on the facing page. Compared with all the numeric machinations we went through, what we see here is satisfyingly simple—and it all adds up. Amazing, yes?!

---

**Summary:** Account for $100,000 U.S. Department of Labor contract awarded to and completed by WsNA.

**1** Record $100,000 as GRANTS & CONTRACT REVENUE and $97,115 as GRANT & CONTRACT EXPENSE on the *Statement of Activities.*

**2** We made a surplus! CHANGE IN NET ASSETS is $2,885 on the *Statement of Activities.* On the *Statement of Financial Position,* add this amount to NET ASSETS W/O DONOR RESTRICTIONS.

**3** We received $100,000 as CASH RECEIPTS from the government, spent only $97,115 as CASH DISBURSEMENTS to finish the project, and have a positive cash flow of $2,885 in ENDING CASH. Add this amount to CASH in the *Statement of Financial Position.* TOTAL ASSETS now equals TOTAL LIABILITIES & NET ASSETS.

**Note:** A nonprofit organization's *profit* is not a dirty word—even though we sanitize using the word *surplus.* The government and most funders expect a well-run nonprofit organization to produce a small profit from its activities necessary to sustain long-term viability.

## STATEMENT OF ACTIVITIES
*for the period*

| REVENUE | WITHOUT DONOR RESTRICTIONS | WITH DONOR RESTRICTIONS | |
|---|---|---|---|
| CONTRIBUTIONS & GIFTS | | | $ 0 |
| PROGRAM SERVICES REVENUE | | | 0 |
| GRANTS & CONTRACTS | ❶ 100,000 | | 100,000 |
| OTHER REVENUE | | | 0 |
| **TOTAL REVENUE** | **$100,000** | **$ 0** | **$100,000** |
| EXPENSES | | | |
| FUNDRAISING | | | $ 0 |
| PROGRAM SERVICES | | | 0 |
| GRANTS & CONTRACTS | ❶ 97,115 | | 97,115 |
| MANAGEMENT & GENERAL | | | 0 |
| **TOTAL EXPENSES** | **$ 97,115** | | **$ 97,115** |
| | CHANGE IN NET ASSETS | ❷ | $ 2,885 |
| | BEGINNING NET ASSETS | | 0 |
| | ENDING NET ASSETS | | $ 2,885 |

## STATEMENT OF FINANCIAL POSITION
*as of the period ending date*

| ASSETS | | LIABILITIES & NET ASSETS | |
|---|---|---|---|
| CASH | ❸ $ 2,885 | ACCOUNTS PAYABLE | |
| ACCOUNTS RECEIVABLE | | SHORT TERM DEBT | |
| INVENTORIES | | LONG TERM DEBT | |
| PREPAID EXPENSES | | ACCRUED EXPENSES | |
| PLEDGES RECEIVABLE | | NET ASSETS: | |
| INVESTMENTS | | W/O DONOR RESTRICTIONS | ❷ 2,885 |
| PP&E (NET) | | WITH DONOR RESTRICTIONS | |
| **TOTAL ASSETS** | **$ 2,885** | **TOTAL LIABILITIES & NET ASSETS** | **$ 2,885** |

## STATEMENT OF CASH FLOWS
*for the period*

**Transaction 22.**
**Statement**
**Entries**

| BEGINNING CASH | $ 0 |
|---|---|
| CASH RECEIPTS | ❸ $ 100,000 |
| CASH DISBURSEMENTS | ❸ 97,115 |
| **CASH FLOW FROM OPERATIONS** | **$ 2,885** |
| PP&E PURCHASES | |
| NET BORROWINGS | |
| INVESTMENT INCOME | |
| **ENDING CASH** | **❸ $ 2,885** |

129

# Chapter 13.
# Capital Transactions & Depreciation

Capital transactions are investments in the physical infrastructure of the organization. Here is how these expenditures in property, plant, and equipment (PP&E) show on the books.

**Transaction 23.** Wealthy donor funds $1.2 million gift to purchase a building to house our Senior Center.

**Transaction 24.** Purchase "Giverson Building" for $1.9 million with a mortgage of $950,000.

**Transaction 25.** Obtain a construction loan and make necessary renovations and improvements.

**Transaction 26.** Pay off construction loan, refinance the mortgage, and set up the depreciation schedule for our new building.

**Transaction 27.** Record a month of occupancy expenses for our new Senior Center.

# T23. Wealthy donor funds $1.2 million gift to purchase a building to house our senior center.

Robert and Mary Giverson, town elders and long-time supporters of WsNA, step up to the plate. They agree to donate $1.2 million to be used to purchase our current Senior Center building. Our CEO makes the pitch that, through their donation, the Giversons will secure the long-term future of the organization. The clincher is when she says we will name the building after the family!

Owning our own building will lower and stabilize our occupancy costs and lessen our cash flow needs. We will be able to house all our operations in a "home" for the organization. The community will see brick and mortar evidence of our long-term commitment to our shared local mission.

We are thrilled as the Giversons hand over the $1.2 million check. The local neighborhood weekly newspaper sends a photographer to memorialize the event and writes a glowing article.

---

**Transaction:** Receive by check a $1,200,000 contribution for use to purchase a building to house WsNA's Senior Center and operations offices.

**1** Deposit the $1,200,000 check in WsNA's bank account and record as a **CASH RECEIPT** on the *Statement of Cash Flows*. **ENDING CASH** on the *Statement of Cash Flows* is always the same as **CASH** on the *Statement of Financial Position,* so add $1,200,000 to **CASH** on that statement.

**2** Record the $1,200,000 donation as **REVENUE WITH DONOR RESTRICTION** on the *Statement of Activities*. The gift agreement specifies that it must be used to purchase a building to house WsNA's operations.

**3** **CHANGE IN NET ASSETS** increases on the *Statement of Activities* by the gift. Record this change as **NET ASSETS WITH DONOR RESTRICTIONS** on the *Statement of Financial Position.*

## STATEMENT OF ACTIVITIES                                  *for the period*

| REVENUE | WITHOUT DONOR RESTRICTIONS | WITH DONOR RESTRICTIONS | |
|---|---|---|---|
| CONTRIBUTIONS & GIFTS | | ❷ $1,200,000 | $1,200,000 |
| PROGRAM SERVICES REVENUE | | | 0 |
| GRANTS & CONTRACTS | | | 0 |
| OTHER REVENUE | | | 0 |
| TOTAL REVENUE | $ 0 | $1,200,000 | $1,200,000 |
| EXPENSES | | | |
| FUNDRAISING | | | $0 |
| PROGRAM SERVICES | | | 0 |
| GRANTS & CONTRACTS | | | 0 |
| MANAGEMENT & GENERAL | | | 0 |
| TOTAL EXPENSES | $ 0 | | $0 |

| | | |
|---|---|---|
| CHANGE IN NET ASSETS | ❸ | $1,200,000 |
| BEGINNING NET ASSETS | | 0 |
| ENDING NET ASSETS | | $1,200,000 |

## STATEMENT OF FINANCIAL POSITION            *as of the period ending date*

| ASSETS | | LIABILITIES & NET ASSETS | |
|---|---|---|---|
| CASH | ❶ $1,200,000 | ACCOUNTS PAYABLE | |
| ACCOUNTS RECEIVABLE | | SHORT TERM DEBT | |
| INVENTORIES | | LONG TERM DEBT | |
| PREPAID EXPENSES | | ACCRUED EXPENSES | |
| PLEDGES RECEIVABLE | | NET ASSETS: | |
| INVESTMENTS | | W/O DONOR RESTRICTIONS | |
| PP&E (NET) | | ❸ WITH DONOR RESTRICTIONS | 1,200,000 |
| TOTAL ASSETS | $1,200,000 | TOTAL LIABILITIES & NET ASSETS | $1,200,000 |

## STATEMENT OF CASH FLOWS   *for the period*

| | | |
|---|---|---|
| BEGINNING CASH | | $0 |

**Transaction 23. Statement Entries**

| | | |
|---|---|---|
| CASH RECEIPTS | ❶ | $1,200,000 |
| CASH DISBURSEMENTS | | |
| CASH FLOW FROM OPERATIONS | | $1,200,000 |
| PP&E PURCHASES | | |
| NET BORROWINGS | | |
| INVESTMENT INCOME | | |
| ENDING CASH | ❶ | $1,200,000 |

# T24. Purchase "Giverson Building" for $1.9 million with a mortgage of $950,000.

The asking price for the property we currently rent for $15,833 per month is $2.5 million, but our building inspector says it is run-down, needs new wiring and a new roof—about $500,000 of immediate work. We offer $1.9 million to buy the building as-is, and the owner accepts! Hurrah and...OMG!

We have $1,200,000 million in the bank from the Giverson's donation but will need more money to finance the deal. We apply for a mortgage through WestSideBankCorp offering a down payment of 50% of the building's purchase price. Fred Friendly, chief loan officer and West-Side neighbor, responds with a proposed 30-year $950,000 mortgage with 4.25% interest and payments of $4,673 each month. After a board vote, our CEO signs on the dotted line, and WestSideBankCorp deposits $950,000 into our account.

---

**Transaction:** Buy building for $1,900,000 with a 50% down payment and a $950,000 mortgage.

**1** Write a $1,900,000 check to our now ex-landlord to purchase the building. Record as **PP&E PURCHASES** on the *Statement of Cash Flows*. Add that amount to **PP&E** on the assets section of the *Statement of Financial Position*.

**2** Receive $950,000 in mortgage financing. Increase **NET BORROWINGS** by that amount on the *Statement of Cash Flows*. Add that amount to **LONG-TERM DEBT** on the *Statement of Financial Position*.

**3** **ENDING CASH** in the *Statement of Cash Flows* is now ($950,000) for these transactions. Enter ($950,000) as **CASH** in the *Statement of Financial Position*.

Now, **TOTAL ASSETS** equals **TOTAL LIABILITIES & NET ASSETS** on the *Statement of Financial Position*.

## STATEMENT OF ACTIVITIES *for the period*

| REVENUE | WITHOUT DONOR RESTRICTIONS | WITH DONOR RESTRICTIONS | |
|---|---|---|---|
| CONTRIBUTIONS & GIFTS | | | $0 |
| PROGRAM SERVICES REVENUE | | | 0 |
| GRANTS & CONTRACTS | | | 0 |
| OTHER REVENUE | | | 0 |
| TOTAL REVENUE | $ 0 | $0 | $0 |
| EXPENSES | | | |
| FUNDRAISING | | | $0 |
| PROGRAM SERVICES | | | 0 |
| GRANTS & CONTRACTS | | | 0 |
| MANAGEMENT & GENERAL | | | 0 |
| TOTAL EXPENSES | $ 0 | | $0 |
| CHANGE IN NET ASSETS | | | $0 |
| BEGINNING NET ASSETS | | | 0 |
| ENDING NET ASSETS | | | $0 |

## STATEMENT OF FINANCIAL POSITION *as of the period ending date*

| ASSETS | | | LIABILITIES & NET ASSETS | | |
|---|---|---|---|---|---|
| CASH | ❸ | ($950,000) | ACCOUNTS PAYABLE | | |
| ACCOUNTS RECEIVABLE | | | SHORT TERM DEBT | | |
| INVENTORIES | | | LONG TERM DEBT | ❷ | 950,000 |
| PREPAID EXPENSES | | - | ACCRUED EXPENSES | | |
| PLEDGES RECEIVABLE | | | NET ASSETS: | | |
| INVESTMENTS | | | W/O DONOR RESTRICTIONS | | |
| PP&E (NET) | ❶ | 1,900,000 | WITH DONOR RESTRICTIONS | | |
| TOTAL ASSETS | | $950,000 | TOTAL LIABILITIES & NET ASSETS | | $950,000 |

## STATEMENT OF CASH FLOWS *for the period*

**Transaction 24.
Statement
Entries**

| BEGINNING CASH | | $0 |
|---|---|---|
| CASH RECEIPTS | | |
| CASH DISBURSEMENTS | | |
| CASH FLOW FROM OPERATIONS | | $0 |
| PP&E PURCHASES | ❶ | $1,900,000 |
| NET BORROWINGS | ❷ | $950,000 |
| INVESTMENT INCOME | | |
| ENDING CASH | ❸ | ($950,000) |

# T25. Obtain a construction loan. Make necessary renovations & improvements.

We will need $500,000 worth of necessary building renovations done and we need it before the next big rain. We also want to make $300,000 worth of interior improvements. All tolled, the renovation cost will be $800,000. We have $250,000 in cash left over from the Giversons' donation and the mortgage financing, but would need and like $500,000 (with a $50,000 cushion) as a short-term construction loan. The bank says okay, but the interest rate on a construction loan will be 7.5% annually, and it will be due in one lump sum of $537,500 and paid within 12 months. We feel the pressure.

BuildBetter General Contractors, Inc. has done work for several of our board members. Coming well recommended, we hire them and cross our fingers. When renovations are complete, we will have a building worth $2,737,500 (original purchase price plus improvements plus construction loan interest).

The construction gods are kind. Work is completed on time and on budget! We pay our contractor $800,000 for a job well done.

---

**Transaction:** Obtain construction financing. Complete renovation of WsNA building and pay the general contractor for his work.

**1** Record the $500,000 construction loan. Add that amount to **NET BORROWINGS** on the *Statement of Cash Flows* and to **SHORT-TERM DEBT** on the *Statement of Financial Position.*

**2** Issue a check for $800,000 to the contractor and record it as a **PP&E PURCHASE** on the *Statement of Cash Flows.* Increase **PP&E (NET)** in the *Statement of Financial Position* by the same amount.

In the *Statement of Cash Flows*, a positive entry in **PP&E PURCHASES** results in lower **ENDING CASH**; a positive entry in **NET BORROWINGS** results in more **ENDING CASH**.

**3** **ENDING CASH** on the *Statement of Cash Flows* is always the same as **CASH** on the *Statement of Financial Position,* so add ($300,000) to **CASH** in that statement

## STATEMENT OF ACTIVITIES

*for the period*

| REVENUE | WITHOUT DONOR RESTRICTIONS | WITH DONOR RESTRICTIONS | |
|---|---|---|---|
| CONTRIBUTIONS & GIFTS | | | $0 |
| PROGRAM SERVICES REVENUE | | | 0 |
| GRANTS & CONTRACTS | | | 0 |
| OTHER REVENUE | | | 0 |
| **TOTAL REVENUE** | $  0 | $0 | $0 |
| **EXPENSES** | | | |
| FUNDRAISING | | | $0 |
| PROGRAM SERVICES | | | 0 |
| GRANTS & CONTRACTS | | | 0 |
| MANAGEMENT & GENERAL | | | 0 |
| **TOTAL EXPENSES** | $  0 | | $0 |

| | |
|---|---|
| **CHANGE IN NET ASSETS** | $0 |
| **BEGINNING NET ASSETS** | 0 |
| **ENDING NET ASSETS** | $0 |

## STATEMENT OF FINANCIAL POSITION

*as of the period ending date*

| ASSETS | | LIABILITIES & NET ASSETS | |
|---|---|---|---|
| CASH ❸ | ($300,000) | ACCOUNTS PAYABLE | |
| ACCOUNTS RECEIVABLE | | SHORT TERM DEBT ❶ | 500,000 |
| INVENTORIES | | LONG TERM DEBT | |
| PREPAID EXPENSES | | ACCRUED EXPENSES | |
| PLEDGES RECEIVABLE | | NET ASSETS: | |
| INVESTMENTS | | W/O DONOR RESTRICTIONS | |
| PP&E (NET) ❷ | 800,000 | WITH DONOR RESTRICTIONS | |
| **TOTAL ASSETS** | **$500,000** | **TOTAL LIABILITIES & NET ASSETS** | **$500,000** |

**Transaction 25. Statement Entries**

## STATEMENT OF CASH FLOWS  *for the period*

| | |
|---|---|
| **BEGINNING CASH** | $0 |
| CASH RECEIPTS | |
| CASH DISBURSEMENTS | |
| **CASH FLOW FROM OPERATIONS** | $0 |
| PP&E PURCHASES ❷ | $800,000 |
| NET BORROWINGS ❶ | $500,000 |
| INVESTMENT INCOME | |
| **ENDING CASH** ❸ | ($300,000) |

137

# T26. Pay off the construction loan, refinance the mortgage, and set up the depreciation schedule for new building.

We refinance the mortgage with only the original down payment of $950,000 adding another $600,000, for a total of $1.55 million of mortgage debt. We simultaneously pay off the high-interest construction loan. Payments on the $1.55 million mortgage are $7,625 per month.

Our accountants say we will need to *depreciate* the value of the building through the *Statement of Activities* over the next 39 years. Our land is appraised at $650,000 but GAAP says land cannot be depreciated. Thus, the depreciable value of building is computed at $2,087,500 ($1,900,000 purchase price, plus renovations of $800,000, plus $37,500 in interest, minus $650,000 land value). Straight-line depreciation (equal amounts for the next 468) months will be $4,460 per month.

Depreciation is a so-called *noncash* expense. The *Statement of Cash Flows* is not affected when we record it monthly as an expense on the *Statement of Activities*. Remember we lowered cash when we bought the building originally. To record it now again would be double counting. Got that?

---

**Transaction:** Pay off the high-interest construction loan. Refinance the mortgage. Do depreciation later.

**❶** Write a check for $537,500 to the bank to pay off the construction loan with interest. Record this payment as **CASH DISBURSEMENT** on the *Statement of Cash Flows*. Lower **SHORT-TERM DEBT** by $500,000 and add $37,500 to **PP&E** on the *Statement of Financial Position*. Interest expense is added ("capitalized") to the cost of purchased property (a non-cash transaction).

**❷** Refinance our mortgage by adding $600,000 in mortgage debt. Record this amount as **NET BORROWINGS** in the *Statement of Cash Flows*. Increase **LONG-TERM DEBT** in the liabilities section of *Statement of Financial Position*.

**❸** **ENDING CASH** is $62,500 on the *Cash Flow Statement* and in **CASH** on the *Statement of Financial Position*.

## STATEMENT OF ACTIVITIES                    *for the period*

| REVENUE | WITHOUT DONOR RESTRICTIONS | WITH DONOR RESTRICTIONS | |
|---|---|---|---|
| CONTRIBUTIONS & GIFTS | | | $0 |
| PROGRAM SERVICES REVENUE | | | 0 |
| GRANTS & CONTRACTS | | | 0 |
| OTHER REVENUE | | | 0 |
| **TOTAL REVENUE** | $ 0 | $0 | $0 |
| **EXPENSES** | | | |
| FUNDRAISING | | | $0 |
| PROGRAM SERVICES | | | 0 |
| GRANTS & CONTRACTS | | | 0 |
| MANAGEMENT & GENERAL | | | 0 |
| **TOTAL EXPENSES** | $ 0 | | $0 |
| | CHANGE IN NET ASSETS | | $0 |
| | BEGINNING NET ASSETS | | 0 |
| | ENDING NET ASSETS | | $0 |

## STATEMENT OF FINANCIAL POSITION         *as of the period ending date*

| ASSETS | | | LIABILITIES & NET ASSETS | | |
|---|---|---|---|---|---|
| CASH | ❸ | $62,500 | ACCOUNTS PAYABLE | | |
| ACCOUNTS RECEIVABLE | | | SHORT TERM DEBT | ❶ | (500,000) |
| INVENTORIES | | | LONG TERM DEBT | ❷ | 600,000 |
| PREPAID EXPENSES | | | ACCRUED EXPENSES | | |
| PLEDGES RECEIVABLE | | | NET ASSETS: | | |
| INVESTMENTS | | | W/O DONOR RESTRICTIONS | | |
| PP&E (NET) | ❶ | 37,500 | WITH DONOR RESTRICTIONS | | |
| **TOTAL ASSETS** | | **$100,000** | **TOTAL LIABILITIES & NET ASSETS** | | **$100,000** |

## STATEMENT OF CASH FLOWS   *for the period*

| | | |
|---|---|---|
| BEGINNING CASH | | $0 |
| CASH RECEIPTS | | |
| CASH DISBURSEMENTS | ❶ | 537,500 |
| **CASH FLOW FROM OPERATIONS** | | **($537,500)** |
| PP&E PURCHASES | | |
| NET BORROWINGS | ❷ | $600,000 |
| INVESTMENT INCOME | | |
| **ENDING CASH** | ❸ | **$62,500** |

**Transaction 26.**
**Statement**
**Entries**

# T27. Record a month of occupancy expenses for our new Senior Center.

We own our own building! No more rent! However, we still have occupancy expenses, they are just structured in a new way. Now, our monthly occupancy costs are total of $14,085 each month:

- $7,625 mortgage payment to the bank,
- $4,460 depreciation, and
- $2,000 in utilities expenses paid to the utilities companies.

As shown in Transaction 9, our rent plus utilities expense was $20,500 before we bought the building. WOW, what a savings. But it gets even better. Depreciation expense will not be made in cash. Rather, it comes from the *Statement of Financial Position* adjustments. The checks we will write for occupancy will be only for mortgage and utility payments totaling $9,625. Those are for real, current cash outflows.

Before we bought the building, our monthly negative cash flow for occupancy expense was $20,500; now it is only $9,625. Many thanks to the Giversons! Finance committee is dancing for joy!

---

**Transaction:** Make monthly mortgage and utility payments. Record these building occupancy expenses plus added depreciation expenses.

**1** Write checks totaling $9,625 including mortgage payment of $7,625 (lowering LONG-TERM DEBT) and $2,000 utility expense. Record this amount as CASH DISBURSEMENT on the *Statement of Cash Flows*.

**2** Record $4,460 depreciation charge plus the $2,000 utility expense totaling $6,460 in MANAGEMENT & GENERAL EXPENSES in the *Statement of Activities*. Lower NET ASSETS W/O RESTRICTIONS by this amount on the *Statement of Financial Position*.

**3** Lower PP&E (NET) by depreciation expense of $4,460 on the *Statement of Financial Position*. *Net* means total cost of PP&E minus total (accumulated) depreciation to date, also called *book value*.

**4** ENDING CASH equals CASH as it must by definition.

## STATEMENT OF ACTIVITIES  *for the period*

| REVENUE | WITHOUT DONOR RESTRICTIONS | WITH DONOR RESTRICTIONS | |
|---|---|---|---|
| CONTRIBUTIONS & GIFTS | | | $ 0 |
| PROGRAM SERVICES REVENUE | | | 0 |
| GRANTS & CONTRACTS | | | 0 |
| OTHER REVENUE | | | 0 |
| **TOTAL REVENUE** | $ 0 | $0 | $ 0 |
| **EXPENSES** | | | |
| FUNDRAISING | | | 0 |
| PROGRAM SERVICES | | | 0 |
| GRANTS & CONTRACTS | | | 0 |
| MANAGEMENT & GENERAL | ❷ 6,460 | | 6,460 |
| **TOTAL EXPENSES** | $ 6,460 | | $ 6,460 |

CHANGE IN NET ASSETS ❷ $ (6,460)

BEGINNING NET ASSETS 0

ENDING NET ASSETS $ (6,460)

## STATEMENT OF FINANCIAL POSITION  *as of the period ending date*

| ASSETS | | LIABILITIES & NET ASSETS | |
|---|---|---|---|
| CASH | ❹ $ (9,625) | ACCOUNTS PAYABLE | |
| ACCOUNTS RECEIVABLE | | SHORT TERM DEBT | |
| INVENTORIES | | LONG TERM DEBT | ❶ (7,625) |
| PREPAID EXPENSES | | ACCRUED EXPENSES | |
| PLEDGES RECEIVABLE | | NET ASSETS: | |
| INVESTMENTS | | W/O DONOR RESTRICTIONS | ❷ (6,460) |
| PP&E (NET) | ❸ (4,460) | WITH DONOR RESTRICTIONS | |
| **TOTAL ASSETS** | $ (14,085) | **TOTAL LIABILITIES & NET ASSETS** | $ (14,085) |

## STATEMENT OF CASH FLOWS  *for the period*

**Transaction 27.**
**Statement**
**Entries**

| BEGINNING CASH | $ 0 |
|---|---|
| CASH RECEIPTS | |
| CASH DISBURSEMENTS | ❶ 9,625 |
| **CASH FLOW FROM OPERATIONS** | $ (9,625) |
| PP&E PURCHASES | |
| NET BORROWINGS | |
| INVESTMENT INCOME | |
| **ENDING CASH** | ❹ $ (9,625) |

# Chapter 14.
# Fundraising Transactions

Fundraising expense is accounted for separately from all other nonprofit organization expenses. The IRS wants to keep close track on these revenue-generating expenses. In addition, excessive fundraising expense is frowned-upon in the nonprofit community. However, what is *excessive*? 10% of monies raised? 20%? 50%? Even with 50% fundraising expense, the organization gets the other 50% to grow and support its mission.

For nonprofits to expand their operations, they need capital to grow. Often, the organization's operating surplus alone does not provide an adequate amount of *growth* capital. Fundraising provides the rest.

**Transaction 28.**  Hire fundraising consultant to plan our annual-fund campaign.

**Transaction 29.**  Pay fundraising consultant for preparing her excellent annual campaign plan.

**Transaction 30.**  Hold an awards dinner followed by a high-end auction of donated antiques.

**Transaction 31.**  Promote "Rainy-Day Club," and give donors an umbrella as a thank-you gift.

**Transaction 32.**  Conduct a trial email fundraising campaign. Money well spent?

# T28. Hire fundraising consultant to plan our annual-fund campaign.

Our director of development (a.k.a. fundraising), Margery Friendly, has been with WsNA from day one. She is known and respected by our significant donors. However, the board thinks that there is more money out there and that an expert would know where to find it. Margery and our chairman decide to hire a consultant experienced in planning annual-fund campaigns. It is time to "up our game," and Margery is happy to have the help.

Roberta Highpoint comes highly recommended by organizations like ours. Her proposal includes an initial planning effort costing $15,000 and then implementation assistance as we go along. She charges a standard rate of $1,000 per day. We agree, sign Roberta's contract, pay her one-half now and will pay the remaining one-half when we accept the final plan. Roberta starts work immediately.

---

**Transaction:** Write our new fundraising consultant a $7,500 check for professional services to be performed.

**1** Record the $7,500 check as a CASH DISBURSEMENT on the *Statement of Cash Flows* and as a PREPAID EXPENSE on the *Statement of Financial Position*.

**2** ENDING CASH on the *Statement of Cash Flows* is always the same as CASH on the *Statement of Financial Position,* so add the ($7,500) to that statement.

**Note:** When Roberta submits her final invoice, we will write her another $7,500 check and the record the total fundraising expense of $15,000 on the *Statement of Activities*, thus lowering NET ASSETS.

## STATEMENT OF ACTIVITIES for the period

| REVENUE | WITHOUT DONOR RESTRICTIONS | WITH DONOR RESTRICTIONS | | |
|---|---|---|---|---|
| CONTRIBUTIONS & GIFTS | | | $ | 0 |
| PROGRAM SERVICES REVENUE | | | | 0 |
| GRANTS & CONTRACTS | | | | 0 |
| OTHER REVENUE | | | | 0 |
| **TOTAL REVENUE** | $  0 | $0 | $ | 0 |
| **EXPENSES** | | | | |
| FUNDRAISING | | | | 0 |
| PROGRAM SERVICES | | | | 0 |
| GRANTS & CONTRACTS | | | | 0 |
| MANAGEMENT & GENERAL | | | | 0 |
| **TOTAL EXPENSES** | $  0 | | $ | 0 |
| | **CHANGE IN NET ASSETS** | | $ | 0 |
| | **BEGINNING NET ASSETS** | | | 0 |
| | **ENDING NET ASSETS** | | $ | 0 |

## STATEMENT OF FINANCIAL POSITION as of the period ending date

| ASSETS | | LIABILITIES & NET ASSETS | |
|---|---|---|---|
| CASH | ❷ $ (7,500) | ACCOUNTS PAYABLE | |
| ACCOUNTS RECEIVABLE | | SHORT TERM DEBT | |
| INVENTORIES | | LONG TERM DEBT | |
| PREPAID EXPENSES | ❶ 7,500 | ACCRUED EXPENSES | |
| PLEDGES RECEIVABLE | | NET ASSETS: | |
| INVESTMENTS | | W/O DONOR RESTRICTIONS | |
| PP&E (NET) | | WITH DONOR RESTRICTIONS | |
| **TOTAL ASSETS** | $  0 | **TOTAL LIABILITIES & NET ASSETS** | $  0 |

## STATEMENT OF CASH FLOWS <i>for the period</i>

| Transaction 28. Statement Entries | | |
|---|---|---|

| | | |
|---|---|---|
| BEGINNING CASH | $ | 0 |
| CASH RECEIPTS | | |
| CASH DISBURSEMENTS | ❶ | 7,500 |
| **CASH FLOW FROM OPERATIONS** | $ | (7,500) |
| PP&E PURCHASES | | |
| NET BORROWINGS | | |
| INVESTMENT INCOME | | |
| **ENDING CASH** | ❷ $ | (7,500) |

# T29. Pay our fundraising consultant for preparing an excellent annual campaign plan.

Roberta submits the plan at a presentation to the board. Margery and the board chair strongly endorse the work. The whole board is thrilled and ready to move forward to implement the plan.

Roberta submits her $15,000 invoice for her work. In T28 we paid Roberta a $7,500 deposit for the work. Now we cut her a check for the remaining $7,500 we owe her.

---

**Transaction:** Accept annual plan document from our consultant and issue a $7,500 check as final payment and record $15,000 fundraising expense paid for professional services ($7,500 in T28 and $7,500 here in T29).

**1** Record the $15,000 cost of the plan as **FUNDRAISING EXPENSE** on the *Statement of Activities*. Lower **NET ASSETS W/O DONOR RESTRICTIONS** on *the Statement of Financial Position* by the same amount.

**2** Record the $7,500 check as a **CASH DISBURSEMENT** on the *Statement of Cash Flows*. **ENDING CASH** on the *Statement of Cash Flows* is always the same as **CASH** on the *Statement of Financial Position,* so add the ($7,500) to that statement.

**3** Reduce prepaid expense by the $7,500 recorded on the *Statement of Financial Position* in T28.

**4** Now, **TOTAL ASSETS** equals **TOTAL LIABILITIES & NET ASSETS** on the *Statement of Financial Position*.

## STATEMENT OF ACTIVITIES    *for the period*

| REVENUE | WITHOUT DONOR RESTRICTIONS | WITH DONOR RESTRICTIONS | |
|---|---|---|---|
| CONTRIBUTIONS & GIFTS | | | $ 0 |
| PROGRAM SERVICES REVENUE | | | 0 |
| GRANTS & CONTRACTS | | | 0 |
| OTHER REVENUE | | | 0 |
| **TOTAL REVENUE** | $ 0 | $0 | $ 0 |
| **EXPENSES** | | | |
| FUNDRAISING | ❶ $ 15,000 | | 15,000 |
| PROGRAM SERVICES | | | 0 |
| GRANTS & CONTRACTS | | | 0 |
| MANAGEMENT & GENERAL | | | 0 |
| **TOTAL EXPENSES** | $ 15,000 | | $ 15,000 |

CHANGE IN NET ASSETS ❶ $ (15,000)
BEGINNING NET ASSETS 0
ENDING NET ASSETS $ (15,000)

## STATEMENT OF FINANCIAL POSITION    *as of the period ending date*

| ASSETS | | LIABILITIES & NET ASSETS | |
|---|---|---|---|
| CASH | ❷ $ (7,500) | ACCOUNTS PAYABLE | |
| ACCOUNTS RECEIVABLE | | SHORT TERM DEBT | |
| INVENTORIES | | LONG TERM DEBT | |
| PREPAID EXPENSES | ❸ (7,500) | ACCRUED EXPENSES | |
| PLEDGES RECEIVABLE | | NET ASSETS: | |
| INVESTMENTS | | W/O DONOR RESTRICTIONS | ❶ (15,000) |
| PP&E (NET) | | WITH DONOR RESTRICTIONS | |
| **TOTAL ASSETS** | ❹ $ (15,000) | **TOTAL LIABILITIES & NET ASSETS** | ❹ $ (15,000) |

## STATEMENT OF CASH FLOWS *for the period*

**Transaction 29. Statement Entries**

| | |
|---|---|
| BEGINNING CASH | $ 0 |
| CASH RECEIPTS | |
| CASH DISBURSEMENTS | ❷ 7,500 |
| **CASH FLOW FROM OPERATIONS** | $ (7,500) |
| PP&E PURCHASES | |
| NET BORROWINGS | |
| INVESTMENT INCOME | |
| **ENDING CASH** | ❷ $ (7,500) |

# T30. Hold an awards dinner followed by a high-end auction of donated antiques.

Every year WsNA holds a cocktail party to thank donors for their support. We give speeches, bestow "Donor of the Year" awards, and conduct an auction of donated antiques and other high-end items. It is all good fun! A cash bar makes it a low cost affair and the auction is at a classy country club, gratis. A colorful local licensed auctioneer, Clem Biddle, writes the catalog, stores the goods at his warehouse, and offers delivery service.

This year, we have assembled a particularly nice selection of items. We issue donation receipts to people putting up the items for auction.

Clem does his magic and total sales amount to $28,675. Our total direct expenses for running the auction were $350 for special invitations and $1,350 for a color auction catalogue, for a total of $1,700. Our surplus is $26,975 for the auction. Well done!

Note, auction item winners may be eligible for a tax deductible contribution for any amount paid over the estimated fair market value for the auctioned goods.

---

**Transaction:** Record auction proceeds and expenses.

**1** Record $28,675 as **FUNDRAISING REVENUE** on the *Statement of Activities* and as a **CASH RECEIPT** on the *Statement of Cash Flows*.

**2** Record $1,700 as **FUNDRAISING EXPENSE** on the *Statement of Activities* and as a **CASH DISBURSEMENT** on the *Statement of Cash Flows*.

**3** **ENDING CASH** on the *Statement of Cash Flows* is always the same as **CASH** on the *Statement of Financial Position*, so add $26,975 on that statement.

**4** Increase **NET ASSET W/O DONOR RESTRICTIONS** on the *Statement of Financial Position* by $26,975 which is the **CHANGE OF NET ASSETS** as shown on the *Statement of Activities*.

## STATEMENT OF ACTIVITIES          *for the period*

| REVENUE | WITHOUT DONOR RESTRICTIONS | WITH DONOR RESTRICTIONS | |
|---|---|---|---|
| CONTRIBUTIONS & GIFTS | | | $ 0 |
| PROGRAM SERVICES REVENUE | | | 0 |
| GRANTS & CONTRACTS | | | 0 |
| OTHER REVENUE | ❶ 28,675 | | 28,675 |
| **TOTAL REVENUE** | **$ 28,675** | **$0** | **$ 28,675** |
| **EXPENSES** | | | |
| FUNDRAISING | ❷ $ 1,700 | | 1,700 |
| PROGRAM SERVICES | | | 0 |
| GRANTS & CONTRACTS | | | 0 |
| MANAGEMENT & GENERAL | | | 0 |
| **TOTAL EXPENSES** | **$ 1,700** | | **$ 1,700** |
| | CHANGE IN NET ASSETS ❹ | | $ 26,975 |
| | BEGINNING NET ASSETS | | 0 |
| | **ENDING NET ASSETS** | | **$ 26,975** |

## STATEMENT OF FINANCIAL POSITION          *as of the period ending date*

| ASSETS | | LIABILITIES & NET ASSETS | |
|---|---|---|---|
| CASH | ❸ $ 26,975 | ACCOUNTS PAYABLE | |
| ACCOUNTS RECEIVABLE | | SHORT TERM DEBT | |
| INVENTORIES | | LONG TERM DEBT | |
| PREPAID EXPENSES | | ACCRUED EXPENSES | |
| PLEDGES RECEIVABLE | | NET ASSETS: | |
| INVESTMENTS | | W/O DONOR RESTRICTIONS ❹ | 26,975 |
| PP&E (NET) | | WITH DONOR RESTRICTIONS | |
| **TOTAL ASSETS** | **$ 26,975** | **TOTAL LIABILITIES & NET ASSETS** | **$ 26,975** |

## STATEMENT OF CASH FLOWS  *for the period*

| | Transaction 30. Statement Entries | | |
|---|---|---|---|

| | | |
|---|---|---|
| BEGINNING CASH | | $ 0 |
| CASH RECEIPTS | ❶ | $ 28,675 |
| CASH DISBURSEMENTS | ❷ | 1,700 |
| **CASH FLOW FROM OPERATIONS** | | **$ 26,975** |
| PP&E PURCHASES | | |
| NET BORROWINGS | | |
| INVESTMENT INCOME | | |
| **ENDING CASH** | ❸ | **$ 26,975** |

# T31. Promote "Rainy-Day Club;" give donors an umbrella as a thank-you!

Roberta says public television stations do it all the time—give away a logo-embellished umbrella to new organization members who donate a certain amount. We decided to try. We promote the "Rainy-Day Club," our new website giving membership opportunity to support emergency relief for residents in need throughout the community. The response is phenomenal and very gratifying.

New memberships are $75.00 and donors receive a free umbrella valued at $23.50 (our cost). We sign up 446 new members and receive $33,450 in revenue. Wow! Our umbrella expense for the promotion is $10,480 total.

We spent 31% of revenue in this promotion. Too high? But then, we do have $22,970 more to advance our mission.

---

**Transaction:** Record fundraising revenue from WsNA membership promotion and expense from umbrella gift.

**1** Record $33,450 as **FUNDRAISING REVENUE** on the *Statement of Activities* and as a **CASH RECEIPT** on the *Statement of Cash Flows.*

**2** Record $10,480 as **FUNDRAISING EXPENSE** on the *Statement of Activities* and as a **CASH DISBURSEMENT** on the *Statement of Cash Flows.*

**3** Increase **NET ASSETS W/O DONOR RESTRICTIONS** on the *Statement of Financial Position* by $22,970, the **CHANGE IN NET ASSETS** on the *Statement of Activities.*

**4** **ENDING CASH** on the *Statement of Cash Flows* is always the same as **CASH** on the *Statement of Financial Position,* so add $22,970 on that statement.

**Note:** Only $51.50 may be tax deductible to new membership donors ($75.00 minus $23.50, the value of the umbrella received in the package deal).

## STATEMENT OF ACTIVITIES　　　　　　　*for the period*

| REVENUE | WITHOUT DONOR RESTRICTIONS | WITH DONOR RESTRICTIONS | | |
|---|---|---|---|---|
| CONTRIBUTIONS & GIFTS | | | $ | 0 |
| PROGRAM SERVICES REVENUE | | | | 0 |
| GRANTS & CONTRACTS | | | | 0 |
| OTHER REVENUE | ❶ 33,450 | | | 33,450 |
| **TOTAL REVENUE** | **$ 33,450** | **$0** | **$** | **33,450** |
| **EXPENSES** | | | | |
| FUNDRAISING | ❷ $ 10,480 | | | 10,480 |
| PROGRAM SERVICES | | | | 0 |
| GRANTS & CONTRACTS | | | | 0 |
| MANAGEMENT & GENERAL | | | | 0 |
| **TOTAL EXPENSES** | **$ 10,480** | | **$** | **10,480** |
| | | CHANGE IN NET ASSETS | ❸ $ | 22,970 |
| | | BEGINNING NET ASSETS | | 0 |
| | | ENDING NET ASSETS | $ | 22,970 |

## STATEMENT OF FINANCIAL POSITION　　　　*as of the period ending date*

| ASSETS | | LIABILITIES & NET ASSETS | |
|---|---|---|---|
| CASH | ❹ $ 22,970 | ACCOUNTS PAYABLE | |
| ACCOUNTS RECEIVABLE | | SHORT TERM DEBT | |
| INVENTORIES | | LONG TERM DEBT | |
| PREPAID EXPENSES | | ACCRUED EXPENSES | |
| PLEDGES RECEIVABLE | | NET ASSETS: | |
| INVESTMENTS | | W/O DONOR RESTRICTIONS | ❸ 22,970 |
| PP&E (NET) | | WITH DONOR RESTRICTIONS | |
| **TOTAL ASSETS** | **$ 22,970** | **TOTAL LIABILITIES & NET ASSETS** | **$ 22,970** |

## STATEMENT OF CASH FLOWS　*for the period*

| | | |
|---|---|---|
| BEGINNING CASH | $ | 0 |

| Transaction 31. Statement Entries |
|---|

| | | |
|---|---|---|
| CASH RECEIPTS | ❶ $ | 33,450 |
| CASH DISBURSEMENTS | ❷ | 10,480 |
| **CASH FLOW FROM OPERATIONS** | **$** | **22,970** |
| | | |
| PP&E PURCHASES | | |
| NET BORROWINGS | | |
| INVESTMENT INCOME | | |
| **ENDING CASH** | ❹ **$** | **22,970** |

# T32. Conduct a trial email fundraising campaign. Money well spent?

Roberta also thinks there may be an opportunity to increase donations specifically from new donors living in the general communities we serve. Email fundraising services are sprouting up to help nonprofits such as ours. They do all the work finding email lists (and deleting any current donors), designing the copy, performing the email blasts, and collecting the cash. Why not give it a try?

After getting a recommendation from Roberta, we sign a contract with GentlePush, Inc. to manage the campaign. Cost is a $5,000 fixed fee, plus a bonus of $5.00 for each new donor generated.

Gosh, it works. We raise a total of $11,250 in donations from 475 new donors. Average donation size is slightly less than $25.00 per donor. The cost of the promotion is the initial $5,000 fixed fee plus $2,375 as the "new donor" bonus. Thus, a total of $7,375 in expense to raise $11,250 in revenue. Seems high to us but...

Rebeca says that if these new folks turn into repeat donors year-after-year, we will reap the benefit of the much lower fundraising expense common for repeat donors. Hmm, perhaps such campaigns are not a bad long-term investment. We shall have to wait and see.

---

**Transaction:** Receive email fundraising revenue and pay expenses to email service provider.

**❶** Record $11,250 as **FUNDRAISING REVENUE** on the *Statement of Activities* and as a **CASH RECEIPT** on the *Statement of Cash Flows*.

**❷** Record $7,375 as **FUNDRAISING EXPENSE** on the *Statement of Activities* and as a **CASH DISBURSEMENT** on the *Statement of Cash Flows*.

**❸** Increase **NET ASSETS W/O DONOR RESTRICTIONS** on the *Statement of Financial Position* by $3,875, the **CHANGE OF NET ASSETS** on the *Statement of Activities*.

## STATEMENT OF ACTIVITIES · *for the period*

| REVENUE | WITHOUT DONOR RESTRICTIONS | WITH DONOR RESTRICTIONS | |
|---|---|---|---|
| CONTRIBUTIONS & GIFTS | ❶ $ 11,250 | | $ 11,250 |
| PROGRAM SERVICES REVENUE | | | 0 |
| GRANTS & CONTRACTS | | | 0 |
| OTHER REVENUE | | | 0 |
| **TOTAL REVENUE** | $ 11,250 | $0 | $ 11,250 |
| **EXPENSES** | | | |
| FUNDRAISING | ❷ $ 7,375 | | 7,375 |
| PROGRAM SERVICES | | | 0 |
| GRANTS & CONTRACTS | | | 0 |
| MANAGEMENT & GENERAL | | | 0 |
| **TOTAL EXPENSES** | $ 7,375 | | $ 7,375 |

| | |
|---|---|
| CHANGE IN NET ASSETS ❸ | $ 3,875 |
| BEGINNING NET ASSETS | 0 |
| ENDING NET ASSETS | $ 3,875 |

## STATEMENT OF FINANCIAL POSITION · *as of the period ending date*

| ASSETS | | LIABILITIES & NET ASSETS | |
|---|---|---|---|
| CASH | $ 3,875 | ACCOUNTS PAYABLE | |
| ACCOUNTS RECEIVABLE | | SHORT TERM DEBT | |
| INVENTORIES | | LONG TERM DEBT | |
| PREPAID EXPENSES | | ACCRUED EXPENSES | |
| PLEDGES RECEIVABLE | | NET ASSETS: | |
| INVESTMENTS | | W/O DONOR RESTRICTIONS ❸ | 3,875 |
| PP&E (NET) | | WITH DONOR RESTRICTIONS | |
| **TOTAL ASSETS** | $ 3,875 | **TOTAL LIABILITIES & NET ASSETS** | $ 3,875 |

## STATEMENT OF CASH FLOWS · *for the period*

**Transaction 32. Statement Entries**

| | |
|---|---|
| BEGINNING CASH | $ 0 |
| CASH RECEIPTS ❶ | $ 11,250 |
| CASH DISBURSEMENTS ❷ | 7,375 |
| **CASH FLOW FROM OPERATIONS** | $ 3,875 |
| PP&E PURCHASES | |
| NET BORROWINGS | |
| INVESTMENT INCOME | |
| **ENDING CASH** | $ 3,875 |

# Chapter 15.
# Restricted Contributions and Contracts

Restricted contributions and gifts and government contracts are handled in a unique way in nonprofit accounting. These transactions will deal with their financial statement presentation. We will introduce a special way of keeping track of these funds by making entries in a special *Restricted Net Assets Worksheet.*

See **Transaction 2.** *Receive a $15,000 gift to write, print, and distribute a booklet* which describes how to record a restricted contribution. In **Transaction 33.** below we will fulfill our obligation to the donor.

**Transaction 33.** Produce and distribute booklet funded by a purpose-restricted donation.

**Transaction 34.** Receive donation and place a portion of funds received into board-restricted Net Assets.

**Transaction 35.** Release board-restricted Net Assets and fund scholarship.

**Transaction 36.** Accept contract from the state DHS to provide meals-on-wheels to shut-ins in our community'

**Transaction 37.** Provide contracted meals-on-wheels services.

# T33. Receive utility bills.

We receive utility bills from our services providers—telephone, electricity, trash removal, etc.—totaling $2,835 for the month.

Electricity, trash removal, heat, light, power, and telephone, are major components of a nonprofit's *overhead* expense. Not flashy, but a "keep-the-door open" expense that needs to be controlled and not so minimized as to interfere with our ability to manage our operations effectively. Staff and volunteers would get pretty crabby when they are asked to work in the dark and cold because we did not pay our utility bills.

---

**Transaction:** Receive $2,835 in bills from our utilities suppliers for payment later in the month.

**1** Record the utilities cost of $2,835 as a **MANAGEMENT & GENERAL EXPENSE** on the *Statement of Activities.*

**2** **CHANGE IN NET ASSETS** on the *Statement of Activities* is a negative $2,835. This amount reduces **NET ASSET W/O DONOR RESTRICTIONS** on the *Statement of Financial Position.*

**3** Increase **ACCOUNTS PAYABLE** $2,835 on the *Statement of Financial Position.* We are going to pay the bills later.

Note that **TOTAL ASSETS** still equals **TOTAL LIABILITIES & NET ASSETS** on the *Statement of Financial Position.*

## STATEMENT OF ACTIVITIES
*for the period*

| REVENUE | WITHOUT DONOR RESTRICTIONS | WITH DONOR RESTRICTIONS | | |
|---|---|---|---|---|
| CONTRIBUTIONS & GIFTS | | | $ | 0 |
| PROGRAM SERVICES REVENUE | | | | 0 |
| GRANTS & CONTRACTS | | | | 0 |
| OTHER REVENUE | | | | 0 |
| **TOTAL REVENUE** | **$ 0** | **$0** | **$** | **0** |
| **EXPENSES** | | | | |
| FUNDRAISING | | | | 0 |
| PROGRAM SERVICES | | | | 0 |
| GRANTS & CONTRACTS | | | | 0 |
| MANAGEMENT & GENERAL | ❶ 2,835 | | | 2,835 |
| **TOTAL EXPENSES** | **$ 2,835** | | **$** | **2,835** |
| | CHANGE IN NET ASSETS | | $ | (2,835) |
| | BEGINNING NET ASSETS | | | 0 |
| | ENDING NET ASSETS | | $ | (2,835) |

## STATEMENT OF FINANCIAL POSITION
*as of the period ending date*

| ASSETS | | | LIABILITIES & NET ASSETS | | |
|---|---|---|---|---|---|
| CASH | | | ACCOUNTS PAYABLE | ❸ $ | 2,835 |
| ACCOUNTS RECEIVABLE | | | SHORT TERM DEBT | | |
| INVENTORIES | | | LONG TERM DEBT | | |
| PREPAID EXPENSES | | | ACCRUED EXPENSES | | |
| PLEDGES RECEIVABLE | | | NET ASSETS: | | |
| INVESTMENTS | | | W/O DONOR RESTRICTIONS | ❷ | (2,835) |
| PP&E (NET) | | | WITH DONOR RESTRICTIONS | | |
| **TOTAL ASSETS** | **$** | **0** | **TOTAL LIABILITIES & NET ASSETS** | **$** | **0** |

## STATEMENT OF CASH FLOWS
*for the period*

**Transaction 33. Statement Entries**

| | | |
|---|---|---|
| BEGINNING CASH | $ | 0 |
| CASH RECEIPTS | | |
| CASH DISBURSEMENTS | | |
| **CASH FLOW FROM OPERATIONS** | **$** | **0** |
| PP&E PURCHASES | | |
| NET BORROWINGS | | |
| INVESTMENT INCOME | | |
| **ENDING CASH** | **$** | **0** |

# T34 Receive a generous donation and place a portion in Board-Restricted Net Assets.

We receive a generous donation of $10,000 from the family of Marylou Teacher in honor of her life-long commitment to teaching young people of the community. Marylou recently retired as a professor of history at the local community college.

The board wishes to honor Marylou and after debate, establishes a scholarship in her name for a local first-in-family college student of the community. Then the board votes to place $5,000 of the gift into board-restricted net assets to fund the scholarship for the coming year. Now as board restricted Net Assets, this $5,000 must be used for scholarship purposes only. By this board vote, our executive director is required to fulfill the board's wishes.

---

**Transaction:** Accept the donation of $10,000 and book as Revenue in the *Statement of Activities* and as an increase in New Assets in the *Statement of Financial Position*.

**1** Record the $10,000 check as CONTRIBUTIONS & GIFTS in the *Statement of Activities* and also as a CASH RECEIPT in the *Statement of Cash Flows*.

**2** ENDING CASH on the S*tatement of Cash Flows* is always the same as CASH on the *Statement of Financial Position*, so add $10,000 to CASH on that Statement.

**3** Record $5,000 as an increase in each of NET ASSETS WITH RESTRICTIONS and also NET ASSETS W/O RESTRICTIONS in the Liabilities & Net Assets section of the *Statement of Financial Position*. The *Statement of Financial Position* is now in balance.

Make appropriate entries in the *Restricted Net Assets Worksheet* below.

| | Fund Description | Amount | Balance |
|---|---|---|---|
| T34 | Scholarship Fund *(Board restricted)* | $5,000 | $5,000 |

## STATEMENT OF ACTIVITIES                                          *for the period*

| REVENUE | | WITHOUT DONOR RESTRICTIONS | WITH DONOR RESTRICTIONS | | |
|---|---|---|---|---|---|
| CONTRIBUTIONS & GIFTS | ❶ | $ 10,000 | | $ | 10,000 |
| PROGRAM SERVICES REVENUE | | | | | 0 |
| GRANTS & CONTRACTS | | | | | 0 |
| OTHER REVENUE | | | | | 0 |
| **TOTAL REVENUE** | | **$ 10,000** | **$0** | **$** | **10,000** |
| **EXPENSES** | | | | | |
| FUNDRAISING | | | | | 0 |
| PROGRAM SERVICES | | | | | 0 |
| GRANTS & CONTRACTS | | | | | 0 |
| MANAGEMENT & GENERAL | | | | | 0 |
| **TOTAL EXPENSES** | | **$ 0** | | **$** | **0** |
| | | | **CHANGE IN NET ASSETS** | **$** | **10,000** |
| | | | **BEGINNING NET ASSETS** | | **0** |
| | | | **ENDING NET ASSETS** | **$** | **10,000** |

## STATEMENT OF FINANCIAL POSITION                         *as of the period ending date*

| ASSETS | | LIABILITIES & NET ASSETS | | |
|---|---|---|---|---|
| ❷ CASH | $ (10,000) | ACCOUNTS PAYABLE | | |
| ACCOUNTS RECEIVABLE | | SHORT TERM DEBT | | |
| INVENTORIES | | LONG TERM DEBT | | |
| PREPAID EXPENSES | | ACCRUED EXPENSES | | |
| PLEDGES RECEIVABLE | | NET ASSETS: | | |
| INVESTMENTS | | W/O DONOR RESTRICTIONS | ❸ | 5,000 |
| PP&E (NET) | | WITH DONOR RESTRICTIONS | ❸ | 5,000 |
| **TOTAL ASSETS** | **$ (10,000)** | **TOTAL LIABILITIES & NET ASSETS** | **$** | **10,000** |

## STATEMENT OF CASH FLOWS                   *for the period*

| | | |
|---|---|---|
| BEGINNING CASH | $ | 0 |
| CASH RECEIPTS ❶ | $ | 10,000 |
| CASH DISBURSEMENTS | | |
| **CASH FLOW FROM OPERATIONS** | **$** | **10,000** |
| PP&E PURCHASES | | |
| NET BORROWINGS | | |
| INVESTMENT INCOME | | |
| **ENDING CASH** | **$** | **10,000** |

> **Transaction 34.**
> **Statement**
> **Entries**

# T35. Release board-restricted Net Assets and fund scholarship.

After reviewing scholarship applications, our executive director selects Sarah Studious as the winner! Sarah is a youngest of three sisters and can really use the money. Everyone is pleased with our selection. As a consolation prize for the four other applicants, we award $250 to each to purchase textbooks next year.

We could take the money out of Teacher Family gift restricted funds, but the executive director chooses to use unrestricted general net assets instead to show the family our support and participation in their generosity.

The board is pleased and so is the family. Perhaps we will ask them for another gift next year to perpetuate the scholarship fund. Previous donors are often the best source of future donations. Cultivate them.

---

**Transaction:** Issue a check for $5,000 to our scholarship winner and four $250 checks to the runners-up.

❶ Record the $6,000 in checks as a **CASH DISBURSEMENT** on the *Statement of Cash Flows*. **ENDING CASH** on the *Statement of Cash Flows* is always the same as **CASH** on the *Statement of Financial Position*, so add ($6,000) to **CASH** on that statement.

❷ In the *Statement of Activities*, record the $6,000 expenditure as a **PROGRAM SERVICES EXPENSE** (for want of a more appropriate account in our simplified statement).

❸ **ENDING NET ASSETS** has decreased by $6,000 on the *Statement of Activities* so lower **NET ASSETS W/O DONOR RESTRICTIONS** by $1,000 and **NET ASSERTS WITH DONOR RESTRICTION** by $5,000 on the *Statement of Financial Position*.

Make appropriate entries in the **Restricted Net Assets Worksheet** below.

| | Fund Description | Amount | Balance |
|---|---|---|---|
| T35 | Scholarship Fund *(Board restricted)* | $5,000 | $5,000 |
| T35 | Scholarship Fund *(Board restricted)* | ($5,000) | $0 |

*Restricted Contributions and Contracts*

## STATEMENT OF ACTIVITIES  *for the period*

| REVENUE | WITHOUT DONOR RESTRICTIONS | WITH DONOR RESTRICTIONS | | |
|---|---|---|---|---|
| CONTRIBUTIONS & GIFTS | | | $ | 0 |
| PROGRAM SERVICES REVENUE | | | | 0 |
| GRANTS & CONTRACTS | | | | 0 |
| OTHER REVENUE | | | | 0 |
| **TOTAL REVENUE** | **$ 0** | **$0** | **$** | **0** |
| **EXPENSES** | | | | |
| FUNDRAISING | | | | 0 |
| ❶ PROGRAM SERVICES | 6,000 | | | 6,000 |
| GRANTS & CONTRACTS | | | | 0 |
| MANAGEMENT & GENERAL | | | | 0 |
| **TOTAL EXPENSES** | **$ 6,000** | | **$** | **6,000** |
| | CHANGE IN NET ASSETS | | $ | (6,000) |
| | BEGINNING NET ASSETS | | | 0 |
| | ENDING NET ASSETS | | $ | (6,000) |

## STATEMENT OF FINANCIAL POSITION  *as of the period ending date*

| ASSETS | | | LIABILITIES & NET ASSETS | | |
|---|---|---|---|---|---|
| ❷ CASH | $ | (6,000) | ACCOUNTS PAYABLE | | |
| ACCOUNTS RECEIVABLE | | | SHORT TERM DEBT | | |
| INVENTORIES | | | LONG TERM DEBT | | |
| PREPAID EXPENSES | | | ACCRUED EXPENSES | | |
| PLEDGES RECEIVABLE | | | NET ASSETS: | | |
| INVESTMENTS | | | W/O DONOR RESTRICTIONS | ❸ | 1,000 |
| PP&E (NET) | | | WITH DONOR RESTRICTIONS | ❸ | 5,000 |
| **TOTAL ASSETS** | **$** | **(6,000)** | **TOTAL LIABILITIES & NET ASSETS** | **$** | **6,000** |

## STATEMENT OF CASH FLOWS  *for the period*

| | | |
|---|---|---|
| BEGINNING CASH | $ | 0 |
| CASH RECEIPTS | | |
| CASH DISBURSEMENTS ❶ | | 6,000 |
| **CASH FLOW FROM OPERATIONS** | **$** | **(6,000)** |
| PP&E PURCHASES | | |
| NET BORROWINGS | | |
| INVESTMENT INCOME | | |
| **ENDING CASH** | **$** | **(6,000)** |

Transaction 35.
Statement
Entries

161

# T36. Accept a contract from the state Department of Human Services to provide meals-on-wheels to shut-ins in the community for next month.

We have a restaurant and commercial kitchen in our senior center to provide nutritious meals to seniors that drop in for lunch or an early dinner. It would be a natural extension to provide meals-on-wheels to seniors and shut-ins. We negotiate with the state Department of Human Services for a trial contract at a cost of $10,000 to provide 35 meals each day for a month. The state issues us a check ro $1,000 as an initial payment.

Normally, when a contract for future services is signed by a nonprofit, no revenue is recorded (unless a deposit is paid by the contractor.) Then as services are performed under the contract, expenses paid by the nonprofit to provide the services are recorded and a corresponding invoice upto the contract value is sent to the contractor for their reimbursement of the nonprofit's expenses. Generally, revenue is recorded by the nonprofit when services are provided and the invoice sent, but prior to actual cash payment.

---

**Transaction:** Accept a $10,000 contract with the DHS and receive a $1,000 prepayment.

**1** Record the $1,000 prepayment as GRANS & CONTRACTS REVENUE with donor restrictions.

**2** Record the $1,000 as a CASH RECEIPT on the *Cash Flow Statement*. Now, ENDING CASH on the *Statement of Cash Flows* is always the same as CASH on the *Statement of Financial Position*, so add ($1,000) to CASH on that statement.

**3** NET ASSETS with donor restrictions increases by $1,000.

Make appropriate entries in the *Restricted Net Assets Worksheet* below.

|  | Fund Description | Amount | Balance |
|---|---|---|---|
| **T36** | DHS Contract *(Meals-On-Wheels)* | $10,000 | $10,000 |
| **T36** | DHS Contract prepayment | ($1,000) | $9,000 |

## STATEMENT OF ACTIVITIES
*for the period*

| REVENUE | WITHOUT DONOR RESTRICTIONS | WITH DONOR RESTRICTIONS | | |
|---|---|---|---|---|
| CONTRIBUTIONS & GIFTS | | | $ | 0 |
| PROGRAM SERVICES REVENUE | | | | 0 |
| GRANTS & CONTRACTS | | 1,000 ❶ | | 1,000 |
| OTHER REVENUE | | | | 0 |
| **TOTAL REVENUE** | $ 0 | $0 | $ | 1,000 |
| **EXPENSES** | | | | |
| FUNDRAISING | | | | 0 |
| PROGRAM SERVICES | | | | 0 |
| GRANTS & CONTRACTS | | | | 0 |
| MANAGEMENT & GENERAL | | | | 0 |
| **TOTAL EXPENSES** | $ 0 | | $ | 0 |
| | CHANGE IN NET ASSETS | | $ | 1,000 |
| | BEGINNING NET ASSETS | | | 0 |
| | ENDING NET ASSETS | | $ | 1,000 |

## STATEMENT OF FINANCIAL POSITION
*as of the period ending date*

| ASSETS | | | LIABILITIES & NET ASSETS | | |
|---|---|---|---|---|---|
| ❷ CASH | $ | 1,000 | ACCOUNTS PAYABLE | | |
| ACCOUNTS RECEIVABLE | | | SHORT TERM DEBT | | |
| INVENTORIES | | | LONG TERM DEBT | | |
| PREPAID EXPENSES | | | ACCRUED EXPENSES | | |
| PLEDGES RECEIVABLE | | | NET ASSETS: | | |
| INVESTMENTS | | | W/O DONOR RESTRICTIONS | | |
| PP&E (NET) | | | WITH DONOR RESTRICTIONS ❸ | | 1,000 |
| **TOTAL ASSETS** | $ | 1,000 | **TOTAL LIABILITIES & NET ASSETS** | $ | 1,000 |

## STATEMENT OF CASH FLOWS
*for the period*

| | | |
|---|---|---|
| BEGINNING CASH | $ | 0 |
| CASH RECEIPTS ❷ | $ | 1,000 |
| CASH DISBURSEMENTS | | |
| **CASH FLOW FROM OPERATIONS** | $ | 1,000 |
| PP&E PURCHASES | | |
| NET BORROWINGS | | |
| INVESTMENT INCOME | | |
| **ENDING CASH** | $ | 1,000 |

**Transaction 36.
Statement
Entries**

# T37. Provide meals-on-wheels to shut-ins in the community for the month.

In fulfillment of the obligations in our contract with the State Department of Social Services, we have delivered meals-on-wheels to department designated recipients.

As is often the case with government contracts, we did not cover all our expenses and had to dip into our unrestricted net assets to fulfill the obligations of the contract. While this work is fully within our mission objectives, we need to limit the contracts we accept to the amounts that we can afford to spend with funds from other philanthropic sources.

**Transaction:** Fulfill DHS contract commitments and issue them an invoice for $9,000 and receive payment. Our total cost was $10,750 so will need to fund $750 from our own assets.

**1** Record the $9,000 as **REVENUE** and $10,750 as a **PROGRAM SERVICES EXPENSE** in the *Statement of Activities*. These two entries result in a ($750) **CHANGE IN NET ASSETS**.

**Note,** in **Transaction 92** we recorded the prepayment of $2,000 as **REVENUE** and here record $9,000 for the total contract amount of $10,000.

**2** Record **CASH DISBURSEMENTS** of $10,750 on the *Statement of Cash Flows* and also reduce **CASH** on the *Statement of Financial Position*.

**3** **NET ASSETS WITH DONOR RESTRICTIONS** decreases by $10,000 (the contract amount, now fulfilled) and **W/O DONOR RESTRICTIONS** by $750, our contribution.

Make appropriate entries in the ***Restricted Net Assets Worksheet*** below.

|  | Fund Description | Amount | Balance |
|---|---|---|---|
| **T37** | DHS Contract payment | ($9,000) | $0 |

## STATEMENT OF ACTIVITIES — *for the period*

| REVENUE | WITHOUT DONOR RESTRICTIONS | WITH DONOR RESTRICTIONS | | |
|---|---|---|---|---|
| CONTRIBUTIONS & GIFTS | | | $ | 0 |
| PROGRAM SERVICES REVENUE | | | | 0 |
| GRANTS & CONTRACTS | | 9,000 ❶ | | 9,000 |
| OTHER REVENUE | | | | 0 |
| **TOTAL REVENUE** | $ 0 | $0 | $ | 9,000 |
| **EXPENSES** | | | | |
| FUNDRAISING | | | | 0 |
| PROGRAM SERVICES | | | | 0 |
| GRANTS & CONTRACTS | ❶ 10,750 | | | 10,750 |
| MANAGEMENT & GENERAL | | | | 0 |
| **TOTAL EXPENSES** | $ 10,750 | | $ | 10,750 |
| | CHANGE IN NET ASSETS | | $ | (1,750) |
| | BEGINNING NET ASSETS | | | 0 |
| | ENDING NET ASSETS | | $ | (1,750) |

## STATEMENT OF FINANCIAL POSITION — *as of the period ending date*

| ASSETS | | LIABILITIES & NET ASSETS | | |
|---|---|---|---|---|
| ❷ CASH | $ (10,750) | ACCOUNTS PAYABLE | | |
| ACCOUNTS RECEIVABLE | | SHORT TERM DEBT | | |
| INVENTORIES | | LONG TERM DEBT | | |
| PREPAID EXPENSES | | ACCRUED EXPENSES | | |
| PLEDGES RECEIVABLE | | NET ASSETS: | | |
| INVESTMENTS | | W/O DONOR RESTRICTIONS | ❸ | (750) |
| PP&E (NET) | | WITH DONOR RESTRICTIONS | ❸ | (10,000) |
| **TOTAL ASSETS** | $ (10,750) | **TOTAL LIABILITIES & NET ASSETS** | $ | (10,750) |

## STATEMENT OF CASH FLOWS — *for the period*

| | | |
|---|---|---|
| BEGINNING CASH | $ | 0 |
| CASH RECEIPTS | | |
| ❷ CASH DISBURSEMENTS | | 10,750 |
| **CASH FLOW FROM OPERATIONS** | $ | (10,750) |
| PP&E PURCHASES | | |
| NET BORROWINGS | | |
| INVESTMENT INCOME | | |
| **ENDING CASH** | $ | (10,750) |

**Transaction 37. Statement Entries**

# Chapter 16.
# Other Common Transactions

A few odds-and-ends. These transactions are not as exciting as for program services and do not add directly to revenue, but they do benefit our mission. For example, without heat, light, and power all our volunteers would be cold and in the dark!

**Transaction 38.** Receive utility bills.

**Transaction 39.** Pay utility bills.

**Transaction 40.** Hire accountants and lawyers for audit and to help us prepare IRS Form 990.

**Transaction 41.** Pay WsNA's annual liability insurance premium and record first quarter's expense.

**Transaction 42.** Unrelated business income.

# T38. Receive utility bills.

We receive utility bills from our services providers—telephone, electricity, trash removal, etc.—totaling $2,835 for the month.

Electricity, trash removal, heat, light, power, and telephone, are major components of a nonprofit's *overhead* expense. Not flashy, but a "keep-the-door open" expense that needs to be controlled and not so minimized as to interfere with our ability to manage our operations effectively. Staff and volunteers would get pretty crabby when they are asked to work in the dark and cold because we did not pay our utility bills.

---

**Transaction:** Receive $2,835 in bills from our utilities suppliers for payment later in the month.

**❶** Record the utilities cost of $2,835 as a **MANAGEMENT & GENERAL EXPENSE** on the *Statement of Activities.*

**❷** **CHANGE IN NET ASSETS** on the *Statement of Activities* is a negative $2,835. This amount reduces **NET ASSET W/O DONOR RESTRICTIONS** on the *Statement of Financial Position.*

**❸** Increase **ACCOUNTS PAYABLE** $2,835 on the *Statement of Financial Position.* We are going to pay the bills later.

Note that **TOTAL ASSETS** still equals **TOTAL LIABILITIES & NET ASSETS** on the *Statement of Financial Position.*

## STATEMENT OF ACTIVITIES                                    *for the period*

| REVENUE | WITHOUT DONOR RESTRICTIONS | WITH DONOR RESTRICTIONS | | |
|---|---|---|---|---|
| CONTRIBUTIONS & GIFTS | | | $ | 0 |
| PROGRAM SERVICES REVENUE | | | | 0 |
| GRANTS & CONTRACTS | | | | 0 |
| OTHER REVENUE | | | | 0 |
| **TOTAL REVENUE** | $ 0 | $0 | $ | 0 |
| **EXPENSES** | | | | |
| FUNDRAISING | | | | 0 |
| PROGRAM SERVICES | | | | 0 |
| GRANTS & CONTRACTS | | | | 0 |
| MANAGEMENT & GENERAL | ❶ 2,835 | | | 2,835 |
| **TOTAL EXPENSES** | $ 2,835 | | $ | 2,835 |
| | **CHANGE IN NET ASSETS** | | $ | (2,835) |
| | **BEGINNING NET ASSETS** | | | 0 |
| | **ENDING NET ASSETS** | | $ | (2,835) |

## STATEMENT OF FINANCIAL POSITION                     *as of the period ending date*

| ASSETS | | | LIABILITIES & NET ASSETS | | |
|---|---|---|---|---|---|
| CASH | | | ACCOUNTS PAYABLE | ❸ $ | 2,835 |
| ACCOUNTS RECEIVABLE | | | SHORT TERM DEBT | | |
| INVENTORIES | | | LONG TERM DEBT | | |
| PREPAID EXPENSES | | | ACCRUED EXPENSES | | |
| PLEDGES RECEIVABLE | | | NET ASSETS: | | |
| INVESTMENTS | | | W/O DONOR RESTRICTIONS | ❷ | (2,835) |
| PP&E (NET) | | | WITH DONOR RESTRICTIONS | | |
| **TOTAL ASSETS** | $ | 0 | **TOTAL LIABILITIES & NET ASSETS** | $ | 0 |

## STATEMENT OF CASH FLOWS     *for the period*

| | | |
|---|---|---|
| BEGINNING CASH | $ | 0 |
| CASH RECEIPTS | | |
| CASH DISBURSEMENTS | | |
| **CASH FLOW FROM OPERATIONS** | $ | 0 |
| PP&E PURCHASES | | |
| NET BORROWINGS | | |
| INVESTMENT INCOME | | |
| **ENDING CASH** | $ | 0 |

**Transaction 38.
Statement
Entries**

## T39. Pay utility bills.

We pay the electric company, telephone company, and the trash removal guys for overhead bills booked in the prior transaction.

Nothing happens to the *Statement of Activities* when an invoice (accounts payable) is actually paid. This statement changed when we originally recorded the expense in T33. Isn't the accrual basis of accounting wonderful?

---

**Transaction:** Cut and mail checks totaling $2,835 in payment for overhead expenses recorded in the previous transaction.

**1** Record check payment of $2,835 as a **CASH DISBURSEMENT** on the *Statement of Cash Flows*.

**2** Reduce **ACCOUNTS PAYABLE** by the same amount on the *Statement of Financial Position*.

**3** **ENDING CASH** on the *Statement of Cash Flows* is always the same as **CASH** on the *Statement of Financial Position*, so add ($2,835) to **CASH** on that statement.

Now, **TOTAL ASSETS** equals **TOTAL LIABILITIES & NET ASSETS** on the *Statement of Financial Position*, as they must by definition.

**Note:** Paying bills has no effect on the *Statements of Activities*. No increase or decrease in **NET ASSETS** has occurred. Yeah, accrual accounting!

## STATEMENT OF ACTIVITIES                    *for the period*

| REVENUE | WITHOUT DONOR RESTRICTIONS | WITH DONOR RESTRICTIONS | | |
|---|---|---|---|---|
| CONTRIBUTIONS & GIFTS | | | $ | 0 |
| PROGRAM SERVICES REVENUE | | | | 0 |
| GRANTS & CONTRACTS | | | | 0 |
| OTHER REVENUE | | | | 0 |
| **TOTAL REVENUE** | $    0 | $0 | $ | 0 |
| **EXPENSES** | | | | |
| FUNDRAISING | | | | 0 |
| PROGRAM SERVICES | | | | 0 |
| GRANTS & CONTRACTS | | | | 0 |
| MANAGEMENT & GENERAL | | | | 0 |
| **TOTAL EXPENSES** | $    0 | | $ | 0 |
| | CHANGE IN NET ASSETS | | $ | 0 |
| | BEGINNING NET ASSETS | | | 0 |
| | ENDING NET ASSETS | | $ | 0 |

## STATEMENT OF FINANCIAL POSITION            *as of the period ending date*

| ASSETS | | | LIABILITIES & NET ASSETS | | |
|---|---|---|---|---|---|
| CASH | ❸ | $    (2,835) | ACCOUNTS PAYABLE | ❷ | $    (2,835) |
| ACCOUNTS RECEIVABLE | | | SHORT TERM DEBT | | |
| INVENTORIES | | | LONG TERM DEBT | | |
| PREPAID EXPENSES | | | ACCRUED EXPENSES | | |
| PLEDGES RECEIVABLE | | | NET ASSETS: | | |
| INVESTMENTS | | | W/O DONOR RESTRICTIONS | | |
| PP&E (NET) | | | WITH DONOR RESTRICTIONS | | |
| **TOTAL ASSETS** | | $    (2,835) | **TOTAL LIABILITIES & NET ASSETS** | | $    (2,835) |

## STATEMENT OF CASH FLOWS   *for the period*

**Transaction 39.**
**Statement**
**Entries**

| | | |
|---|---|---|
| BEGINNING CASH | $ | 0 |
| CASH RECEIPTS | | |
| CASH DISBURSEMENTS ❶ | | 2,835 |
| **CASH FLOW FROM OPERATIONS** | $ | (2,835) |
| PP&E PURCHASES | | |
| NET BORROWINGS | | |
| INVESTMENT INCOME | | |
| **ENDING CASH** | ❸ $ | (2,835) |

171

# T40. Hire accountants and lawyers for annual audit and to help us prepare Form 990.

It is time to file WsNA's nonprofit *IRS Form 990 Return of Organization Exempt from Income Tax*. It is the most important annual federal government filing for nonprofits, analogous to the *IRS Form 1040, U.S. Individual Income Tax Return* for individuals and the *IRS Form 1120 U.S. Corporation Income Tax Return* for for-profit companies.

Form 990 is not a simple and easy document to complete for many nonprofits. Form 990-EZ is easier but can only be used by smaller nonprofit organizations with less than $200,000 in revenue and less than $500,000 in net assets. Anyway, we are bigger and since our CEO will need to sign the form under penalties of perjury,[1] we contract with our accountants to prepare, and with our lawyers to review the filing before actually executing (signing) it. All in all, it is a $4,000 expense.

---

**Transaction:** Record a $4,000 expense for the preparation by accountants and legal review of Form 990.

**1** Record check payment of $4,000 as a CASH DISBURSEMENT on the *Statement of Cash Flows*.

**2** ENDING CASH on the *Statement of Cash Flows* is always the same as CASH on the *Statement of Financial Position,* so add ($4,000) from CASH on that statement.

**3** Record the payment as a MANAGEMENT & GENERAL EXPENSE on the *Statement of Activities*. Also lower NET ASSETS W/O DONOR RESTRICTIONS on the *Statement of Financial Position* by the same amount.

**Note,** an article in our by-laws states that all board members must be given a review copy of the Form 990. A Board vote formally accepting the document must be made before filing.

---

[1] Signature line so states: "Under penalties of perjury, I declare that I have examined this return, including accompanying schedules and statements, and to the best of my knowledge and belief, it is true, correct, and complete."

**STATEMENT OF ACTIVITIES** *for the period*

| REVENUE | WITHOUT DONOR RESTRICTIONS | WITH DONOR RESTRICTIONS | | |
|---|---|---|---|---|
| CONTRIBUTIONS & GIFTS | | | $ | 0 |
| PROGRAM SERVICES REVENUE | | | | 0 |
| GRANTS & CONTRACTS | | | | 0 |
| OTHER REVENUE | | | | 0 |
| **TOTAL REVENUE** | $ 0 | $0 | $ | 0 |
| **EXPENSES** | | | | |
| FUNDRAISING | | | | 0 |
| PROGRAM SERVICES | | | | 0 |
| GRANTS & CONTRACTS | | | | 0 |
| MANAGEMENT & GENERAL | ❸ 4,000 | | | 4,000 |
| **TOTAL EXPENSES** | $ 4,000 | | $ | 4,000 |
| | CHANGE IN NET ASSETS | | $ | (4,000) |
| | BEGINNING NET ASSETS | | | 0 |
| | ENDING NET ASSETS | | $ | (4,000) |

**STATEMENT OF FINANCIAL POSITION** *as of the period ending date*

| ASSETS | | LIABILITIES & NET ASSETS | |
|---|---|---|---|
| CASH | ❷ $ (4,000) | ACCOUNTS PAYABLE | |
| ACCOUNTS RECEIVABLE | | SHORT TERM DEBT | |
| INVENTORIES | | LONG TERM DEBT | |
| PREPAID EXPENSES | | ACCRUED EXPENSES | |
| PLEDGES RECEIVABLE | | NET ASSETS: | |
| INVESTMENTS | | W/O DONOR RESTRICTIONS | ❸ (4,000) |
| PP&E (NET) | | WITH DONOR RESTRICTIONS | |
| **TOTAL ASSETS** | $ (4,000) | **TOTAL LIABILITIES & NET ASSETS** | $ (4,000) |

**STATEMENT OF CASH FLOWS** *for the period*

| | | |
|---|---|---|
| BEGINNING CASH | $ | 0 |
| CASH RECEIPTS | | |
| CASH DISBURSEMENTS | ❶ | 4,000 |
| **CASH FLOW FROM OPERATIONS** | $ | (4,000) |
| PP&E PURCHASES | | |
| NET BORROWINGS | | |
| INVESTMENT INCOME | | |
| **ENDING CASH** | ❷ $ | (4,000) |

**Transaction 40. Statement Entries**

173

# T41. Pay WsNA's annual liability insurance premium. Record the first quarter's expense.

LightningStrike Insurance Brokers, LLC provides WsNA a package of building insurance, business interruption insurance, and general liability insurance at an annual cost of $28,000.

LightningStrike also finds us D&O (directors and officers) insurance to allow WsNA to indemnify our board members and officers from any personal liability while serving WsNA. That cost is an additional $1,450. The total bill for insurance is $29,450 annually. Simply a cost of doing business, nonprofit or not. Part of overhead.

When we signed up for coverage, the broker said that WsNA could enjoy a hefty discount (10%) if we pay for the whole year now. We pay the discounted $26,505 annual bill, book the first quarter expense of $6,626 through the *Statement of Activities,* and place the remaining three-quarters of insurance coverage as a prepaid expense on the *Statement of Financial Position.*

---

**Transaction:** Issue check to LightingStrike for WsNA's entire annual insurance expense of $26,505. Record first quarter's expense of $6,626.

**1** Record the $26,505 check as a **CASH DISBURSEMENT** on the *Statement of Cash Flows.* **ENDING CASH** on the *Statement of Cash Flows* is always the same as **CASH** on the *Statement* of *Financial Position*, so add ($26,505) to **CASH** on that statement.

**2** Record the quarterly cost of insurance of $6,626 as a **MANAGEMENT & GENERAL EXPENSE** on the *Statement of Activities.*

**3** **CHANGE IN NET ASSETS** on the *Statement of Activities* is a negative $6,626. This amount reduces **NET ASSETS W/O DONOR RESTRICTIONS** on the *Statement of Financial Position.*

**4** Increase **PREPAID EXPENSES** by $19,879 ($26,505 annual payment minus $6,626 quarterly expense) on the *Statement of Financial Position.*

## STATEMENT OF ACTIVITIES                              *for the period*

| REVENUE | WITHOUT DONOR RESTRICTIONS | WITH DONOR RESTRICTIONS | | |
|---|---|---|---|---|
| CONTRIBUTIONS & GIFTS | | | $ | 0 |
| PROGRAM SERVICES REVENUE | | | | 0 |
| GRANTS & CONTRACTS | | | | 0 |
| OTHER REVENUE | | | | 0 |
| **TOTAL REVENUE** | $ 0 | $0 | $ | 0 |
| **EXPENSES** | | | | |
| FUNDRAISING | | | | 0 |
| PROGRAM SERVICES | | | | 0 |
| GRANTS & CONTRACTS | | | | 0 |
| MANAGEMENT & GENERAL | ❷ 6,626 | | | 6,626 |
| **TOTAL EXPENSES** | $ 6,626 | | $ | 6,626 |
| | CHANGE IN NET ASSETS | ❷ | $ | (6,626) |
| | BEGINNING NET ASSETS | | | 0 |
| | ENDING NET ASSETS | | $ | (6,626) |

## STATEMENT OF FINANCIAL POSITION                    *as of the period ending date*

| ASSETS | | | LIABILITIES & NET ASSETS | | |
|---|---|---|---|---|---|
| CASH | ❶ | $ (26,505) | ACCOUNTS PAYABLE | | |
| ACCOUNTS RECEIVABLE | | | SHORT TERM DEBT | | |
| INVENTORIES | | | LONG TERM DEBT | | |
| PREPAID EXPENSES | ❹ | 19,879 | ACCRUED EXPENSES | | |
| PLEDGES RECEIVABLE | | | NET ASSETS: | | |
| INVESTMENTS | | | W/O DONOR RESTRICTIONS | ❸ | (6,626) |
| PP&E (NET) | | | WITH DONOR RESTRICTIONS | | |
| **TOTAL ASSETS** | | $ (6,626) | **TOTAL LIABILITIES & NET ASSETS** | | $ (6,626) |

## STATEMENT OF CASH FLOWS   *for the period*

| | | |
|---|---|---|
| BEGINNING CASH | | $ 0 |
| CASH RECEIPTS | | |
| CASH DISBURSEMENTS | ❶ | 26,505 |
| CASH FLOW FROM OPERATIONS | | $ (26,505) |
| PP&E PURCHASES | | |
| NET BORROWINGS | | |
| INVESTMENT INCOME | | |
| ENDING CASH | ❶ | $ (26,505) |

Transaction 41.

**Statement Entries**

# T42. Unrelated Business Income Tax.

What follows is mostly paraphrased [except the stuff in brackets] from IRS guidance publications. Enjoy.

For nonprofit organizations, an activity is an "unrelated business," and subject to unrelated business income tax, if it meets three requirements:

- It is a trade or business [like an ice cream shoppe].

- It is regularly carried on [seven days a week in the summer, five day per week in the winter and every Thursday night with bingo—see below].

- It is not "substantially related" to furthering the exempt purpose of the organization. [WsNA provides valuable services to seniors, but not necessarily free ice cream.]

WsNA has no current UBIT, but if we did, we would need a different set of financial statements to record its results and a set of additional IRS tax returns to file.

'Certain types of income are not considered unrelated business income, such as income from dividends; interest; royalties; rental of real property; research for a federal, state, or local government; and charitable contributions, gifts, and grants. In addition, unrelated business income does not include income derived from: the work of unpaid volunteers; the sale of donated goods [antiques from the auction, cars, etc.]; trade shows and conventions; a business carried on for the convenience of its members, students, officers, or employees (for example, a school cafeteria); and *income from legal gaming.*

**Bingo!** Yes, that's right, if these games meet the criteria set by the IRS and qualify for the "bingo exemption." WsNA could offer bingo games on Thursday nights, make a bundle from the seniors playing, and not pay any taxes on profits. Income received from gambling operations by a nonprofit organization is not unrelated business income. Gosh.

This is our last transaction example. Thanks for making it this far. *Pat yourself on the back!*

## STATEMENT OF ACTIVITIES · *for the period*

| REVENUE | WITHOUT DONOR RESTRICTIONS | WITH DONOR RESTRICTIONS | | |
|---|---|---|---|---|
| CONTRIBUTIONS & GIFTS | | | $ | 0 |
| PROGRAM SERVICES REVENUE | | | | 0 |
| GRANTS & CONTRACTS | | | | 0 |
| OTHER REVENUE | | | | 0 |
| **TOTAL REVENUE** | $ 0 | $0 | $ | 0 |
| **EXPENSES** | | | | |
| FUNDRAISING | | | | 0 |
| PROGRAM SERVICES | | | | 0 |
| GRANTS & CONTRACTS | | | | 0 |
| MANAGEMENT & GENERAL | | | | 0 |
| **TOTAL EXPENSES** | $ 0 | | $ | 0 |
| | **CHANGE IN NET ASSETS** | | $ | 0 |
| | **BEGINNING NET ASSETS** | | | 0 |
| | **ENDING NET ASSETS** | | $ | 0 |

## STATEMENT OF FINANCIAL POSITION · *as of the period ending date*

| ASSETS | | | LIABILITIES & NET ASSETS | | |
|---|---|---|---|---|---|
| CASH | | | ACCOUNTS PAYABLE | | |
| ACCOUNTS RECEIVABLE | | | SHORT TERM DEBT | | |
| INVENTORIES | | | LONG TERM DEBT | | |
| PREPAID EXPENSES | | | ACCRUED EXPENSES | | |
| PLEDGES RECEIVABLE | | | NET ASSETS: | | |
| INVESTMENTS | | | W/O DONOR RESTRICTIONS | | |
| PP&E (NET) | | | WITH DONOR RESTRICTIONS | | |
| **TOTAL ASSETS** | $ | 0 | **TOTAL LIABILITIES & NET ASSETS** | $ | 0 |

## STATEMENT OF CASH FLOWS · *for the period*

**Transaction 42. Statement Entries**

| | | |
|---|---|---|
| **BEGINNING CASH** | $ | 0 |
| CASH RECEIPTS | | |
| CASH DISBURSEMENTS | | |
| **CASH FLOW FROM OPERATIONS** | $ | 0 |
| PP&E PURCHASES | | |
| NET BORROWINGS | | |
| INVESTMENT INCOME | | |
| **ENDING CASH** | $ | 0 |

# Section D.
# Planning, Budgeting, Reporting & Oversight

# Chapter 17.
# Measuring Financial Performance

A nonprofit organization must decide how to measure its performance, both performance to mission and financial performance in support of the mission. In for-profit companies, there is a concrete, accepted measurement—profits. Things are not so simple for nonprofit organizations.[1]

While achieving mission goals defines ultimate success for all nonprofits, this book focuses mainly on financial measures of success. As I have been preaching *ad nauseam*, an organization faithfully adhering to its mission but operating with sloppy resource (financial) management is failing, as is a beautifully run financial operation that strays from its mission. Efficient and effective stewardship of monies received in support of mission is the hallmark of a responsible nonprofit organization.

## Performance Measures

How does the organization know it is doing a good job? It uses measurement tools and performance standards to answer some important questions. There is no single set of right things to measure for every organization. Management and board must

---

[1] See *Managing the Nonprofit Organization: Principles and Practices* by Peter F. Drucker, HarperCollins Publishers, New York, 1990, p142.

choose whatever is best for its organization's own circumstances.
To review my points from the introduction of this book:

- *Are we doing the right thing?* Is our spending congruent
  with our mission? Do we put our money where our mission
  is? Do we allow misdirection and mission creep?

- *Are we being effective?* Over time, are we reaching our
  goals? How are we sure? How do we measure and demonstrate our success?

- *Are we being efficient?* Are we getting the most bang for
  our buck? If not, we are squandering our donors' money—
  shame on us.

- *Do we have adequate resources?* Are our available
  financial and human resources sufficient to impact and
  support our mission? Are we biting off more than we
  can chew?

*How will we know?* We have the measuring tools of absolute
numbers, timelines, ratios, benchmarks, and words (narration).
Specific indicators to monitor, display, and analyze may include
the status of:

- *Finances:* revenue and expense, cash flow, reserves,
  budget vs. actuals, contracts/grants success;

- *Fundraising:* depth and breadth of donor and community
  support, fundraising, program support, donor demographics;

- *Programs:* reaching defined milestones and goals on-time
  and on-budget, client and customer participation and satisfaction levels;

- *Operations:* balance between program expense, management expense, fundraising expense, financial controls, infrastructure and facilities levels, overhead level for efficient
  overall operations;

- *Human Resources:* staff levels and skills, turn-over rates,
  growth of staff, and compensation comparisons.

Often, efficiency and, sometimes, effectiveness can be measured
quantitatively, while impact may require a qualitative approach.
More on this topic later, but for now...

## Measure, Measure, Measure

Nonprofit organizations need rigorous impact evaluation because they lack the market signals that the for-profit world enjoys. "Businesses know something works when customers buy the product...but if you give people social services for free, you may never learn about bad service because the customer doesn't have a choice."[2]

Using measurement tools to guide nonprofit public charity work is crucial to ensuring the efficient use of limited resources. An evidence-based approach coupled with computer-assisted data collection, analysis, and presentation techniques means that the effectiveness of programs can be constantly assessed during execution.

## Numbers vs. Narratives

Although *quantitative analysis* is a powerful financial tool, it rarely tells a complete story without the help of *qualitative analysis*. The idea behind quantitative analysis is to measure things; the idea behind qualitative analysis is to understand them.

Financial statements and other numeric reports are especially suited to quantitative analysis. Qualitative analysis often focuses on observations. Qualitative analysis can provide a depth and richness that quantitative analysis often lack.

Numbers may alert board and management to a problem. Narrative is needed to discover the story behind the bad numbers. For example, high employee turnover is easily measured quantitatively. However, the reasons for high turnover are best analyzed qualitatively, such as low staff motivation or bad management.

Qualitative analysis is sometimes discounted as only a "gut feeling." However, properly done, it can be a rigorous approach to measurement. In fact, narrative may consume much more time and energy than quantitative analysis but often reveals more action elements and a greater commitment to action.

For board members, just walking around and talking with clients, staff, and management can be as informative, or more so, than regularly reviewing financial statements and monitoring budgets. Best is both.

---

[2] Dina Pomeranz, Assistant Professor, Harvard Business School, as quoted in http://harvardmagazine.com/2015/07/doing-good-scientifically.

## Charts, Tables & Dashboards

Data presented in tables can be detailed, but depending on its complexity, can be difficult to read and understand. Information presented in charts and graphics may be easier to digest. See a happy marriage of the two shown on the next page. Qualitative data does not translate well into charts and the relevant stories will still need to be told with narration.

The CFO, accounting staff, and certainly the auditors will want to look at numbers in table form. Board members and some management may have easier access to the information if presented in graphic form called a *dashboard*, filled with charts.

Dashboards are succinct, easily readable performance indicators graphically presented that allow viewing organizational status at a glance. Dashboards are especially useful to show trends over time and are often a starting point for further discussion. See Chapter 18.

## Budget vs. Actual

"Budget vs. Actual" analysis is the most commonly used and valuable short-term method of performance evaluation in any organization. Not being intimately involved in the annual budgeting process or not closely watching performance-to-budget is probably the most damaging weakness of many nonprofit boards.

Management and staff usually prepare an annual budget and present it to the board for discussion and approval. Weak and ineffectual boards will often just rubber-stamp management's recommendations. Big mistake!

Budgets are one area where the board is ultimately responsible. They must not slack from their responsibilities to ensure "money is where their mission is." Management and staff may have pet priorities and special interests. One such special interest—keeping their jobs—can be an impediment to thoughtful change from the status quo. Budgets are so important, we have devoted a whole chapter to them. See Chapter 19.

## Outcome Measurement

Another layer of nonprofit performance measurement is *outcome measurement*. The complexity of this approach comes from the existential realization that "You get what you measure." Another way of saying the same thing is "If you do not measure a

# Children's Project *(501(c)(3) Corporation)*

## Statement of Activities

| Revenue | 2015 | 2014 |
|---|---|---|
| Contributions - Home | $26,697 | $75,100 |
| Contributions - School | 262,207 | 0 |
| Contributions - Unrestricted | 0 | 15,886 |
| other | 76,527 | 0 |
| **Total Revenue** | **$365,431** | **$90,986** |

| Expenses | 2015 | 2014 |
|---|---|---|
| Grants - Home | $22,110 | $0 |
| Grants - School | 277,747 | 0 |
| Office & Administration | 15,082 | 75 |
| Fundraising | 7,665 | 0 |
| **Total Expenses** | **$322,604** | **$75** |
| *Change in Net Assets* | $42,827 | $90,911 |
| *Beginning Net Assets* | $90,911 | $0 |
| *Ending Net Assets* | $42,827 | $90,911 |

2015 Revenue ($)

other, $76,527 21%

Contributions - Home, $26,697 7%

Contributions - School, $262,207 72%

2015 Expenses ($)

Office & Administration, $15,082 5%

Fundraising, $7,665 2%

Grants - Home, $22,110 7%

Grants - School, $277,747 86%

hoped-for outcome, how do you know you have accomplished it through your efforts?" Deterministically, if you do not measure outcomes, you will not reach them.[3] Seems obvious, but not that easy to accomplish. How much we spend delivering a program is relatively easy to determine; how well these expenditures result in the direct, intended beneficial effects on our stakeholders can be problematic to ascertain.

How does our program add value? What meaningful, positive change has been accomplished by our intervention and is it sustainable? A nutrition program may count the number of meals it delivers to housebound clients. "However, this number is not a measure of whether the clients actually ate the meals, enjoyed the meals, or whether the meals made a significant difference in the client's condition."[3]

Think about it.

## Transparency

What is there to hide? Nonprofits do not have a need for trade secrets as for-profit companies do. The secret sauce formula gives a for-profit manufacturer a competitive advantage. However, if a nonprofit organization discovers a better way to serve its clients, it has a duty to share. The Federal government makes it easy by requiring openness via Form 990.

One exception is the anonymous donor. Even then, several people within the organization must know about the donor and the donation(s): the CEO, the chief of development, the chief of finance and select accounting personnel. All have a responsibility to the organization and the donor to keep the donor's name confidential. However, knowledge of these gifts must be preserved in order to solicit future donations.

---

[3] Adapted from *The Nonprofit Outcomes Toolbook: A complete Guide to Program Effectiveness, Performance Measures, and Results* by Robert M. Penna, John Wiley & Sons, Inc., NJ 2011.

# Chapter 18.
# Ratios & Benchmarks

Now that we have accurate and consistent financial statements, what should we do with them? Huh? There is more? Yep.

Compute ratios! Ratio analysis is comparing one number on the organization's financial statements with another. Ratio analysis is particularly useful when:

- **comparing** your organization's financial performance with that of another similar organization. This comparison technique is called *benchmarking*. Are they getting better results than we are? Why? What do they do better than we do?

- **comparing** recent performance of your organization with that of past years. Are we doing better than we did last year? What are we doing better now and can we do more of it?

- **identifying** areas of weak financial performance in the organization. What is out of line? How can we improve?

For example, if your organization spent $356,812 on fundraising (see Ⓑ below and on the next page) in the year and total revenue (see Ⓐ below and on the next page) was $1,400,496 you would compute the *Fundraising Expense Ratio* as:

$$\text{Fundraising Expense Ratio} = \frac{\$356,812\,\text{B}}{\$1,400,496\,\text{A}} = 25\%$$

## STATEMENT OF ACTIVITIES    *for the period*

| REVENUE | WITHOUT DONOR RESTRICTIONS | WITH DONOR RESTRICTIONS | | |
|---|---|---|---|---|
| CONTRIBUTIONS & GIFTS | | | $ | 0 |
| PROGRAM SERVICES REVENUE Ⓙ | | | | 0 |
| GRANTS & CONTRACTS Ⓝ | | | | 0 |
| OTHER REVENUE | | | | 0 |
| TOTAL REVENUE Ⓐ | $ 0 | $ 0 | $ | 0 |
| EXPENSES | | | | |
| FUNDRAISING Ⓑ | | | $ | 0 |
| PROGRAM SERVICES Ⓜ | | | | 0 |
| GRANTS & CONTRACTS | | | | 0 |
| MANAGEMENT & GENERAL Ⓟ | | | | 0 |
| TOTAL EXPENSES Ⓗ | $ 0 | | $ | 0 |
| | CHANGE IN NET ASSETS Ⓒ | | $ | 0 |
| | BEGINNING NET ASSETS | | | 0 |
| | ENDING NET ASSETS | | $ | 0 |

## STATEMENT OF FINANCIAL POSITION    *as of the period ending date*

| ASSETS | | | LIABILITIES & NET ASSETS | | |
|---|---|---|---|---|---|
| ⌐ CASH Ⓖ | | | Ⓕ ⌐ ACCOUNTS PAYABLE Ⓛ | | |
| \| ACCOUNTS RECEIVABLE Ⓚ | | | ⌊ SHORT TERM DEBT | | |
| Ⓔ \| INVENTORIES | | | LONG TERM DEBT Ⓘ | | |
| \| PREPAID EXPENSES | | | ACCRUED EXPENSES | | |
| ⌊ PLEDGES RECEIVABLE | | | NET ASSETS: | | |
| INVESTMENTS | | | W/O DONOR RESTRICTIONS | | |
| PP&E (NET) | | | WITH DONOR RESTRICTIONS | | |
| TOTAL ASSETS Ⓓ | $ 0 | | TOTAL LIABILITIES & NET ASSETS | $ | 0 |

This ratio tells you how much is spent on raising money for the year relative to the total amount of revenue that comes into the organization. A ratio of 25% means the organization spends $2.50 on fundraising for every $10 of total revenue received. Such a ratio might be considered high, indicating an inefficient or ineffective fundraising effort. Or maybe not so high if the organization is young, with few repeat donors. *Most nonprofit organizations spend between 10% to 25% of revenue on fundraising expense.*

～

To recap, ratio analysis relies on information contained in a company's financial statements. Ratios are calculated comparing one line item in a financial statement—or a combination of line items—to another line item. Ratios are often presented as a percentage. Depending on the line items chosen to compare, an organization's efficiency, liquidity, profitability, and solvency can be evaluated. In addition, trends of these ratios over time can show whether performance is improving or deteriorating.

To be useful for financial analysis, ratios must be: (1) calculated using accurate financial reports presented consistently from period-to-period, (2) viewed both at a single point and as a trend over time, and (3) used in comparing with benchmarks of similar organizations. Ratio analysis is often used by sophisticated donors to determine management's competence when deciding whether to fund the organization.

What follows are commonly used ratios to evaluate a nonprofit organization's financial performance, financial strength, financial risk, and organizational efficiency.

### Financial Performance

Financial performance measures are the return-on profitability ratios. I know, I know, nonprofit organizations do not generate profits. However, they do have the analogous increase in net assets (revenues minus expenses) and call it a surplus.

The following ratios measure management's ability to generate a surplus from the organization's activities. An organization that generates a surplus from its program services activities is less dependent on fickle outsiders for support.

*Percent Return on Revenue* ratio is the standard measure of generating a surplus. For each $1.00 of revenue, what is left over after all expenses have paid? *Seldom is this ratio greater than 5% for nonprofits.*

$$\% \text{ Return on Revenue} = \frac{\text{CHANGE IN NET ASSETS C}}{\text{REVENUE A}}$$

*Percent Return on Assets* ratio shows how effective we are in generating a surplus using the financial assets employed by the organization.

$$\% \text{ Return on Assets} = \frac{\text{CHANGE IN NET ASSETS C}}{\text{TOTAL ASSETS D}}$$

Consistent surplus generation by a nonprofit organization is an indicator of strong financial management. Breakeven results do not allow for the breathing room necessary for when things do not go according to plan. Ideally, surpluses should contribute to savings, such as for a future rainy day or a strategic opportunity. *However, less than half of nonprofits regularly report a surplus.*[1]

If a new opportunity comes along and your current organization and financial position does not have the capacity to address it, what will you do? A surplus really helps. An organization's program operations need not bring in a surplus on their own. Effective fundraising and the resulting community philanthropy can fill the gap. Contributions with donor restrictions often do not really help establish a nonprofit's overall strength and often do not even cover full overhead and thus can be a financial drain.

### Financial Strength

Financial strength ratios come in two flavors: (1) *liquidity ratios* indicating necessary cash on hand, and (2) *leverage ratios* showing that the organization is not carrying too much debt.

Liquidity ratios measure the ease with which the organization can pay its bills when due. Is there enough cash coming into the organization from contributions and program services revenue and other sources for the organization to meet payment obligations? The two most used liquidity ratios are the *Current Ratio* and *Days Cash on Hand.*

**Current Ratio** measures the organization's ability to pay its bills in the short-term. CURRENT ASSETS are the money the organization plans to collect in the next year; CURRENT LIABILITIES are money the organization expects to pay out in the next year. See pages 53 and 54 for more detailed definitions.

$$\text{Current Ratio} = \frac{\text{CURRENT ASSETS E}}{\text{CURRENT LIABILITIES F}}$$

*A current ratio of between 1½ and 2½ is ideal for a nonprofit organization, providing an adequate safety margin.* A current ratio of less than 1 could mean that the organization may suffer a major liquidity crisis if negative unforeseen events transpire.

---

[1] *Top Indicators of Nonprofit Financial Health,* Nonprofit Finance Fund, NYC. Accessed as: http://www.nonprofitfinancefund.org/blog/top-indicators-nonprofit-financial-health.

**Days Cash on Hand** compares the amount of cash the organization has in the bank with how many days that cash will last at the organizations' daily spending rate.

$$\text{Days Cash On Hand} = \frac{\text{CASH } G}{(\text{TOTAL EXPENSES } H \div 365)}$$

Three months of expenses that can be covered with available unrestricted cash on hand is usually adequate liquidity, depending on the organization's funding volatility, facility needs, and the general economic environment. *About half of all nonprofits have over 90 days of cash on hand. Half do not.*[1]

**Debt Ratio** compares the amount of TOTAL DEBT with TOTAL ASSETS. Debt is a critical financial tool that can help organizations manage the ebbs and flows of cash for operations, facility purchases and upgrades, and more. However, as liabilities bump up against an organization's ability to pay off those obligations, they can become a real problem.

$$\text{Debt Ratio} = \frac{\text{TOTAL DEBT } I}{\text{TOTAL ASSETS } D}$$

Nonprofit organizations can often carry a manageable amount of debt to extend its ability to serve its mission. *A debt ratio of 10% to 15% is common.* A higher ratio, say 35% to 50% is most often too high. Such a high debt means that debt service costs will rob the organization of resources and limit its flexibility.

———

Increasing financial liquidity and strength are worthy goals. Any organization can have periods of illiquidity—being without sufficient funds on hand to pay all of its bills on time. However, if this illiquidity is a common occurrence or goes on for an extended period, the organization risks bankruptcy.

Further, what happens if you have to replace a hot water heater? Formal reserves for facility improvements and replacements are a good sign. Absent formal reserves, are there appropriate levels of liquidity to respond?

## Financial Risk

***Reliance on Revenue Source*** is a key measure of financial risk—how many of your eggs are being carried in one basket. Reliance on a single income source is risky because it could go away. Sigh.

$$\text{Reliance on a Revenue Source} = \frac{REVENUE\ SOURCE\ \text{N}}{TOTAL\ REVENUE\ \text{A}}$$

There is nothing inherently wrong with revenue source concentration. However, management needs to pay very close attention and focus support on its limited funding sources and demonstrate the reliability of the sources over time. Lower overall risk to the organization's long-term viability is found with a broad base of support from individuals, foundations, and government agencies through contributions and gifts, program services revenue, contracts, and grants.

***Self-Sufficiency Ratio*** means how well you generate revenue on your own through program services. Another good measure of lower financial risk is management's ability to bring in recurring dollars. This skill requires an ability to predict an adequate level of income with a fair amount of certainty, based on historical performance and an understanding of market dynamics.

$$\text{Self-Sufficiency Ratio} = \frac{EARNED\ REVENUE\ \text{J}}{TOTAl\ EXPENSES\ \text{H}}$$

Organizations with earned income, such as that from retail program services to individuals, generally have more autonomy and flexibility than those without. A self-sufficiency ratio is computed as shown above. *The higher the percentage, the lower the risk.*

## Organizational Efficiency

How efficiently are we using the assets entrusted to us to advance our mission? Spending ratios including program expense ratio and its mirror, the administrative expense (overhead) ratio, are useful in assessing organizational efficiency. The fundraising expense ratio is useful here also.

***Receivable Days*** indicates how fast the organization collects money due.

$$\text{Receivable Days} = \frac{\text{ACCOUNTS RECEIVABLE K}}{(\text{TOTAL REVENUE A} \div 365)}$$

***Payable Days*** indicates how fast the organization pays its own bill from others. *Generally between 30 days and 45 days is normal and acceptable for both measures.*

$$\text{Payable Days} = \frac{\text{ACCOUNTS PAYABLE L}}{(\text{TOTAL EXPENSES H} \div 356)}$$

If receivables get older and more delinquent, they are more likely to be written off as a bad debt which will directly lower net assets. If payables increase, the organization is just being sloppy, antagonizing vendors, or in a cash flow crisis. *A good goal is less than 45 days.*

***Overhead Ratio*** is the percentage of a nonprofit's total expenses that is devoted to its administrative and fundraising costs. There is no *right* percentage here. Organizations have different strategies of operation and function in different realms. But, we can agree that fundraising and administrative expenses are essential in sustaining the organization.

$$\text{Overhead Ratio} = \frac{ADMIN. \text{ P } + FUNDRAISING \text{ B}}{TOTAl \text{ } EXPENSES \text{ H}}$$

Underspending in infrastructure, management, and in general operations can threaten effectiveness. Inadequate fundraising expense results in less philanthropic revenue for the organization. *Generally, an overhead rate of over 35% is considered excessive.*

$$\text{Program Expense Ratio} = \frac{PROGRAM \text{ } EXPENSES \text{ M}}{TOTAl \text{ } EXPENSES \text{ H}}$$

***Program Expense Ratio***, the mirror to the overhead ratio, is the percentage of program services expenses to total expenses. Low administration and overhead expenses, while theoretically a good idea, can force managers to underinvest in good governance, planning, compliance and risk management, program evaluation, data collection, and staff training. Also, it focuses on the short-term performance rather than building long-term relationships and strengths. Low fundraising expenses can rob the organization of revenue necessary to make mission impact. Perversely, foundation contracts often do not designate sufficient overhead amounts to cover a nonprofit's full costs of running the program. The necessary money has to come from somewhere, often the organization's general revenue sources. Sigh. It costs the organization to accept these contracts and grants.

———

The ultimate questions that ratio analysis helps answer are:

1. Overall, how healthy is our organization today? Is it healthier today than it was three years ago? Why or why not?

2. How effective are our programs in serving our mission?

3. Are our programs sustainable, that is, generating resources to meet today's needs without compromising the future?

Look at the ratio examples shown on the facing page. The ratio values are all over the place. But then, the organizations listed are dissimilar. Pick a few organizations in the same charitable and geographic area as yours and compare (benchmark) your ratio values to theirs. Ideas for improvement?

| ** | Fundraising Expense Ratio | Administrative Ratio * | Days Accounts Receivable | Days Accounts Payable | Days Cash on Hand | Debt Ratio | Current Ratio | Return (surplus) on Assets | Return (surplus) on Revenue |
|---|---|---|---|---|---|---|---|---|---|
| March of Dimes | 14% | 23% | 10 | 19 | 0.0 | 22 | 0.6 | -13% | -5% |
| Massachusetts Audubon Society | 9% | 18% | 10 | 22 | 0.0 | 62 | 1.0 | 2% | 16% |
| Girl Scouts of America | 28% | 13% | 21 | 52 | 0.0 | 59 | 1.5 | 1% | 2% |
| Massachusetts Historical Society | 32% | 30% | 64 | 23 | 0.2 | >1,000 | 12.3 | -2% | -51% |
| American Diabetes Association | 31% | 30% | 8 | 18 | 0.0 | 30 | 3.5 | 11% | 5% |
| Boston Fund | 2% | 10% | 1 | 17 | 0.0 | 67 | 4.9 | 0% | -2% |
| American Cancer Society | 21% | 26% | 2 | 16 | 0.0 | 71 | 0.5 | 0% | 0% |
| Community Servings (Boston) | 18% | 19% | 19 | 26 | 1.1 | 170 | 8.1 | -8% | -13% |
| WGBH (Boston Public TV) | n/a | 28% | 24 | 81 | 0.9 | 54 | 3.5 | -2% | -3% |
| Dana Farber Cancer Institute | 6% | 20% | 35 | 45 | 0.2 | 5 | 1.3 | -4% | -4% |
| Cambridge Center for Adult Education | 21% | 13% | 2 | 55 | 0.0 | 70 | 4.9 | 15% | 11% |

* includes Management & General and Fundraising Expenses

** data from latest year available (2013, 2014, or 2015)

# Chapter 19.
# Nonprofit "Dashboards"

*Dashboards* are a simple, often colorful, graphic representation of key performance indicators. They convey financial and operating information in an easy to understand and difficult to ignore or misinterpret format. See below for a simple but compelling graphic presentation of revenue by source.

Nonprofit organizations use dashboards to summarize and present their operations data to stakeholders less familiar with numeric financial statement formats. In dashboards, this financial information is supplemented with quantitative and qualitative graphics to give an interesting and complete presentation of performance to mission—*at a glance.*

## Symbolic Representation of Performance

Dashboards can be both fun and informative. They can be designed to rivet attention to what is truly important and timely for the board, management, and staff to review.

Smiley faces that turn into frowny faces are hard to ignore. A 5-star performance is obviously better than a 2-star performance. Numbers are dry; symbols are not. *Use colors too!*

## Key Performance Indicators

Key performance indicators (KPIs) are quantifiable measurements of a nonprofit organization's health and success. KPIs for an organization are usually benchmarked against peer organizations and are commonly recognized business model ratios. Different types of nonprofit organizations will use different KPIs, for example, visitor and membership data for a museum, enrollment for a day care center, patients served for a clinic. Dashboards are an ideal way to present these KPIs to stakeholders of the organization—both people who need to know and people who care!

Major benefits of a dashboard format for financial reports is that it levels the playing field with the financial literates and the less literate and highlights agreed upon measures of organizational success. Dashboards make it easy to show performance over time and compare results with budget.

Dashboards encourage conversation and development of action items. Dashboards may wave red flags that cannot be ignored. A selection of KPIs are shown on the facing page. Select a few that are important for your organization. Imagine how they could be presented graphically.

### Key Performance Indicators

**Finance KPIs**
Revenue, expense, & surplus levels
Actual vs. budget
Revenue dependence by type
Cash flow and liquidity
Ratios:
    Financial performance
    Financial strength
    Financial risk
    Organizational efficiency

**Fundraising KPIs**
Annual campaign performance to-date
Event results
Capital campaign performance
Revenue received/expense—efficiency ratio

**Program Services KPIs**
Clients served
Client satisfaction
Revenue & expense
Costs per client

**Contracts & Grants KPIs**
Schedules & milestones
Financial measures
Outcome measures & deliverables
Contract awards

**Human Resources KPIs**
Payroll
Headcounts:
    New hires
    Resignations
    Terminations
Volunteers:
    Number
    Hours

**Operations KPIs**
Spending levels
Overhead coverage

## Steps in making a good Dashboard:

- Define the audience for the specific dashboard.
- Select key performance indicators important to that audience.
- Decide how to best present KPIs in a user-friendly, visual format—line charts, column charts, pie charts, and special symbols and emoticons. Use color.
- If appropriate, show actual vs. budgets and any special targets.
- Show current status of programs and initiatives; show trends over time. Highlight unexpected results.
- Focus on only the limited number of KPIs that are most important to follow.
- Combine numbers with graphs to get the best of both. See example on page 173.

~

See the sample WsNA dashboard on the facing page. We have graphically presented KPI data and trends for the prior eight quarters of performance:

- organizational headcount and staff turnover
- payable days and receivable days
- revenue, budget and surplus generation
- revenue by sources
- client visits by type

Also useful is a short narrative discussion (one page maximum length) of good things ☺ happening and bad things ☹ happening within the organization.

# Chapter 20.
# Planning, Budgeting,
# & Strategy

Plan + Budget = Success...or, at least a good chance of success.

- *The Annual Budget* is for operations. How will we pay for what we are going to do this year? If we do not know how we are going to afford to get where we want to go, we will never get there.

- *The Strategic Plan* defines long-term goals, strategies and actions necessary to achieve our mission. Questions are asked, then answered in the strategic plan. What does success look like? Where should we focus our efforts? What investments need to be made? Note, the chief determinants of what a nonprofit organization will become are the investments (expenses) it makes today.

Often included in a strategic plan is a 3-5 year financial forecast—a look into intermediate-term futures. Where can necessary resources be found? What can we do to ensure their availability?

> ## "When a man does not know what harbor he is making for, no wind is the right wind."
> —Seneca the Younger, tutor and adviser to Nero

The actual budgeting/planning process is perhaps the most important group effort that a thoughtful board, management, and staff can accomplish in pursuit of mission. Without these efforts, the organization in the short term will be unfocused and ineffective and in the long term will be flying blind.

Note, accounting and financial types and modern accounting software tend to "overcomplexify" budgets, down to trivial line items, counting every paper clip. They then produce a voluminous document for approval by the board, saying, "This is our budget."

*Wrong!* What they have presented are the detailed line-item monthly spreadsheets that go into our accounting program. The accounting staff needs them to control expenses, but they are not designed for anybody else to review.

Send the spreadsheets back and ask that the budget data be presented in a prospective *Statement of Functional Expenses* format. That is a document the board and management can discuss, modify and approve. If the budget or the plan is not presented in a way that everyone in the organization can understand, it is not a document that will serve its purpose of guidance and fiscal control. Use graphs and colors too!

## Operating Plan & Annual Budget

*How to prepare a good annual budget is beyond the scope of this book, but we can describe the attributes of a good budget.* At its most basic level, a budget is simply a formatted list of:

- estimated revenue including contributions, grants, program service fees, memberships, ticket sales, and other sources,

- estimated expenses including those spent day-to-day such as salaries, supplies, office expense, and all others,

- proposed expenditures for capital equipment like furniture, computers, and other long-lived assets.

A good budget is a layered, working document for the board and for operating managers within the organization. It is the foundation for the most useful management tool, actual versus budget analysis.

A well-drawn budget will include:

- **outcomes**—the targets that have to be achieved
- **steps**—the sequential steps needed to get there,

- **schedules** — the timeline for getting things done,
- **resources** — the people and other resources employed,
- **revenues and expenses** — what all this will cost and how we will pay for it.
- **restricted funds**—money usable only for a restricted purpose that needs to be tracked separately from other funds.

Looking at proposed money coming in as revenue and subtracting expected money going out as expenses and capital expenditures will allow you to see if your organization will have enough funds to cover all your planned activities. If not, you will need to rein in your plans and modify your budget to lowered expectations.

### Strategic Plan

*How to write a good strategic plan is beyond the scope of this book, but we can outline the major attributes of a good plan.*

- Strategy is of the highest importance to success of the organization and is a basic responsibility of the board and CEO.
- Strategy is always actionable. We plan and implement actions to make our strategies real.
- Strategy is always measurable. We will know if our strategies work. Strategy is forward thinking and shapes the future.
- Strategy is systematic, realistic, inclusive and, hopefully, creative.
- Strategy is realistically constrained by resource availability but will use all available resources effectively and efficiently.

Strategic planning is about predicting the future, and predicting the future is a risky business.

---

## "It is tough making predictions, especially about the future."

—attributed to **Yogi Berra**, catcher for the Yankees, but first said by Niels Bohr, physicist and Nobel laureate

---

A good strategic plan can:

- formalize your ideas, structure your priorities, and test your viability,
- help identify responsibilities and help you work together as a group and with partners,
- help you ask the right questions, provide some of the answers, and identify areas where you need to find out more,
- provide you with a map to guide your progress, and stop you from getting sidetracked,
- and importantly, demonstrate to funders that you have done your homework and know what you're doing with their money.

⌒

There are all sorts of cute techniques to assist managers to think strategically. Most of these techniques were first developed in the for-profit arena, but thoughtfully employed, can work for nonprofit organizations too. Try a **SWOT** analysis (strengths, weaknesses, oportunities, and threats), or a **PEST** analysis (political, economic, social, and technology), or, perhaps, a **STEER** analysis (sociocultural, technological, economic, ecological and regulatory). These techniques can broaden understanding of the situation and allow for a creative look at planning the future.

⌒

The facing page outlines the *planning hierarchy* of goals and actions directed at an ultimate mission or purpose. Thinking with these categories in mind can clarify your answer to the question, "What are we doing, and why are we doing it?

# The Planning Hierarchy

**Mission**—purpose, reason for being.

**Vision**—aspirations going forward.

**Goals**—major tasks to accomplish.

**Strategies**—designed to reach goals.

**Actions**—required to implement strategies.

**Tactics**—day-to-day efforts in support of actions.

# Chapter 21.
# Financial Reporting
# with Form 990

Nonprofit organizations report to the federal government annually using IRS Form 990. If you do not file, the organization could lose its nonprofit status. It is important to do it right. It is the law. *U.S. Code › Title 26 › Subtitle F › Chapter 61 › Subchapter A › Part III › Subpart A › § 6033 - Returns by Exempt Organizations* so states, "...every organization exempt from taxation... shall file an annual return, stating specifically the items of gross income, receipts, and disbursements, and such other information for the purpose of carrying out the internal revenue laws as the Secretary [of the Treasury] may by forms or regulations prescribe, and shall keep such records, render under oath such statements, make such other returns, and comply with such rules and regulations as the Secretary may from time to time prescribe..."

## Form 990

Actually, a Form 990 is no more confusing or difficult to complete than is an individual's personal tax return Form 1040. *Gulp!* Many people with simple financial lives can complete their own. Others of us use a tax-preparation service. Same goes for nonprofit organizations.

IRS reporting forms come in different flavors for different sizes and types on nonprofit organizations. Use the original **Form 990** for organizations with annual revenue of over $200,000 or total assets over $500,000. While the actual return is only 16 pages long, with required schedules and descriptive narrative the filing can easily reach over 75 pages.

**Form 990-EZ** is simpler and for use by organizations with annual revenue of less than $200,000 and total assets of less than $500,000. Even simpler, small organizations with annual revenue of less than $50,000 can electronically file a **Form 990-N**, called the e-postcard.

In addition to requiring exhaustive financial information, the Form 990 questions require organizations to disclose significant information about their governance procedures and policies, governing documents, relationships with their organization leaders and with third parties, and much more.

In contrast to an individual's IRS Form 1040 or a for-profit company's IRS Form 1120, which are private and confidential, a nonprofit organization's Form 990 is available for public observation at the nonprofit's offices and on the internet. There will be many people looking over your shoulder at the filings.

### Uses of Form 990

Many different groups and individuals use the organization's Form 990 for various purposes. One such use is the staff looking at *"Part VII Compensation of Officers, Directors, Key Employees"* to see what the boss makes!

The IRS uses Form 990 information to assess the organization's compliance with applicable tax laws. Charity "watchdog" groups use information in Form 990 to evaluate and rate nonprofit organizations on efficiency and effectiveness. Grant funding organizations and donors review the ratings of such watchdog groups.

The highly public nature of Form 990 presents an opportunity for the organization to share positive information about its mission and purpose, the positive impact of its activities, and the effectiveness of its programs. Free publicity!

∼

The facing page shows the table of contents of the IRS Form 990. Subsequent pages show sections of Form 990 for the financial statements we are focusing on in this book. After the summary page is Part VIII Statement of Revenue (partial Statement of Activities), Part IX Statement of Functional Expenses and Part X Balance Sheet (Statement of Financial Position).

**FORM 990: Return of Organization Exempt from Income Tax**
Filing Tax Year
Organization's legal name, address, and telephone number
Employer Identification Number (assigned by IRS)
Principal officer's name and address
**Part I Summary**
Brief description of mission, governance, most significant activities,
volunteers, revenue, and expenses
**Part II Signature Block**
Officer signature and paid-preparer signature
**Part III Statement of Program Service Accomplishments**
Program written descriptions and revenue, expense, and grants summaries
**Part IV Checklist of Required Schedules**
Commonly filed schedules will vary by organization type, for example:
Schedule A. Public Charity Status and Public Support
Schedule B. Contributors
Schedule C. Political Campaign and Lobbying Activities
Schedule D. Supplemental Financial Statements
Schedule G. Information Regarding Fundraising or Gaming
Schedule J. Compensation Information
Schedule M. Noncash Contributions
Schedule O. Program and Mission Details
**Part V. IRS Filings and Tax Compliance**
**Part VI. Governance, Management, and Disclosure**
**Part VII Compensation of Officers, Directors...Key Employees**
**Part VIII. Statement of Revenue**
Revenue amount by type:
Contributions, gifts, and fundraising events revenue
Program service revenue
Foundation grants and contracts
Government grants and contracts
Noncash income
Investment income
Other revenue
**Part IX. Statement of Functional Expenses**
Expense amount by type and by function:
Program service
Management & general overhead
Fundraising
**Part X. Balance Sheet**
Assets
Liabilities & Net assets
**Part XI Financial Statements Preparation and Reporting**
Accounting method used, cash or accrual
Statements compiled, reviewed, or audited by independent accountant?

# Form 990 Summary and Signature Page

| Form **990** | **Return of Organization Exempt From Income Tax** | OMB No. 1545-0047 |
|---|---|---|
| | Under section 501(c), 527, or 4947(a)(1) of the Internal Revenue Code (except private foundations) | **2015** |
| Department of the Treasury<br>Internal Revenue Service | ▶ Do not enter social security numbers on this form as it may be made public.<br>▶ Information about Form 990 and its instructions is at www.irs.gov/form990. | **Open to Public Inspection** |

**A** For the 2015 calendar year, or tax year beginning _____ , 2015, and ending _____ , 20___

| B Check if applicable: | C Name of organization | D Employer identification number |
|---|---|---|
| ☐ Address change | Doing business as | |
| ☐ Name change | Number and street (or P.O. box if mail is not delivered to street address)  Room/suite | E Telephone number |
| ☐ Initial return | | |
| ☐ Final return/terminated | City or town, state or province, country, and ZIP or foreign postal code | |
| ☐ Amended return | | G Gross receipts $ |
| ☐ Application pending | F Name and address of principal officer: | H(a) Is this a group return for subordinates? ☐ Yes ☐ No<br>H(b) Are all subordinates included? ☐ Yes ☐ No<br>If "No," attach a list. (see instructions) |

**I** Tax-exempt status: ☐ 501(c)(3) ☐ 501(c) ( ) ◀ (insert no.) ☐ 4947(a)(1) or ☐ 527

**J** Website: ▶ _____ H(c) Group exemption number ▶

**K** Form of organization: ☐ Corporation ☐ Trust ☐ Association ☐ Other ▶ **L** Year of formation: **M** State of legal domicile:

## Part I  Summary

| | | |
|---|---|---|
| Activities & Governance | 1 | Briefly describe the organization's mission or most significant activities: |
| | 2 | Check this box ▶☐ if the organization discontinued its operations or disposed of more than 25% of its net assets. |
| | 3 | Number of voting members of the governing body (Part VI, line 1a) . . . . . . . . **3** |
| | 4 | Number of independent voting members of the governing body (Part VI, line 1b) . . . . **4** |
| | 5 | Total number of individuals employed in calendar year 2015 (Part V, line 2a) . . . . . **5** |
| | 6 | Total number of volunteers (estimate if necessary) . . . . . . . . . . . **6** |
| | 7a | Total unrelated business revenue from Part VIII, column (C), line 12 . . . . . . **7a** |
| | b | Net unrelated business taxable income from Form 990-T, line 34 . . . . . . . **7b** |

| | | | Prior Year | Current Year |
|---|---|---|---|---|
| Revenue | 8 | Contributions and grants (Part VIII, line 1h) . . . . . . . | | |
| | 9 | Program service revenue (Part VIII, line 2g) . . . . . . . | | |
| | 10 | Investment income (Part VIII, column (A), lines 3, 4, and 7d) . . . . | | |
| | 11 | Other revenue (Part VIII, column (A), lines 5, 6d, 8c, 9c, 10c, and 11e) . . . | | |
| | 12 | Total revenue—add lines 8 through 11 (must equal Part VIII, column (A), line 12) | | |
| Expenses | 13 | Grants and similar amounts paid (Part IX, column (A), lines 1–3) . . . . . | | |
| | 14 | Benefits paid to or for members (Part IX, column (A), line 4) . . . . . | | |
| | 15 | Salaries, other compensation, employee benefits (Part IX, column (A), lines 5–10) | | |
| | 16a | Professional fundraising fees (Part IX, column (A), line 11e) . . . . . | | |
| | b | Total fundraising expenses (Part IX, column (D), line 25) ▶ _____ | | |
| | 17 | Other expenses (Part IX, column (A), lines 11a–11d, 11f–24e) . . . . | | |
| | 18 | Total expenses. Add lines 13–17 (must equal Part IX, column (A), line 25) | | |
| | 19 | Revenue less expenses. Subtract line 18 from line 12 . . . . . . | | |
| | | | Beginning of Current Year | End of Year |
| Net Assets or Fund Balances | 20 | Total assets (Part X, line 16) . . . . . . . . . . | | |
| | 21 | Total liabilities (Part X, line 26) . . . . . . . . . . | | |
| | 22 | Net assets or fund balances. Subtract line 21 from line 20 . . . . | | |

## Part II  Signature Block

Under penalties of perjury, I declare that I have examined this return, including accompanying schedules and statements, and to the best of my knowledge and belief, it is true, correct, and complete. Declaration of preparer (other than officer) is based on all information of which preparer has any knowledge.

| Sign Here | ▶ Signature of officer | Date |
|---|---|---|
| | ▶ Type or print name and title | |

| Paid Preparer Use Only | Print/Type preparer's name | Preparer's signature | Date | Check ☐ if self-employed | PTIN |
|---|---|---|---|---|---|
| | Firm's name ▶ | | | Firm's EIN ▶ | |
| | Firm's address ▶ | | | Phone no. | |

May the IRS discuss this return with the preparer shown above? (see instructions) . . . . . . . . . . ☐ Yes ☐ No

For Paperwork Reduction Act Notice, see the separate instructions.  Cat. No. 11282Y  Form **990** (2015)

# Form 990 Part VIII Statement of Revenue

Form 990 (2015) — Page **9**

**Part VIII** Statement of Revenue

Check if Schedule O contains a response or note to any line in this Part VIII . . . . . . . . . . ☐

| | | | (A) Total revenue | (B) Related or exempt function revenue | (C) Unrelated business revenue | (D) Revenue excluded from tax under sections 512-514 |
|---|---|---|---|---|---|---|
| **Contributions, Gifts, Grants and Other Similar Amounts** | 1a | Federated campaigns . . . **1a** | | | | |
| | b | Membership dues . . . . **1b** | | | | |
| | c | Fundraising events . . . . **1c** | | | | |
| | d | Related organizations . . . **1d** | | | | |
| | e | Government grants (contributions) **1e** | | | | |
| | f | All other contributions, gifts, grants, and similar amounts not included above **1f** | | | | |
| | g | Noncash contributions included in lines 1a-1f: $ | | | | |
| | h | **Total.** Add lines 1a–1f . . . . . . ▶ | | | | |
| **Program Service Revenue** | 2a | Business Code | | | | |
| | b | | | | | |
| | c | | | | | |
| | d | | | | | |
| | e | | | | | |
| | f | All other program service revenue . | | | | |
| | g | **Total.** Add lines 2a–2f . . . . . . . ▶ | | | | |
| **Other Revenue** | 3 | Investment income (including dividends, interest, and other similar amounts) . . . . . . ▶ | | | | |
| | 4 | Income from investment of tax-exempt bond proceeds ▶ | | | | |
| | 5 | Royalties . . . . . . . . . . . ▶ | | | | |
| | | (i) Real | (ii) Personal | | | |
| | 6a | Gross rents . . | | | | |
| | b | Less: rental expenses | | | | |
| | c | Rental income or (loss) | | | | |
| | d | Net rental income or (loss) . . . . . ▶ | | | | |
| | 7a | Gross amount from sales of assets other than inventory | (i) Securities | (ii) Other | | |
| | b | Less: cost or other basis and sales expenses . | | | | |
| | c | Gain or (loss) . . | | | | |
| | d | Net gain or (loss) . . . . . . . . ▶ | | | | |
| | 8a | Gross income from fundraising events (not including $ of contributions reported on line 1c). See Part IV, line 18 . . . . . **a** | | | | |
| | b | Less: direct expenses . . . . **b** | | | | |
| | c | Net income or (loss) from fundraising events . ▶ | | | | |
| | 9a | Gross income from gaming activities. See Part IV, line 19 . . . . . **a** | | | | |
| | b | Less: direct expenses . . . . **b** | | | | |
| | c | Net income or (loss) from gaming activities . . ▶ | | | | |
| | 10a | Gross sales of inventory, less returns and allowances . . . **a** | | | | |
| | b | Less: cost of goods sold . . . **b** | | | | |
| | c | Net income or (loss) from sales of inventory . . ▶ | | | | |
| | | Miscellaneous Revenue | Business Code | | | |
| | 11a | | | | | |
| | b | | | | | |
| | c | | | | | |
| | d | All other revenue . . . . . | | | | |
| | e | **Total.** Add lines 11a–11d . . . . . . . ▶ | | | | |
| | 12 | **Total revenue.** See instructions. . . . . . ▶ | | | | |

Form **990** (2015)

# Nonprofit Accounting & Financial Statements

## Part IX Statement of Functional Expenses

| Part IX | Statement of Functional Expenses | | | | |
|---|---|---|---|---|---|
| Section 501(c)(3) and 501(c)(4) organizations must complete all columns. All other organizations must complete column (A). | | | | | |
| Check if Schedule O contains a response or note to any line in this Part IX . . . . . . . . . . . . . ☐ | | | | | |
| **Do not include amounts reported on lines 6b, 7b, 8b, 9b, and 10b of Part VIII.** | | **(A)** Total expenses | **(B)** Program service expenses | **(C)** Management and general expenses | **(D)** Fundraising expenses |
| 1 | Grants and other assistance to domestic organizations and domestic governments. See Part IV, line 21 . . | | | | |
| 2 | Grants and other assistance to domestic individuals. See Part IV, line 22 . . . . . | | | | |
| 3 | Grants and other assistance to foreign organizations, foreign governments, and foreign individuals. See Part IV, lines 15 and 16 . . . | | | | |
| 4 | Benefits paid to or for members . . . . | | | | |
| 5 | Compensation of current officers, directors, trustees, and key employees . . . . . | | | | |
| 6 | Compensation not included above, to disqualified persons (as defined under section 4958(f)(1)) and persons described in section 4958(c)(3)(B) . . | | | | |
| 7 | Other salaries and wages . . . . . . . | | | | |
| 8 | Pension plan accruals and contributions (include section 401(k) and 403(b) employer contributions) | | | | |
| 9 | Other employee benefits . . . . . . . | | | | |
| 10 | Payroll taxes . . . . . . . . . . . . | | | | |
| 11 | Fees for services (non-employees): | | | | |
| a | Management . . . . . . . . . . . | | | | |
| b | Legal . . . . . . . . . . . . . . | | | | |
| c | Accounting . . . . . . . . . . . . | | | | |
| d | Lobbying . . . . . . . . . . . . . | | | | |
| e | Professional fundraising services. See Part IV, line 17 | | | | |
| f | Investment management fees . . . . . | | | | |
| g | Other. (If line 11g amount exceeds 10% of line 25, column (A) amount, list line 11g expenses on Schedule O.) . . | | | | |
| 12 | Advertising and promotion . . . . . . | | | | |
| 13 | Office expenses . . . . . . . . . . | | | | |
| 14 | Information technology . . . . . . . . | | | | |
| 15 | Royalties . . . . . . . . . . . . . | | | | |
| 16 | Occupancy . . . . . . . . . . . . | | | | |
| 17 | Travel . . . . . . . . . . . . . . | | | | |
| 18 | Payments of travel or entertainment expenses for any federal, state, or local public officials | | | | |
| 19 | Conferences, conventions, and meetings . | | | | |
| 20 | Interest . . . . . . . . . . . . . . | | | | |
| 21 | Payments to affiliates . . . . . . . . | | | | |
| 22 | Depreciation, depletion, and amortization . | | | | |
| 23 | Insurance . . . . . . . . . . . . . | | | | |
| 24 | Other expenses. Itemize expenses not covered above (List miscellaneous expenses in line 24e. If line 24e amount exceeds 10% of line 25, column (A) amount, list line 24e expenses on Schedule O.) | | | | |
| a | ........................................... | | | | |
| b | ........................................... | | | | |
| c | ........................................... | | | | |
| d | ........................................... | | | | |
| e | All other expenses | | | | |
| 25 | **Total functional expenses.** Add lines 1 through 24e | | | | |
| 26 | **Joint costs.** Complete this line only if the organization reported in column (B) joint costs from a combined educational campaign and fundraising solicitation. Check here ▶ ☐ if following SOP 98-2 (ASC 958-720) . . . . | | | | |

Form **990** (2015)

## Part X Balance Sheet *(Statement of Financial Position)*

| | | | (A) Beginning of year | (B) End of year |
|---|---|---|---|---|
| | | Form 990 (2015) | | Page 11 |
| **Part X** | | **Balance Sheet** | | |
| | | Check if Schedule O contains a response or note to any line in this Part X . . . . . . . . . . . ☐ | | |

**Assets**

| # | Description | | (A) Beginning of year | (B) End of year |
|---|---|---|---|---|
| 1 | Cash — non-interest-bearing . . . . . . . . . . . . . | 1 | | |
| 2 | Savings and temporary cash investments . . . . . . . . . . | 2 | | |
| 3 | Pledges and grants receivable, net . . . . . . . . . . . | 3 | | |
| 4 | Accounts receivable, net . . . . . . . . . . . . . . | 4 | | |
| 5 | Loans and other receivables from current and former officers, directors, trustees, key employees, and highest compensated employees. Complete Part II of Schedule L . . . . . . . . . . . . | 5 | | |
| 6 | Loans and other receivables from other disqualified persons (as defined under section 4958(f)(1)), persons described in section 4958(c)(3)(B), and contributing employers and sponsoring organizations of section 501(c)(9) voluntary employees' beneficiary organizations (see instructions). Complete Part II of Schedule L . . . . . . . | 6 | | |
| 7 | Notes and loans receivable, net . . . . . . . . . . . . | 7 | | |
| 8 | Inventories for sale or use . . . . . . . . . . . . . | 8 | | |
| 9 | Prepaid expenses and deferred charges . . . . . . . . . | 9 | | |
| 10a | Land, buildings, and equipment: cost or other basis. Complete Part VI of Schedule D   **10a** | | | |
| b | Less: accumulated depreciation . . .   **10b** | 10c | | |
| 11 | Investments — publicly traded securities . . . . . . . . . | 11 | | |
| 12 | Investments — other securities. See Part IV, line 11 . . . . . | 12 | | |
| 13 | Investments — program-related. See Part IV, line 11 . . . . . . | 13 | | |
| 14 | Intangible assets . . . . . . . . . . . . . . . . | 14 | | |
| 15 | Other assets. See Part IV, line 11 . . . . . . . . . . . | 15 | | |
| 16 | **Total assets.** Add lines 1 through 15 (must equal line 34) . . . . . | 16 | | |

**Liabilities**

| # | Description | | (A) | (B) |
|---|---|---|---|---|
| 17 | Accounts payable and accrued expenses . . . . . . . . . | 17 | | |
| 18 | Grants payable . . . . . . . . . . . . . . . . . | 18 | | |
| 19 | Deferred revenue . . . . . . . . . . . . . . . . | 19 | | |
| 20 | Tax-exempt bond liabilities . . . . . . . . . . . . . | 20 | | |
| 21 | Escrow or custodial account liability. Complete Part IV of Schedule D . | 21 | | |
| 22 | Loans and other payables to current and former officers, directors, trustees, key employees, highest compensated employees, and disqualified persons. Complete Part II of Schedule L . . . . . . | 22 | | |
| 23 | Secured mortgages and notes payable to unrelated third parties . . | 23 | | |
| 24 | Unsecured notes and loans payable to unrelated third parties . . . | 24 | | |
| 25 | Other liabilities (including federal income tax, payables to related third parties, and other liabilities not included on lines 17-24). Complete Part X of Schedule D . . . . . . . . . . . . . . . . | 25 | | |
| 26 | **Total liabilities.** Add lines 17 through 25 . . . . . . . . . | 26 | | |

**Net Assets or Fund Balances**

| # | Description | | (A) | (B) |
|---|---|---|---|---|
| | **Organizations that follow SFAS 117 (ASC 958), check here ▶ ☐ and complete lines 27 through 29, and lines 33 and 34.** | | | |
| 27 | Unrestricted net assets . . . . . . . . . . . . . . | 27 | | |
| 28 | Temporarily restricted net assets . . . . . . . . . . . | 28 | | |
| 29 | Permanently restricted net assets . . . . . . . . . . . | 29 | | |
| | **Organizations that do not follow SFAS 117 (ASC 958), check here ▶ ☐ and complete lines 30 through 34.** | | | |
| 30 | Capital stock or trust principal, or current funds . . . . . . . | 30 | | |
| 31 | Paid-in or capital surplus, or land, building, or equipment fund . . . | 31 | | |
| 32 | Retained earnings, endowment, accumulated income, or other funds . | 32 | | |
| 33 | Total net assets or fund balances . . . . . . . . . . . | 33 | | |
| 34 | Total liabilities and net assets/fund balances . . . . . . . . | 34 | | |

Form **990** (2015)

# Section E.
# Conclusion

# Chapter 22.
# What Can Go Wrong?

A lot can go wrong. *Bad things happen to good nonprofit organizations every day.* Maybe the worst financial disaster that can happen is bankruptcy. Or, perhaps losing nonprofit status and most of your donors. Or, perhaps a financial scandal. For board members, the worst might be being held personally liable by the IRS for the unpaid employment taxes of the bankrupt organization. It is a potential minefield out there, really.

Subtler, but still as potentially devastating, disasters can come from losing your way, mission shift, starving the organization of resources, or ignoring the needs of stakeholders. Squandering nonprofit resources and donor contributions should be a crime. Unfortunately, it is not...yet, anyway.

Scoundrel leaders, dishonest employees, or crooked contractors can severely damage or even destroy the organization's capacity to serve the mission. Malpractice in nonprofit organizations is particularly contemptible; losses touch the people served, the volunteers, the honest employees, and the donors.

∼

For nonprofit organizations, everything revolves around money in some important way. Starting with a special tax status and a charter of charity, the 501(c)(3) organization assembles financial resources to be used in promoting a social mission.

## Financial Fraud

If proper financial controls are not in place in a nonprofit organization, financial fraud by trusted employees is a ticking time bomb. Leaving the cookie jar open and unattended is an invitation for simple garden-variety theft and full-blown embezzlement.

Who steals money from a charity? Mary in accounting raiding petty cash $10 at a time until, after a few years, the total amount exceeds that for felony theft. Self-dealing and private inurement by the chairman of the board or the CEO can involve larger sums.

How often does this happen? More than you think. When discovered, it is usually hushed up. What nonprofit organization wants to admit to its donors that their donations have been stolen by a staff member?

Note, use of restricted revenue in contradiction to the donor's wishes is financial fraud and leaves the organization and its leaders open to civil suit and damage awards. It is the board's and CEO's responsibility to assure donors that their donations are being used for the purpose stated in the donation agreement.

A nonprofit organization is most susceptible to financial fraud if it has inadequate financial systems and procedures, lax controls with few checks and balances, no outside accountants, and then compounds the problem by ignoring signs. Sound familiar? I hope not.

Prevention of financial fraud is an area where accountants can really help, both in setting up systems and procedures to prevent fraud and also in auditing to identify any fraudulent behavior.

No *self-dealing* and *private inurement* is the cardinal rule specifically for nonprofits. No one individual is to profit from the organization. Conflicts of interest need to be recognized, disclosed, and dealt with directly and publicly.

### Excessive Fundraising Expenditures

Most issues of fundraising ethics revolve around how much is proper for a nonprofit to spend on fundraising events and on how to compensate fundraising professionals. There is no real consensus in the nonprofit community as to how much is too much expense relative to the amounts raised. Legislators and the courts have not set statutory limits on fundraising expenses, though misleading potential donors is illegal. An alternate view is that spending a great deal of money to raise sums needed to accomplish some great goal should be applauded, not condemned. Ultimately, it is up to donors to decide what goals they want to support, what approach they believe will best serve those goals, and which organizations show the greatest promise of using available resources to pursue them. Donors need only ask, more frequently and more carefully, for evidence that the work is being done well. Responsible nonprofits will be able to provide it.

## Waste & Inefficiency

Do not be ineffective, inefficient, or misguided.

* *Ineffective:* not producing any significant or desired effect.

  *Synonyms:* unsuccessful, unproductive, counterproductive, fruitless, futile, purposeless, useless, worthless, ineffectual, inefficient, inefficacious, inadequate, feeble, inept, lame

* *Inefficient:* not achieving maximum productivity, wasting or failing to make the best use of time or resources

  *Synonyms:* unproductive, incompetent, inept, incapable, unfit, unskillful, inexpert, amateurish, unprofessional, disorganized, unprepared, negligent, lax, sloppy, slack, careless, useless, good-for-nothing, uneconomical, wasteful, unproductive, slow, deficient, unsystematic.

* *Misguided:* heading in the wrong direction.

  *Synonyms:* Mistaken (often stubbornly so), wrong-headed, luddite (using ineffective old technology), fighting the last war, reactionary, lose your way.

Nonprofits are traditionally conservative and most board members are older experienced folks—the main reasons nonprofit organizations do not embrace technological advances in productivity, communications, marketing, and all sorts of good things. I recommend hiring some youngsters to help, really!

## Ethical Behavior in Nonprofit Organizations

All nonprofit organization should have a "Statement of Ethical Behavior" that is read and signed by each employee and volunteer before they join the organization.

Ethics in an organization is top-down. Regardless of the written statement, the CEO and her lieutenants set the stage for ethical behavior in the organization. The board, CEO, and senior managers must demonstrate ethical behavior every day.

The best test for what constitutes ethical behavior is whether it follows two rules: one golden and one black & white:

1. *Golden Rule.* How would you like to be treated? Simply treat others that way.

2. *Front Page Rule.* If an action were to be disclosed and reported on the front page of the local newspaper, would you or the organization be embarrassed? Then just do not do it.

There is really nothing more to add.

### Reporting Malfeasance[1]

Finally, what if you are in the bowels of the organization and you suspect and are troubled by a real criminal or ethical problem? What should you do? Who should you contact?

1. Ask yourself, "Do I really want to do this?" There are real professional and personal risks in reporting potential malfeasance. "What if I am wrong?"

2. Contact the Attorney General of your state or, if your report is concerning a federal contract, contact the local office of the federal prosecutor (State's Attorney for your state) or the FBI.

3. Be as specific as you can be about the conduct you regard as illegal or wrong. Provide, in writing, specific and factual information: who, what, where, when and how, attaching any pertinent documentation and offer to provide any other information needed.

4. Sign the above with your real name, unless you have a VERY good reason not to.

---

[1] Paraphrased from statements made by Dave Horn, former Assistant Attorney General in the Consumer Protection Division of the Office of the Attorney General for Washington State *(speaking for himself).*

3. Your opinions and "gut sense" should not be a part of a formal report but, if you truly believe them relevant, you may choose to add a separate document with this information. Resist the impulse to shame and blame in this format.

4. Be patient. If your complaint has merit AND the agency you contacted has sufficient resources, it will be pursued.

5. Look for another job. Life is too short to work in an organization you cannot respect.

# Chapter 23.
# Twenty Important
# Lessons Learned

**Act on all the principles below.** I mean actually really follow them, not just talk about them. You know.

———

**(1)** USE THE ACCOUNTING NUMBERS. You have learned the essentials of nonprofit accounting and financial reporting. This new numeric knowledge will make you a better board member, manager, or staff person. Ultimately however, it is not enough to just learn the mechanics. This knowledge is just a tool; it's the beginning. To be effective you must know how to use the numbers to improve your organization and its service to mission. While a public charity is not a for-profit business, it must act in a business-like fashion if it is to prosper. The laws of economics still apply to charitable organizations.

**(2)** MEASURE EFFECTIVENESS & EFFICIENCY. A competent management team must continuously search for better ways of conducting its activities. Using the numbers to guide charity work is crucial to ensuring the efficient use of limited resources. The board's role is as an overseer, demanding management demonstrates its worth.

**(3)** DEMONSTRATE COMPETENCE TO YOUR DONORS. Most people, including big donors, think nonprofit managers are nice people who do not manage their organizations very well. Remember, it is your donors' money that you are spending. You want more money from them? Show them how well you support their mission.

**(4)** PUT YOUR MONEY WHERE YOUR MISSION IS. Use thoughtful budgets coupled with well-drawn spending controls to make sure your organization's efforts are focused on the best programs to serve the mission. Both misdirected programs and "mission creep" can seriously impede progress.

**(5)** ANSWER THE QUESTION: "CAN WE AFFORD IT?" Board members must be realistic and hard-nosed when answering such questions. If you are not watching revenue coming in and expenses going out, the organization may get into financial trouble. Of course, an alternative is to just raise more and more money.

**(6)** NO SCANDALS; NO MALFEASANCE; NO FRAUD. Nonprofits cannot afford to allow a hint of scandal to taint their organizations. Nothing will dry up funding and damage your organization's efforts more than scandal. If you do not have adequate financial controls, your most trusted, long-term staff will be tempted to steal from you. Do not tempt them—it is your responsibility.

**(7)** YOU ARE A FIDUCIARY (LIKE IT OR NOT). Board members are *fiduciaries* of the organizations they serve. Fiduciary duties are a combination of legal and ethical responsibilities within a long-standing tradition that is well established in law and practice. Fiduciaries hold the organization's interests and mission before their own.

While board service is a voluntary act of social responsibility, board members are expected to devote time, attention, knowledge, and skill to their fiduciary duties. More than ever before, board members and managers can expect to be accountable for their decisions and their actions.

**8** PAY ATTENTION; DO YOUR HOMEWORK. The *Duty of Care* requires board members to carry out their responsibilities in good faith, and using that degree of diligence, care, and skill which ordinarily prudent persons would reasonably exercise under similar circumstances in like positions.

A board member cannot just "coast." A board member must act in a manner that he or she reasonably believes to be in the best interests of the institution.[1]

**9** REMEMBER, IT IS NOT ABOUT YOU. The *Duty of Loyalty* requires board members to act in good faith in the interests of the organization and its nonprofit or public purposes, rather than their own interests or the interests of another person or organization. A fiduciary must not act out of expedience, avarice, or self-interest.[1]

**10** IT IS ALL ABOUT MISSION. The *Duty of Obedience* obligates board members to act always to advance the stated mission of the organization. This duty also requires that board members assure themselves that the organization is always operating according to law and government regulations. Further, board members are themselves expected to act in a manner that is consistent with the mission, goals and values of the organization.[1]

**11** BE OPEN. As a board member of a public charity, you are holding a public trust. What secrets do you need to keep? Certainly, those of your clients you serve, but that is the law. Otherwise, why not be an open book? IRS Form 990 requires much disclosure. The public supports you financially; they want to know. Tell them.

**12** LISTEN TO *ALL* THE STAKEHOLDERS. Honor and cherish all the stakeholders of your organization: clients (those directly served by the organization), staff, volunteers, management, other board members, federal government (often your biggest donor and your biggest purchaser of services), state government (incorporator and overseer) and the community.

---

[1] Adapted from the Association of Governing Board Members of Universities and Colleges (AGB) *Statement of Fiduciary Duties.* July 2015.

Weigh competing interests fairly and with the wisdom of Solomon. Further, realize that more stakeholders now expect to participate in decision making and we now have the tools to easily gather and disseminate relevant information to them. The result will be an explosion of participation. The implications for future nonprofit governance, organization, and leadership are considerable.[2]

**(13)** **BE BOTH A SHEPHERD AND A STEWARD.** Nonprofit board members oversee all the actions of the organization for which they serve. Directors—working without compensation—are shepherds of the organization's mission and are ultimately responsible for the organization's success. As stewards, directors are especially responsible for the financial viability necessary to achieve the organization's mission.

**(14)** **STRUCTURE THE BOARD'S ROLE CORRECTLY.** The board is the only group in the organization whose *first* loyalty is to mission. Everybody else wants something. Management and employees want jobs, clients want services, vendors want orders, and so forth.

The board gets to decide strategy and ratify plans. The board determines key service offerings and budgets. Management, on the other hand, runs operations and executes to plan on budget. Do not step on each other's toes. Roles are separate, as are the skills required for success. Boards should not just "rubber-stamp" management actions but not micromanage them either. Amen!

**(15)** **FUNDRAISE.** Better yet, network! Ask your friends for money to support the organization. Give generously of your time and your money. 100% of the board must donate and rich board members should make sizable donations. Fundraising should be a constant and pressing concern for all board members.

---

[2.] Adapted from *The Participatory Revolution in Nonprofit Management* by Gregory D Saxton. Nonprofit Quarterly, August 2012.

**(16)** **HIRE THE RIGHT CEO.** Hiring the organization's CEO is—after mission—the penultimate responsibility of the board. The CEO is the leader of the organization as well as its primary voice. The board acts as a body; the CEO is *en pointe*. While a strong CEO is necessary to the success of mission, fire the CEO who does not realize that the board is his/her boss. If board is not active, the CEO will control everything and the mission too. Not a good idea.

**(17)** **PROFIT IS NOT A DIRTY WORD.** A nonprofit organization just calls it by another name, surplus. If your organization is not making a surplus from your operations, you are not running operations efficiently (that is, you are wasting money). All well-run nonprofit organizations should have at least a small surplus. Make sure that your organization does.

**(18)** **COMMUNICATE.** The organization's Annual Report may be fancy, but its IRS Form 990 tells the real story. Make sure it is informative. Donors in the know rely on Form 990 for the true scoop.

The auditors and management may prepare the Form 990, but every member of the board must read and understand it and vote (unanimous!) its approval before submission to the IRS. Form 990 is signed by the head of the organization under "penalty of perjury." Take it seriously.

**(19)** **SET POLICY, PRIORITIES & BUDGETS.** The board controls the purse strings by approving thoughtful budgets that reflect the financial realities the organization faces. Assure that the budget is congruent with and advances the organization's mission. Then, follow your progress closely as the year evolves. Correct if necessary.

If you are not watching how funds are spent, the organization may be spending them inefficiently, to the detriment of mission. If the CEO is not providing the board with well-presented and understandable financial and operations information, fire that CEO and hire one who does.

**AVOID FINANCIAL CATASTROPHE.** Basically, only two things can put your organization out of business: losing your nonprofit status or running out of cash (going bankrupt). It is your fiduciary duty as a board member to avoid both.

In some instances you may be personally liable for board actions (or inactions). For example, if the organization does not pay its payroll withholding tax on employees' salary and wages, the IRS can and will come after you personally for payment. Normal legal shields of corporate structure of the organization may not protect your personal assets from being seized. Watch out.

――――

Overall, how healthy is our organization today? Is it healthier today than it was three years ago? Why or why not? How effective are our programs serving mission? Are they sustainable, generating resources to meet today's needs without compromising the future? Remember, surplus (profit), like program impact, is fundamental to sustainability.

That's all folks. Thank you.

"Ask most nonprofit organizations operating today to name their largest problem, and they will tell you that it is a lack of money. In the charitable sector, however, lack of money is rarely their single problem. Organizations with outstanding leadership, sound management, strong mission, effective programs and services reflecting that mission, and welcoming attitudes toward new constituents (donors, volunteers, and clients alike) do not suffer money problems."

Renata J. Rafferty
Chandler House Press 1999

# Appendix A.
# Implementing New Rules

The important changes made to nonprofit accounting and financial reporting by FASB in 2017 and by the Office of Management and Budget in 2019 are now fully operational. The major changes for 2017 (the first since 1993) are described in Addendum to the 2nd Edition of this book which follows at the end of this chapter. Here we will discuss added changes in reporting made by the Office of Management and Budget for implementation in 2019.

## Liquidity

Going forward, nonprofit organizations should provide both qualitative and quantitative information about liquidity (availability of cash) and its use:

- Qualitative information that communicates how the NFP manages its liquid resources available to meet cash needs for general expenditures within one year of the Statement of financial Position date.

- Quantitative information that communicates the availability of the NFP's financial assets to meet cash needs for general expenditures within one year of the Statement of Financial Position date.

The main question to be answered is, "Does organization have ample resources to fund activities over the next 12 months? Note however, there is no prescribed presentation format for the information required. Each organization should decide on a format that best fits its particular situation.

The new guidance requires enhanced financial statement disclosures regarding an organization's liquidity and availability of resources. Both qualitative and quantitative information are required. The *qualitative component* describes the organization's liquidity management plan, or how liquid assets are managed to meet cash needs for general expenditures within one year following the balance sheet date. *Quantitative information* regarding those assets and their availability to meet current-year needs may be presented either on the face of the statement of financial position or in the notes to the financial statements.

## Why?

Regulatory agencies feel that potential donors, grantors, creditors and other not-for-profit constituents want to know that the organizations they are evaluating have sufficient resources to meet financial obligations as they come due. The new guidance increases transparency in the financial statements and promotes a more thorough and accurate understanding of the organization's ability to fund operations.

---

**Liquidity (money in the bank for use in emergencies) is an underrated virtue in the nonprofit world. Liquidity gives the organization the financial strength to ride out a storm of either lower than expected donations, loss of a contract, unexpected management issues, or a dramatic change in the environment (think Covid-19).**

---

Having a liquidity management plan is a best practice. An organization's liquidity management plan or process will depend on its sophistication and size, the type and complexity of its activities, and its specific liquidity risks, and the general availability of funds from contributions and debt draw-down.

## Addendum to the 2nd Edition

During 2017 some important changes were implemented by FASB in nonprofit accounting and financial statement reporting.[1]

(The last big change was in 1993.) These changes are really important for accountants — but not so much for us nonfinancial folks. So, it is okay to chill, but be generally aware of what has happened and how the new presentation formats relate to the previous ones. Here are some highlights:

1. The new nonprofit *Statement of Financial Position* will distinguish between only two classes of net assets. Unlike the past three classes of net assets (unrestricted, temporarily restricted and permanently restricted), there will only be two: (a) NET ASSETS WITHOUT DONOR RESTRICTIONS and (b) NET ASSETS WITH DONOR RESTRICTIONS.

2. In the *Statement of Activities*, expenses associated with revenue without donor restrictions will be classified as either program operations related or as management and general overhead related.

3. A *Statement of Functional Expenses* will be required in nonprofit reporting, rather than optional.

4. Organizations may use the direct or indirect method of cash flow reporting in the *Statement of Cash Flows* (see Chapter 6), making it easier to review with the newly redesigned *Statement of Activities.*

5. More detailed quantitative and qualitative disclosures will be required which will be useful in assessing the organization's liquidity and cash flow in both the short and long run.

～

FASB's goals in making these changes are three-fold:

1. To provide more consistency between nonprofit and for-profit accounting and financial reporting. Many nonprofit financial statement users have a for-profit background and the new rules will assist in their understanding in the implementation of nonprofit standards,

2. To focus on reporting so that stakeholders can better appreciate the need for program-related and general overhead expense, and

3. To provide early insight on potential cash flow issues in the organization.

---

[1]FASB Accounting Standards Update 2016-14 Not-for-Profit Entities (Topic 958) Presentation of Financial Statements of Not-for-Profit Entities August 2016

# Appendix B.
# Debits and Credits

I seldom use the words "debit" and "credit" in this book. However, trained accountants and bookkeepers use these words all the time when making entries into the organization's ledgers and financial statements.

The concepts of debits and credits can be confusing to most non-financial managers. The terms, while useful to accountants, are not necessary for this book's overview purposes.

### The Olden Days

Back in the olden days when systematic accounting and statement presentation was first developed, the monks would write down each and every transaction as they occurred. Literally, "the books" of an organization were just that, the books containing an organization's financial records! The concept of debits and credits was invented to:

(a) structure the layout of the books for everyone to understand,

(b) aid the monks in classifying and recording transactions properly, and

(c) help catch manual transcribing errors.

The term debit comes from the Latin word *debitum*, meaning "what is due," and credit comes from the Latin *creditum*, defined as "something entrusted to another or a loan." The logic is that when you increase assets, the change in the asset account is a debit, because something must be due to pay for that increase (i.e. the cost of the asset in cash that would be entered as a credit in the cash account).

## Double-Entry Bookkeeping

Debits and credits are terms first coming into used 500 years ago. Luca Pacioli, a Franciscan monk, developed the concepts underlying double entry bookkeeping. The monks would prepare books (called ledgers) with one account on each page. They would write down a description of the transaction and then put the transaction dollar amount in one of two columns at the right on the page.

The first column was labeled debit and the next column was labeled credit. Note, there was often a third column on the page with a running total for the account.

---

## "Do not end your workday until your debits equal your credits."
— **Luca Pacioli**, Franciscan monk, the "Father of Accounting"

---

Every accounting transaction had to have a credit entry on one account page and a debit entry on another account page. Hence, double entry bookkeeping. Thus, when a transaction is entered with these two entries, the financial statement will remain in balance according to the general equation of accounting: Assets = Liabilities + Equity.

Double entry and debits and credits are still used by bookkeepers when they manually record financial transactions in the organization's record books. This double-entry system reduces clerical errors. Since the books must always balance, the total debits must always equal the total credits after you post the journal entries to the ledger accounts. If the amounts do not balance, you have made an error and you must find and correct it.

Bookkeepers and accountants still find the concept of debit and credit useful and standard accounting courses still teach this basic debit/credit structure. However, you will not find it used in this book because debit and credit nomenclature is:

(a) often counterintuitive and thus confusing for nonaccountants,
(b) not necessary to have a grasp of financial statement required for non-financial managers, and
(c) computerization of accounting records has made catching mistakes when manually entering numbers less necessary.

Accounting is done with computer's now and database rules govern where amounts are placed in virtual ledgers. But since bookkeepers and accountants use these terms debit and credit all the time, in this appendix we will attempt to give you just enough understanding to be able to converse intelligently with the accounting types in your organization.

**Transaction Entries** A double-entry bookkeeping system uses journal books (with chronological entries) and ledger books (with separate account-by-account pages), to record the transaction descriptions and associated debit and credit amounts. The so-called General Journal contains a record of all transaction in chronological order with a unique sequence number to forever remember them and tie the transaction to entries in the account ledgers. Makes finding errors easier.

---

**Whether a DEBIT increases or decreases an account depends on the type of account. The basic principle is that the account receiving benefit is "debited" and the account giving benefit is "credited." For instance, an increase in an asset account is a debit. An increase in a liability or equity account is a CREDIT. An increase in a sales account is a debit. An increase in an expense account is a credit.**

---

Transactions are first entered in a journal and then posted to ledger accounts. These accounts show income, expenses, assets (property a business owns), liabilities (debts of a business), and net worth (excess of assets over liabilities). In the double-entry system, each account has a left side column for debits and a right side column for credits. It is self-balancing because you record every transaction as a debit entry in one account and as a credit entry in another. Whether a debit increases or decreases an account depends on the type of account. The basic principle is that the account receiving benefit is "debited" and the account giving benefit is "credited."

For instance, an increase in an asset account is a debit. An increase in a liability or equity account is a credit. An increase in a sales account is a debit. An increase in an expense account is a credit. As an example: paying off a debt "benefits" the liability section of the Balance Sheet. The entry lowers the reported numeric value. Thus, the entry is a debit.

**Effects of Debits and Credits** There are five basic account types: assets, liabilities, sales/income and expense. Making account entries will either increase or decrease the account balances. Entries made on the left column (debit) in a T-Account Ledger, will either increase or decrease the balance as shown below by account type. For each debit entry there must be a compensating credit entry (made on the right column). This debit/credit concept is easiest to remember by thinking about:

1. *Balance Sheet* equation and keeping it in balance,

### Assets = Liability + Equity

2. *Income Statement* equation and the relationship of increases in sales revenue, expenses, and income.

### Sales – Costs + Expenses = Income

**Transaction Examples** Following are journal entries for selected transaction examples in this book. Refer to the Transaction No. detail pages earlier in the book.

**Recording a Contribution (Transaction 1)**

| Account | DEBIT | CREDIT |
|---|---|---|
| Cash | 1,000 | |
| Revenue | | $1,000 |

**Recording a Payment to a Vendor (Transaction 9)**

| Account | DEBIT | CREDIT |
|---|---|---|
| Cash | (20,500) | |
| Net Assets | | (20,500) |

**Receive Supplies (Transaction 11)**

| Account | DEBIT | CREDIT |
|---|---|---|
| n/a | | |
| n/a | | |

**Pay for supplies (Transaction 2)**

| Account | DEBIT | CREDIT |
|---|---|---|
| Inventory | $1,255 | |
| Accounts Payable | | $1,255 |

**Use Supplies (Transaction 13)**

| Account | DEBIT | CREDIT |
|---|---|---|
| Cash | ($1,255) | |
| Accounts Payable | | ($1,225) |

**Obtain a Loan (Transaction 25)**

| Account | DEBIT | CREDIT |
|---|---|---|
| Cash | | $500,000 |
| Net Borrowings | $500,000 | |

## Still Confused?

Me too. Don't worry too much. You are not the bookkeeper or accountant. You can still understand financial statements and use them to run your business without being able to credit or debit!

**Revenue Accounts**
*4000 Series*

## STATEMENT OF ACTIVITIES

*for the period*

| | WITHOUT DONOR RESTRICTIONS | WITH DONOR RESTRICTIONS | | |
|---|---|---|---|---|
| **REVENUE** | | | | |
| CONTRIBUTIONS & GIFTS | | | $ | 0 |
| PROGRAM SERVICES REVENUE | | | | 0 |
| GRANTS & CONTRACTS | | | | 0 |
| OTHER REVENUE | | | | 0 |
| **TOTAL REVENUE** | $ 0 | $0 | $ | 0 |

**Expense Accounts**
*7000 & 8000 Series*

| **EXPENSES** | | | |
|---|---|---|---|
| FUNDRAISING | | | 0 |
| PROGRAM SERVICES | | | 0 |
| GRANTS & CONTRACTS | | | 0 |
| MANAGEMENT & GENERAL | | | 0 |
| **TOTAL EXPENSES** | $ 0 | $ | 0 |

| | | |
|---|---|---|
| CHANGE IN NET ASSETS | $ | 0 |
| BEGINNING NET ASSETS | | 0 |
| ENDING NET ASSETS | $ | 0 |

**Asset Accounts**
*1000 Series*

## STATEMENT OF FINANCIAL POSITION

*as of the period ending date*

| **ASSETS** | | **LIABILITIES & NET ASSETS** | | |
|---|---|---|---|---|
| CASH | | ACCOUNTS PAYABLE | | |
| ACCOUNTS RECEIVABLE | | SHORT TERM DEBT | | |
| INVENTORIES | | LONG TERM DEBT | | |
| PREPAID EXPENSES | | ACCRUED EXPENSES | | |
| PLEDGES RECEIVABLE | | NET ASSETS: | | |
| INVESTMENTS | | W/O DONOR RESTRICTIONS | | |
| PP&E (NET) | | WITH DONOR RESTRICTIONS | | |
| **TOTAL ASSETS** | $ 0 | **TOTAL LIABILITIES & NET ASSETS** | $ | 0 |

**Net Asset Accounts**
*3000 Series*

**Liability Accounts**
*2000 Series*

## STATEMENT OF CASH FLOWS *for the period*

| | | |
|---|---|---|
| **BEGINNING CASH** | $ | 0 |
| CASH RECEIPTS | | |
| CASH DISBURSEMENTS | | |
| **CASH FLOW FROM OPERATIONS** | $ | 0 |

**Other Accounts**
*9000 Series*

| | | |
|---|---|---|
| PP&E PURCHASES | | |
| NET BORROWINGS | | |
| INVESTMENT INCOME | | |
| **ENDING CASH** | $ | 0 |

# Appendix C.
# Chart of Accounts

Every time a document comes into the organization that effects its finances (donations, bills, supply payments, and so forth), it is logged into the general journal (chronological) and a single account ledger or multiple ledgers. All original documents are then filed for further reference.

This process is the primary system of accounting control for the organization. It provides a complete "audit trail" of financial activities and form the basis for the production of financial statements for the organization.

∼

The figure on the left page shows the financial statement grouping according to standard **"Chart of Accounts"** described on the next few pages. First recorded in pen and ink (see chapter 99), accounting is now done with computers and database rules govern where amounts are placed in virtual ledgers.

For ease in coding and data entry, the Chart of Accounts individual account numbers are divided into groupings of income (4000), expenses (7000 & 8000), assets (1000 — the property a business owns), liabilities (2000 — debts of a business), and net worth (3000; excess of assets over liabilities). On data entry, these account numbers can be augmented with **Statements of Functional Expenses Activity Codes** (see page 247) to make generation of that now required statement easy to prepare automatically.

## Sample Chart of Accounts

Key to any successful accounting system is a well designed and appropriate-to-the-organization chart of accounts. The sample below has 50 or so accounts. It is best to use a simple, minimal chart of accounts to start. More accounts with more detail can be added later if necessary. Gaps in the numbering sequence are designed to accommodate added accounts.

Shown in the right-hand columns in the table below are the locations of account summations to be entered on **IRS Form 999 Return of Organization Exempt from Income *Tax*** and on **Form 990EZ** (see Chapter21 for a description of Form 990).

| Account Number | — Statement of Financial Position — <br> *4 Digit Account Descriptions* | Form 990 Line# | Form 990EZ Line# |
|---|---|---|---|
| | **Asset Accounts – 1000 Series** | | |
| 1100 | Cash, Unrestricted Account | 45 | 22 |
| 1150 | Cash, Restricted account | | |
| 1190 | Petty Cash | 46 | 22 |
| 1200 | Accounts Receivable | 50 | 24 |
| 1290 | Doubtful Accounts Receivable Allowance | | |
| 1300 | Inventory for Sale | 52 | 24 |
| 1350 | Inventory for Use | | |
| 1400 | Prepaid Expenses | 46 | 22 |
| 1500 | Pledges, Gifts, & Grants Receivable | 48 | 24 |
| 16XX | Investment Account(s) | 54-56 | 22 |
| 1700 | Fixed Assets at Cost | 57a | 23-24 |
| 1750 | Accumulated Depreciation | 57b | 23-24 |
| 1900 | other Assets | 58 | 24 |
| *sum* | **Total Assets** | 59 | 25 |
| | **Liability Accounts – 2000 Series** | | |
| 2100 | Accounts Payable | 60 | 26 |
| 2200 | Accrued Expenses | 60 | 26 |
| 2300 | other Short-Term Liabilities | 65 | 26 |

| Account Number | — Statement of Activities —<br>*4 digit Account Descriptions* | Form 990 Line # | Form 990EZ Line # |
|---|---|---|---|
| 2700 | Short-Term Debt | 65 | 26 |
| 2800 | Long-Term Debt | 64 | 26 |
| 2900 | other Long-Term Liabilities | 64 | 26 |
| *sum* | **Total Liabilities** | 66 | 26 |
| | | | |
| 3100 | Unrestricted Net Assets | | |
| 3200 | Restricted Net Assets, Board Designated | | |
| 3500 | Restricted Net Assets, by Donor or Funder | | |
| *sum* | **Total Net Assets** | 21, 73 | 21, 27 |
| | | | |
| *sum* | **Total Liabilities & Net Assets** | 74 | n/a |
| | | | |
| | **Revenue Accounts – 4000 Series** | | |
| 4100 | Contributions & Gifts Without Restrictions | 1a | 1 |
| 4110 | Membership Revenue | | |
| 4120 | Ticket/Admission Revenue | | |
| 4130 | Event Revenue | | |
| 4140 | Other Unrestricted Revenue | | |
| 4200 | Contributions & Gifts With Restrictions | 1a | 1 |
| 4300 | Program Revenue - Nongovernment | 2 | |
| 4350 | Program Revenue - Government | 1c | |
| 4400 | Grants/Contract Revenue – Nongovernment | 1a | 1 |
| 4450 | Grants/Contract – Government | 1c | |
| 4500 | Investment Revenue | | |
| 4600 | Revenue Released from Restrictions | n/a | n/a |
| 4910 | other Contributed Revenue | | |
| 4930 | other Earned Revenue | | |
| 4950 | Unrelated Business Revenue | | |
| *sum* | **Total Revenue** | 59 | 25 |
| | | | |

| Account Numbers | — Statement of Activities Accounts — 4 Digit Account Descriptions | Form 990 Line # |
|---|---|---|
| | | |
| | **Personnel Expense – 7000 Series** | |
| 7100 | Officer's Compensation | 25 |
| 7130 | Salaries & Wages | 26 |
| 7160 | Employee Benefits | 27, 28 |
| 7190 | Payroll Taxes | 29 |
| 7200 | Contract Services | |
| 7300 | Temporary Help | 43 |
| 7400 | Professional Fees | |
| 7900 | other Personnel Expense | |
| *sum* | **Total Personnel Expense** | |
| | | |
| | **Non-Personnel Expense – 8000 Series** | |
| 8110 | Supplies | 33 |
| 8120 | Telephone | 34 |
| 8130 | Postage | 35 |
| 8210 | Occupancy & Rent | 36 |
| 8229 | Equipment Rental & Maintenance | 37 |
| 8310 | Printing & Publications | 38 |
| 8410 | Travel | 39 |
| 8420 | Conferences & Meetings | 40 |
| 8800 | Interest Paid | 41 |
| 8850 | Depreciation | 42 |
| 8900 | Contracted Services | |
| 8950 | other Non-Personnel Expense | |
| *sum* | **Total non-Personnel Expense** | |
| | | |
| *sum* | **Total Expenses** | 44 |
| | | |

| Account Numbers | — Other Accounts —<br>*4 Digit Account Descriptions* | Form 990 Line # |
|---|---|---|
| 9100 | PP&E Purchases | |
| 9200 | Short-Term Debt Takedown | |
| 9250 | Long-Term Debt Takedown | |
| 9300 | From Board Restricted NA into Revenue | |
| 9350 | From Donor Restricted NA into Revenue | |
| 9800 | Adjusting Journal Entries | |
| 9900 | other | |

| Activity Codes | — Statement of Functional Expenses —<br>*3 Digit Activity Code Account Suffix* |
|---|---|
| 110 | Program A Expense |
| 120 | Program B Expense |
| 130 | Program C Expense |
| 195 | other Program |
| 20X | Unrelated Business(es) Income |
| 210 | G&A Department |
| 220 | Fundraising Department |
| 295 | other Department |
| 895 | Public Relations and Outreach |
| 3XX | Special Event(s) |
| 4XX | Contract(s) |
| 411 | Membership Revenue |
| 412 | Ticket Revenue |
| 413 | Event Revenue |
| 89X | Services Legal, accounting, etc. |
| 9XX | Location |

**Note:** Other examples of a nonprofit chart of accounts may have more accounts showing finer details. However, best to start simple.

# Appendix D.
# Accounting Systems

A very small nonprofit organization may process a dozen transactions a month. That level of activity can easily be recorded and track with manual systems like a journal and ledger book, an Excel spreadsheet and a check book. At the other end of size, national nonprofit organizations can easily be as complex as for-profit Fortune 500 corporation, processing a million transaction each day! Most nonprofit organizations fall in the middle, too large for manual accounting systems but too big for the massive accounting superstructures required to run a megacorporation.

## Large Organizations

Large nonprofit organizations have available to them of all the resources of knowledgeable consultants and big accounting firms. They can afford the 1-2% of revenue expense accounting and control functions and processes can cost. They can have 100 clerks to process donations or afford the bank charges a bank lockbox costs. I don't pretend to offer here the caliber of advice they can receive from their paid advisors.

## Organizations of a "Certain" size

So what to do if you are trying to manage the finances of a "middling" nonprofit organization? You will need:

- a dedicated staff to record and process financial transactions,

- accountants on staff to manage the group and financial managers to plot financial strategy for the organization and prepare and analyze management reports,
- an auditing firm to prepare financial statements to present to the board and to compile the information required to submit to the IRS on their Form 990,
- a computer system and all the hassles that entails. and
- specialized software to run the computer system and support systems to teach you how to use it and to fix it when it breaks (and it will).

Note, all the above may cost over 5% of a midsized organization's revenue. Don't skimp on this expense. It will subject the organization to fraud.

∼

My advice is to initially hire a local consultant or accounting firm to set up a system for you and to hire and train the staff. Regard this expense as an investment for the future just as you would view a building. Perhaps solicit donations to cove this initial expense.

Then keep the organization on as a retained consultant, for check-ups and troubleshooting.

Do the best you can and good luck!

# Further Reading

## Websites

**Greater Washington Society of CPAs** *(nonprofitaccounting basics.org)* serves more than 3,000 CPA and Non-CPA members in the District of Columbia, Maryland, and Virginia. It presents a useful website on the basics of nonprofit accounting.
Probably the best place to go for additional information on finance and accounting for nonprofit organizations. Gives an interpretation of important nonprofit accounting concepts with greater detail higher than is in this book—but it is still highly readable.

**National Assembly of State Arts Agencies** *(nasaa-arts.org)* NASAA is the membership organization that unites, represents, and serves the nation's state and jurisdictional arts agencies. Each of the 56 states and jurisdictions has created an agency to support excellence in and access to the arts.
NASAA's website is an excellent source of information about nonprofit accounting and financial reporting.

**Nonprofits Assistance Fund** *(nonprofitsassistancefund.org)* Nonprofits Assistance Fund provides financial assistance helping nonprofits answer immediate questions, increase financial understanding, and aid in developing effective financial practices.
*You can actually telephone them and they will answer questions!* Nonprofits can schedule one hour sessions in-person or by phone. "Please call us at 612.278.7180."

**National Council of Nonprofits** *(councilofnonprofits.org)* The Council is a trusted resource and advocate for America's charitable nonprofits. Through their powerful network of State associations and 25,000-plus members—the nation's largest network of nonprofits—they serve as a central coordinator and mobilizer to help nonprofits achieve greater collective impact in local communities across the country. They identify emerging trends, share proven practices, and promote solutions that benefit charitable nonprofits and the communities they serve.

**GuideStar USA, Inc.** *(guidestar.org)* is an information service specializing in reporting on U.S. nonprofit companies. Their database contains over 5 million IRS Forms 990 on 1.9 million organizations.

GuideStar is a 501(c)(3) nonprofit organization whose mission is "to revolutionize philanthropy by providing information that advances transparency, enables users to make better decisions, and encourages charitable giving." GuideStar gathers and disseminates information about every nonprofit organization in the U.S. This information is presented in a "consistent easy-to-understand format. GuideStar remains neutral, presenting gathered information for analysis by individuals, companies, and organizations."

**National Center for Charitable Statistics** *(nccs.urban.org)*, The Urban Institute, Washington DC 20037  866.518.3874

The National Center for Charitable Statistics (NCCS) is the national repository of data on the nonprofit sector in the U.S. "Its mission is to develop and disseminate high quality data on nonprofit organizations and their activities for use in research on the relationships between the nonprofit sector, government, the commercial sector, and the broader civil society."

## Books

**Center for Nonprofit Boards** *(boardsource.org)* A leading resource for practical information, tools, and best practices, training and leadership development of nonprofit organizations. BoardSource publishes a series of useful monographs on nonprofit financial governance including:

*The Financial Responsibilities of Nonprofit Boards* by Andrew Lang CPA; BoardSource; 2nd edition (January 2009).

*Legal Responsibilities of Nonprofit Boards* by Bruce R. Hopkins JD, LLM; BoardSource; 2nd edition (January 2009).

*Financial Committees of the Nonprofit Board* by Thomas A. McLaughlin; BoardSource; (November 2003).

*Understanding Nonprofit Financial Statements* by Stephen Berger, CPA; BoardSource; 3rd edition (February 2008)

*The Nonprofit Dashboard: Using Metrics to Drive Mission Success* by Lawrence Butler; BoardSource, 2nd edition (August 2012).

**Jossey-Bass** (an imprint of Wiley) and Wiley itself are leading publishers of books of interest to nonprofit organizations. They publish detailed works written for financial professionals.

*Wiley Not-for-Profit GAAP 2013: Interpretation and Application of Generally Accepted Accounting Principles* by Richard F. Larkin and Marie DiTommaso, John Wiley and Sons; 10th edition (2013).

A detailed and definitive compilation of GAAP (Generally Accepted Accounting Principles) for nonprofit organizations. Only your organization's auditor will understand, but it is the rulebook—600 pages with small type.

*The Simplified Guide to Not-for-Profit Accounting, Formation and Reporting* by Laurence Scot. Wiley; 2010.

A straightforward guide to nonprofits with an emphasis on nonprofit accounting and control. For laypeople.

*The Nonprofit Board Answer Book: A Practical Guide for Board Members and Chief Executives* by BoardSource, Jossey-Bass; 3rd edition (2011).

An easy to read, practical guide for board members and CEOs of nonprofit organizations. Eighty-five short, informative chapters; soup-to-nuts. For laypeople.

*Zone of Insolvency: How Nonprofits Avoid Hidden Liabilities and Build Financial Strength* by Ron Mattocks. Wiley: 2008.

A well-documented analysis of why so many nonprofits operate on the edge of insolvency and what an active board can do to save these organizations. Good read for lay-board members.

# Index

# About the Author

**Thomas R. Ittelson** is an expert at translating complicated financial topics in an accessible way to non-financial folks. He is a natural scientist by training (biochemistry), turned business-person. Writing accounting books came later.

After working initially as a technical writer, Tom moved into sales, marketing, and business development. He became market-ing manager for a scientific instrumentation company, followed by senior management positions as director of European market-ing, based in Strasbourg France, and vice president of marketing for a successful start-up company.

That experience encouraged Tom to become an entrepreneur himself. As founder, CEO, and treasurer of a venture capital-backed, high-tech metallurgy company, Tom learned accounting and financial reporting skills — on the job!

With his combined expertise in entrepreneurial business de-velopment, biotechnology, accounting, and finance, Tom became a sought-after consultant to both venture capitalists and scien-tific entrepreneurs. His over 35 high-tech start-up business plans help raise more than $500,000,000 in equity capital.

To help the scientific, but non-financially minded CEOs of these start-up companies, Tom wrote the best-selling for-profit accounting textbook of its kind, *Financial Statements: A Step-By-Step Guide to Understanding and Creating Financial Reports*, published by Career Press, Wayne NJ. Over 200,000 copies are currently in print.

Now, with several nonprofit board memberships under his belt — and realizing that most nonprofit board members, managers, and staff are no more financially savvy than scientist entrepreneurs — Tom is directing his efforts toward helping the nonprofit community.

His audacious "mission?" Simply to significantly increase the efficiency and effectiveness of U.S. public charities by improving financial literacy within these organizations. To that end, Tom has written thee other nonprofit financial governance books useful for everyone. Immensely helpful information made accessible in an informal and witty way. No prior accounting knowledge is necessary. *"Accounting books that are actually as enjoyable as they are useful."*

*A Picture Book of Nonprofit Financial Statements* by Thomas R. Ittelson, 60 pages, 2017.
ISBN: 978-0997108941

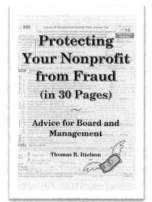

*Understanding Financial Statements (in 30 Pages): A Short tutorial for Board, Management, and Staff* by Thomas R. Ittelson, 30 pages, 2020, ISBN: 978-1970050400

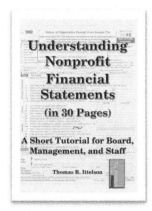

*Protecting Your Nonprofit From Fraud (in 30 Pages): Advice for Board and Management* by Thomas R. Ittelson, 30 pages 2020
ISBN: 978-1-970050-01-1

All three books are available on Amazon.com in paperback or Kindle formats or in quantity from the publisher.

Tom is available as a speaker and teacher for group presentations, in-house seminars, and training courses for nonprofit boards, managers, and staff. Contact him at:

**ittelson@mercurygroup.com**

Information contained in this book can be customized for a particular organization. Specialized teaching materials are available from the author and the publisher. For additional information and/or quantity pricing of this book for nonprofit organizations, please contact the publisher at:

**info@mercurygroup.com**

# Notes

Made in the USA
Middletown, DE
03 November 2022

14043723R00159